The Talmud of the Land of Israel

Chicago Studies in the History of Judaism
Edited by
William Scott Green
Calvin Goldscheider

The University of Chicago Press
Chicago and London

Talmud Yerushalmi. English

The Talmud of the Land of Israel

A Preliminary Translation and Explanation

Volume 8 Maaser Sheni

Translated by
Roger Brooks

The Talmud of the Land of Israel
A Preliminary Translation and Explanation
Jacob Neusner, General Editor

Roger Brooks is the Elie Wiesel Professor of Judaic Studies at Connecticut College. He is the translator of *Yerushalmi Peah*, the second volume in this series.

The University of Chicago Press, Chicago 60637
The University of Chicago Press, Ltd., London

Printed in the United States of America

02 01 00 99 98 97 96 95 94 93 1 2 3 4 5 6

ISBN (cloth): 0-226-57665-5

Acknowledgment is made to TANAKH: *A New Translation of THE HOLY SCRIPTURES According to the Traditional Hebrew Text* (Philadelphia: Jewish Publication Society, 1985), for permission to reprint translations of several verses from the Hebrew Bible.

Library of Congress Cataloging-in-Publication Data

Talmud Yerushalmi. Ma'aser sheni. English.
Maaser sheni / translated by Roger Brooks.
p. cm. — (Chicago studies in the history of Judaism) (The Talmud of the land of Israel ; v. 8)
Includes bibliographical references and indexes.
1. Talmud Yerushalmi. Ma'aser sheni—Commentaries. I. Brooks, Roger. II. Title. III. Series. IV. Series: Talmud Yerushalmi. English. 1982 ; v. 8.
BM498.5.E5 1982 vol. 8
[BM506.M13E5]
296.1'2407 s—dc20
[296.1'24] 92-25277
CIP

(∞) The paper used in this publication meets the minimum requirements of the American National Standard for Information Sciences—Permanence of Paper for Printed Library Materials, ANSI Z39.48-1984.

For my Mother

Beverly Brooks

Contents

Preface

Tractate Maaser Sheni, translated in this book, explains a small part of the rabbinic tax system of late antiquity. Brought to closure sometime between 400 and 450 C.E. in the Land of Israel, this text addresses ordinary farmers and estate holders, who interact on a regular, if infrequent, basis with the Israelite religious and governmental authorities in the holy city of Jerusalem. As the Bible had required, each Israelite who farmed the land was responsible for allotting one-tenth of each crop, bringing that food to Jerusalem, and consuming it in accord with special regulations. At the root of this transfer of produce from farm and estate to the city limits of Jerusalem was the notion that the Land belonged not to Israelite farmers, but to God, who therefore had the right to tell the Israelite farmer how to dispose of the Land's bounty. Israelites worked the soil as tenant farmers and benefited from the Land through God's munificence. Each crop they reaped constituted a reaffirmation of God's gift of the Land to them alone.

In return for this gift, the rabbinic authors of Tractate Maaser Sheni (following biblical commands) deemed the product of the Land of Israel subject to a variety of taxes and transfer payments. Thus Israelite farmers, within the rabbinic system of agriculture, were required to hand over a portion of their crops to priests, who served as God's representatives in the holy Temple. A separate portion of the Land's produce was to be set aside for poor people, who otherwise would not share equally in the benefit of God's Holy Land. The current tractate specifies how these farmers were to support the local economy of Jerusalem, visiting the city with fairly large sums of money derived from the sale of their tithe, which they were required to spend on food in the capital. All of these tax regulations flowed directly out of the rabbis' conviction that God alone owned and controlled the entire Land of Israel. As a whole, the economic measures under discussion thus promoted fidelity to God alone and submission to God's will, expressed through biblical law.

In translating and commenting upon the text below, I have enjoyed and benefited from the aid of many kind colleagues. In particular, I extend my thanks to Jacob Neusner, general editor of this series, whose translations of the bulk of the Talmud of the Land of Israel and most other early rabbinic texts invigorate this generation's work in grappling with the classics. I also extend my thanks to Peter Haas, who generously made available to me his preliminary draft of Tractate Maaser Sheni. The press's reader reviewed the manuscript line by line, suggesting improvements on nearly every page. I of course retain responsibility for any errors that remain.

As I begin new academic challenges, I would be remiss if I did not also extend my gratitude to numerous new colleagues, here at Connecticut College, who in so short a time have already enriched my life. No one could ask for better co-workers. My love and appreciation for easing my transition also go to my wife, Gayle, and my daughters, Shira Yael and Jessica Hadas. I cannot express how much you mean to me.

This volume is dedicated to my mother, Beverly Brooks, as a small token for all she has done for me over so many years.

Roger Brooks
New London, Connecticut

September 9, 1991
Rosh Ha-Shanah, 5752

Introduction

The rabbis who wrote and edited Tractate Maaser Sheni (Second Tithe) believed that all estate holders and farmers in the Land of Israel were responsible for maintaining the economic health of the Israelite nation. Building an entire system of levies out of Scripture's disjointed rulings, the rabbis laid forth a triad of economic measures constructed to equalize all members of Israelite society, to support the Jerusalem Temple in both its sacrificial cult and staff of Levites and priests, and to stimulate the economy of the holy city of Jerusalem, capital then as now of the Israelite world. The various types of poor-relief, including the corner offering, gleanings, forgotten sheaves, poor person's tithe, separated grapes and defective clusters, are treated in Tractate Peah.[1] Several tractates within the rabbinic corpus are designed to specify the various governmental revenues, which include preeminently first tithe and heave offering. And finally, a portion of all crops, known as second tithe (from which this tractate takes its name), was to be circulated through the markets of Jerusalem, so as to spur regular economic activity.

The Scriptural Background of Maaser Sheni

This practice stemmed from the rabbinic understanding of a few passages found in the Hebrew Bible. The biblical law-codes specified requirements for dissipating the holiness inherent in

1. See Brooks, *Support for the Poor,* and idem, *Talmud of the Land of Israel: Tractate Peah.*

produce grown from the Land of Israel, requirements designed, among other goals, to guarantee a regular flow of cash through the city's markets and eating establishments.

Deuteronomy 14:22–26 explains the heart of this economic stimulation measure:

> *You shall set aside every year a tenth part of all the yield of your sowing that is brought from the field. You shall consume the tithes of your new grain and wine and oil, and the firstlings of your herds and flocks in the presence of the LORD your God, in the place where He will choose to establish His name, so that you may learn to revere the LORD your God forever.*
>
> *Should the distance be too great for you, should you be unable to transport them, because the place where the LORD your God has chosen to establish His name is far from you and because the LORD your God has blessed you, you may convert them into money. Wrap up the money and take it with you to the place that the LORD your God has chosen, and spend the money on anything you want—cattle, sheep, wine, or other intoxicant, or anything you may desire. And you shall feast there, in the presence of the LORD your God, and rejoice with your household.*

These few verses line by line systematically express every thought of importance to the proper designation and consumption of this tithe produce.

1. This tax is levied on all crops grown within the boundaries of the Land of Israel, at a marginal rate of 10 percent of the net yield. The analogous designation of a number of animals born in a herd (the tithe of cattle) is one subject of Tractate Bekhorot.

2. The farmer derives full benefit from the tax separated, in that he and his household may eat and drink the tax payment, thereby discharging their responsibility toward God.

3. Before eating the produce, however, farmers must transport the food to Jerusalem, God's chosen capital. In doing so, the Israelite community rededicates itself to God and God's sovereignty alone.

4. In the usual case, when 10 percent of the crop is far too much for easy transport to Jerusalem, the householder may redeem the tithe produce for cash, which itself then takes the place of the tithe: this money must be taken to Jerusalem, and its full value spent on provisions to be joyously eaten within the city.

5. As is the case with any personal transaction regarding consecrated goods, however, this transaction is subject to a 20 percent penalty: *"If anyone wishes to redeem any of his own tithes, he must add one-fifth to them"* (Lev. 27:31).

Rabbinic thought, as we shall see, embellishes and explains these rules, but hardly originates beyond arranging Scripture's otherwise clear statements.

In addition to Deuteronomy 14:22–26, one other passage is of importance in the rabbinic essay that now stands before us. Because the tithe produce is to be eaten by its owner within Jerusalem, the rabbis here include rules about another agricultural tax—fourth-year produce—subject to the same regulation. Leviticus 19:23–25 specifies that farmers must care for the Land's orchards, by harvesting them only after they are well established:

> *When you enter the Land and plant any tree for food, you shall regard its fruit as forbidden. Three years it shall be forbidden for you, not to be eaten. In the fourth year all its fruit shall be set aside for jubilation before the* LORD*; and only in the fifth year may you use its fruit—that its yield to you may be increased: I the* LORD *am your God.*

Jubilantly eating the fourth-year harvest before the LORD apparently reminded the rabbis strongly of the tithe eaten in Jerusalem. This produce too, or its redemption price, was to be consumed only in Jerusalem by the farmer and household.

Having treated these two economic measures, the rabbis take up one final portion of Scripture, Deuteronomy 26:12–19, which specifies the Confession required of each Israelite after properly disposing of the tithes designated from the crops:

> *When you have set aside in full the tenth part of your yield—in the third year, the year of the tithe—and have given it to the Levite, the stranger, the fatherless, and the widow, that they may eat their fill in your settlements, you shall declare before the* LORD *your God:*
>
> *"I have cleared out the consecrated portion from the house; and I have given it to the Levite, the stranger, the fatherless, and the widow, just as You commanded me; I have neither transgressed nor neglected any of Your commandments; I have not eaten of it while in mourning; I have not cleared out any of it while I was unclean, and I have not deposited any of it with the dead. I have obeyed the* LORD *my God; I have done just as You commanded me. Look down from Your heavenly abode, from*

> *heaven, and bless Your people Israel and the soil You have given us, a land flowing with milk and honey, as You swore to our fathers."*
>
> *The* LORD *your God commands you this day to observe these laws and rules; observe them faithfully with all your heart and soul. You have affirmed this day that the* LORD *is your God, that you will walk in His ways, that you will observe His laws and commandments and rules, and that you will obey Him. And the* LORD *has affirmed this day that you are, as He promised you, His treasured people who shall observe all His commandments, and that He will set you, in fame and renown and glory, high above all the nations that He has made; and that you shall be, as He promised, a holy people to the* LORD *your God.*

This last paragraph makes explicit the rationale for following proper tithing procedures, the thoroughgoing recognition of God's sovereignty over both the People and the Land of Israel.

The Mishnah's Tractate Maaser Sheni

The rabbis began systematic thought regarding these scriptural economic measures in the earliest extant literature of the rabbinic movement, a law code called the Mishnah,[2] edited at the end of the second century of the Common Era. The Mishnah's treatise on second tithe (also entitled Tractate Maaser Sheni)[3] systematically explained each part of the scriptural requirement to set aside this tithe for Jerusalem.

The Mishnah's principal interest in treating this topic was to assure that the entire tenth of the crop in fact would be disposed of properly, with not even a small bit wasted or handled inappropriately. Accordingly, within the Mishnah's essay entitled "Second Tithe," the rabbis specified how to handle the consecrated tithe, without loss or destruction, defining both permitted and improper means of "consuming" the tithe. In addition, the tractate legislated at some length the proper procedures should a farmer wish to redeem the tithe produce—as farmers surely would wish to do. Again, given the interest in preserving the entire tenth of the crop, the rabbis took care to assure that the exchange of sanctified produce for money, and the purchase of food to eat with that money, preserved the full value of the tithe. Market prices, bidding procedures, and the timely deposit of consecrated coins with Jerusalemite shopkeepers thus occupied an important place in the rabbis' essay.

2. See Neusner, *The Mishnah.*
3. See Haas, *Maaser Sheni.*

Early rabbinic thought on this tithing procedure, in other words, did little to expand upon Scripture. Yet in attending so carefully to the biblical command, attempting to preserve every bit of consecration inherent in the tithe, the rabbis also indicated a broader attitude toward the Land of Israel and its product. Since God was the ultimate owner of the entire Land, everything that grew upon it or was nourished by it, from crops to herds, took on a special status. God's ownership of all such produce marked it as *holy,* or consecrated (*qadosh*); at any rate, all was unavailable for immediate profane use. Israelite farmers, for their part, farmed this land as sharecroppers, and through their hard labor earned a portion of the same consecrated crops. The question that animates most of the Mishnah's laws on the farm stems directly from this dual claim: how may the Israelite take for personal use what belongs, at least in part, to God?

The answer, found first in Scripture itself, but coming to fullest expression in the Mishnah's Division of Agriculture, lay in concentrating all of God's ownership claim in a small part of the crop. By the power of verbal designation, in other words, the farmer could separate a "tithe," which would then be deemed most holy. This tithe then would belong to God alone, while the remainder of the yield would be devoid of consecration. The Israelite then would have sole possession of this portion of the food and could use it in any manner, for sale, consumption, barter, or gift. This simple exchange—a relatively small amount of utterly holy food standing in for the partially consecrated crop—underlies virtually every agricultural donation mentioned in the Bible and developed by the rabbis. The individual farmer had to effect a number of such transfers in order to remove all consecrated status from the crop, including first tithe, heave offering, second tithe, dough offering, fourth-year produce, first fruits, the many and varied poor offerings, and others. In all, this amounted to a hefty percentage of the crop, between 22 percent and 26 percent, as estimated by Richard Sarason.[4]

The Talmud of the Land of Israel's Tractate Maaser Sheni

The Mishnah's discussions—not just of the economy (the Division of Agriculture), but also of home and village life (the Divisions of Appointed Times, Women, and Damages) and of the

4. Sarason, *Tractate Demai,* p. 9.

Temple Cult (the Divisions of Holy Things and Purities)—gave rise to the greatest proportion of later rabbinic literature. In the case at hand, the Talmud of the Land of Israel, redacted some 200 years after the Mishnah, took the form of a Mishnah-commentary. Each tractate of the Talmud corresponded directly to one of the Mishnah's treatises; each passage within such a treatise led the rabbis to compose a short essay explaining, expanding, or citing materials relevant to the passage at hand.

In particular, Tractate Maaser Sheni confirmed the emphases found in the Mishnah. Central to all of its discussions was the notion that no part of the consecrated tithe should be lost, for if this were to happen, farmers would inadvertantly be stealing God's portion of the crop. In citing the Mishnah tractate paragraph by paragraph, the overwhelming majority of the Talmud's units of discourse responded in some measure to the Mishnah-passage cited, whether by explaining an obscure phrase or an underlying legal theory, or by supplying illustrative materials and stories. Tractate Maaser Sheni's principal concern, point after point, is to explain the text of the Mishnah in its own right, or to compare the portion of Mishnah under discussion with some other passage, taken from another tractate or even from another early rabbinic document. Tractate Maaser Sheni contains 134 units of discourse; of these, 71 percent engage primarily in exegesis of the passage of Mishnah at hand. The others cite and comment upon passages of the Tosefta, a late-third-century supplement to the Mishnah (25 percent of the whole), or move beyond the Mishnah's narrow confines to other, more speculative issues (4 percent of the whole). These figures nicely parallel those for other portions of the Talmud.[5]

In order to make clear Tractate Maaser Sheni's overall topics and its variety of relationships to the Mishnah, I now provide a full outline of the tractate. In its overall composition, of course, the Talmud's tractate narrowly follows that of the Mishnah. (An annotated outline of Mishnah Tractate Maaser Sheni, which forms the basis of the outline below, can be found in Haas, *Maaser Sheni, pp. 3–8*). In the Talmud's outline, therefore, I proceed passage by passage, showing both the issues and content of the Talmud's various units; in addition, in order to distinguish sections of the Talmud that complement or explain the Mishnah

5. See Brooks, *Talmud of the Land of Israel: Tractate Peah*, pp. 5, 21; see also Neusner, *The Talmud of the Land of Israel*, vol. 35, p. 51.

from those that have their own agenda, in the outline below I have used three separate typefaces: *italic* text represents units that adhere closely to the Mishnah's agenda; **boldface** represents units that primarily cite materials taken from the Tosefta or other early rabbinic literature; finally, here I have used ***boldface italics*** to represent the Talmud on its own, in passages essentially independent of the Mishnah's agenda.

I. Improper Disposition of Second Tithe (cf. M. M.S. 1:1–1:7)

A. Improper use of consecrated food (cf. M. M.S. 1:1–2)

1. Produce in the status of second tithe may not be sold, given as a pledge, or used as a counterweight, but it may be given as a gift (cf. M. M.S. 1:1).

Y. M.S. 1:1

I. **Scriptural basis of prohibition on sale of second tithe; T. M.S. 1:1**

II–III. *Judah and Meir; Yudan and Meir dispute over sale and use of second tithe in debts*

IV. **Illustration of taking second tithe as pledge; T. M.S. 1:1, 3:9–10**

V. *Questions on use of second-tithe coins as weights*

VI–VII. *Permitted "trades" and gifts; Meir's view*

2. These same rules apply to tithe of cattle (cf. M. M.S. 1:2).

Y. M.S. 1:1 (cont.)

VIII. *Scriptural and analogic bases of rules of tithe of cattle*

IX. *Use of tithe of cattle as betrothal gift*

X. *Theft of tithe of cattle*

XI. *Use of firstlings as betrothal gifts (cf. M. Qid. 2:8)*

B. Improper use of consecrated coins (cf. M. M.S. 1:2–7)

1. The farmer may not consecrate coins which are defaced,

out of circulation, or inaccessible (cf. M. M.S. 1:2 cont.).

Y. M.S. 1:1 (cont.)

XII. Dosa and Rabbis dispute: deconsecration of second tithe with poorly minted coins (M. Ed. 3:2), bathhouse tokens (T. M.S. 1:4–6

2. *The farmer may not purchase with consecrated money inedible items such as hides or jugs unless these are an intrinsic part of the food they accompany (cf. M. M.S. 1:3–4).*

Y. M.S. 1:2

I. *Scriptural basis for prohibition*

II. *Examples of packing materials*

III. *Extension of prohibition (M. Ḥul. 1:7)*

IV–V. *Origin of prohibition on purchasing domesticated animals as second tithe; dispute between Jeremiah and Zeira (M. Men. 7:5)*

3. *The farmer may not purchase edible items that are not foods, such as water or salt (cf. M. M.S. 1:5).*

Y. M.S. 1:3

I. *Inconsistency between M. M.S. 1:6 and 1:7: dispute between Ḥiyya bar Joseph and Samuel*

II. *Dispute between Aqiva and Ishmael about purchase of items that do not grow from the earth*

4. *The farmer may not purchase foods outside Jerusalem (cf. M. M.S. 1:5 cont.–1:6).*

Y. M.S. 1:3 (cont.)

III. **Prohibition on purchase of second-tithe foods outside Jerusalem: Ḥaggai + Avina, Jeremiah, and Zeira; T. M.S. 3:14 and scriptural basis**

5. The farmer may not purchase items which he cannot eat, drink, or use as a lotion (cf. M. M.S. 1:7).

Y. M.S. 1:3 (cont.)

IV. *Forbidden purchases nonetheless valid post facto*

II. Proper Disposition of Second Tithe (cf. M. M.S. 2:1–4:12)

A. Proper use of consecrated food (cf. M. M.S. 2:1–4)

1. Consecrated food must be used in its normal way (cf. M. M.S. 2:1).

Y. M.S. 2:1

I. *Scriptural basis of permission to eat, drink, and anoint with second tithe; T. Toh. 2:5, M. Shevi. 3:1, M. Shevu. 3:4, M. Yoma 8:3, Sifra Emor 6:8*

II–III. *Illustrations of extraordinary uses of second tithe required by law*

IV. **Permitted anointing: analogy with Sabbath law; T. Shab. 12:13**

2. If consecrated food and unconsecrated food are mixed together, the value of the consecrated food is determined by its proportion in the mixture (cf. M. M.S. 2:1 cont.).

Y. M.S. 2:1 (cont.)

V. *Comparison with Judah's view at M. Ter. 10:1*

VI. **Yoḥanan and Simeon b. Laqish dispute: is an increase in the second tithe's volume required or an improvement in its flavor; M. Beṣ. 5:4, T. M.S. 1:16.**

3. Simeon and sages dispute over the proper use of oil (cf. M. M.S. 2:2).

Y. M.S. 2:2

I. **Leniency regarding heave offering; T. Ter. 10:10**

4. *An appendix to the forgoing in which the Houses dispute the proper use of fenugreek and vetches (cf. M. M.S. 2:3–4).*

Y. M.S. 2:2 (cont.)

II. **Fenugreek designated as heave offering and second tithe compared; T. M.S. 2:1**

III. *Simeon b. Gamaliel: second-tithe vetches brought in and out of Jerusalem must be used for dough and brought in again; M. M.S. 3:5.*

IV. *Jonah disputes Ṭarfon's rule: not all unclean statuses are equivalent.*

B. *Proper transference of the status of second tithe to and from coins (cf. M. M.S. 2:5–9)*

1. *From coins to coins (cf. M. M.S. 2:5–9)*

a. *Consecrated and unconsecrated coins mixed together: coins randomly picked from the batch are deemed consecrated in place of the original money (cf. M. M.S. 2:5).*

Y. M.S. 2:3

I. *Mixtures of coins contrasted with mixtures of liquids*

b. *Consecrated and unconsecrated coins mixed together: the status of the consecrated coins is transferred to a fresh batch of coins (cf. M. M.S. 2:6).*

Y. M.S. 2:3 (cont.)

II. **Proper procedures for this transfer; use of gold and copper coins for silver; T. M.S. 2:5, Y. B.M. 4:5, M. Dem. 1:2, T. M.S. 2:7**

c. *Houses dispute: may the farmer exchange silver coins for gold coins (cf. M. M.S. 2:7).*

III. *Scriptural basis for Shammaite position that one may not use gold coins; M. M.S. 2:8, M. Ed. 1:9*

d. Transfer of status outside Jerusalem (cf. M. M.S. 2:8)

Y. M.S. 2:4

I. *Deconsecration of less than one* selac's *worth of second tithe*

e. Transfer of status inside Jerusalem (cf. M. M.S. 2:9)

Y. M.S. 2:4 (cont.)

II. *Identity of sages alluded to in Mishnah*

III. *Rationale for depositing second-tithe money with a shopkeeper*

2. *From coins to produce (cf. M. M.S. 2:10–3:4)*

a. Consecrated coins may be spent a little at a time (cf. M. M.S. 2:10).

Y. M.S. 2:4 (cont.)

IV. *Preventing spread of ritual impurity to second-tithe food*

b. The farmer may not purchase as second tithe produce in the status of heave offering, since this is in a consecrated status (cf. M. M.S. 3:1–2).

Y. M.S. 3:1

I. *Contrived distinction between gifts and sales*

II–IV. ***Other contrived distinctions: M. Shevi. 8:4, M. Shab. 23:1***

V–VI. *Examples of sales and gifts*

Y. M.S. 3:2

I–II. *Food with dual consecrated status: heave offering and second tithe*

III. **Food with dual consecrated status: sabbatical-year produce and second tithe; Passover sacrifices and firstlings; T. Pes. 9:20, M. Shab. 1:10–11**

IV. **The added fifth when redeeming one's own produce applies only once.**

V. Food with dual consecrated status: communion-meal offerings and second tithe

c. The status of second tithe may be transferred from one person's coins to another person's produce (cf. M. M.S. 3:3).

Y. M.S. 3:3

I. *Second-tithe produce must not be transferred to someone unscrupulous about ritual uncleanness.*

d. The status of second tithe may be transferred from a farmer's coins to his own produce (cf. M. M.S. 3:4).

3. From produce to coins (cf. M. M.S. 3:5–4:8)

a. After the produce has been in Jerusalem (cf. M. M.S. 3:5–13)

i. Produce brought into Jerusalem no longer may be sold (cf. M. M.S. 3:5).

Y. M.S. 3:3 (cont.)

II. *Second tithe brought in and out of Jerusalem must be used for dough and brought in again.*

ii. Houses' dispute: does this rule apply to produce which is unprocessed (cf. M. M.S. 3:6).

Y. M.S. 3:3 (cont.)

III–VI. **The city limits "seize" second-tithe produce brought within them; T. M.S. 2:11.**

VII. *The law accords with the opinion of Simeon b. Judah.*

VIII. *Differentiation between two types of doubtful statuses*

iii. Appendix on determining the boundaries of Jerusalem (cf. M. M.S. 3:7–8)

Y. M.S. 3:4

I. *Stringency involving buildings straddling holy and profane regions*

iv. Houses' dispute: does this rule apply to consecrated produce rendered unclean (cf. M. M.S. 3:9).

Y. M.S. 3:5

I. *Scriptural basis of prohibition on sale of second tithe brought into Jerusalem*

II–III. *Differentiation between primary and secondary sources of uncleanness*

v. The application of this rule to food purchased for use as second tithe and which becomes unclean (cf. M. M.S. 3:10–11)

Y. M.S. 3:6

I. *Scriptural basis of Judah's rule that unclean second tithe should be buried*

II. *Comparison between second-tithe animals and animals dedicated for the upkeep of the Temple; M. Tem. 7:3, Sifra Beḥukotai Parshata 4:2, M. Meil. 3:5*

vi. The purchase in Jerusalem of inedible items (cf. M. M.S. 3:12–13)

Y. M.S. 3:6

III. *Scriptural basis of allowing transport of second tithe in an unconsecrated container*

IV. **Glossed version of M. M.S. 3:12 involving the householder's explicit declaration of tithes; T. M.S. 2:18**

V–VI. *Clarification of Shammaite view that jugs containing second tithe will necessarily become consecrated*

b. Before the produce has been in Jerusalem (cf. M. M.S. 4:1–8)

i. Produce is sold at local market prices (cf. M. M.S. 4:1).

ii. Produce is sold at the lowest prevailing price (cf. M. M.S. 4:2).

Y. M.S. 4:1

I. *Leniency: if prices rise, one still sells at the lower rate.*

iii. Produce, the price of which is unknown, is auctioned (cf. M. M.S. 4:2 cont.).

Y. M.S. 4:1 (cont.)

II. **Estimates must be made as if the produce were unconsecrated, to assure full value; T. M.S. 4:11**

III. **Barter allowed within one species**

IV–V. **Stories involving undervaluing second-tithe produce; T. M.S. 3:5**

iv. An added fifth of the food's value is paid when the farmer transfers the status of second tithe to his own coins (cf. M. M.S. 4:3).

Y. M.S. 4:2

I. *Rationale for giving priority to an independent bid*

II. *Produce worth less than a* peruṭah *is exempt from the added fifth.*

III. *Contrast between second tithe and other items consecrated to the Temple, if redeemed for more than actual worth*

IV. *Rules involving added fifth and gifts represent the view of R. Meir.*

v. An appendix on how the added fifth legally may be avoided (cf. M. M.S. 4:4–5)

Y. M.S. 4:3

I. *Scriptural basis of leniency regarding second tithe: Eleazar and Yose bar Ḥanina*

II–III. *Added fifth applies only if the same person owns the second tithe and the redemption money, excluding slaves and minors; M. Giṭ. 5:5, M. Eruv. 7:6, M. B.M. 8:3*

IV. *Historical origin of rules permitting circumventing added fifth*

vi. *What if the agreed-upon selling price is different from the produce's market value (cf. M. M.S. 4:6).*

Y. M.S. 4:4

I. **Simeon b. Gamaliel's divergent ruling that excess profits from sale of second tithe remain unconsecrated; T. Arakh. 4:4**

II. *Extra profits do not require the added fifth.*

vii. *Does selling consecrated produce require an oral declaration (cf. M. M.S. 4:7).*

Y. M.S. 4:4 (cont.)

III. *Examples of explicit statements*

IV. *Oral declaration unnecessary if sale is uninterrupted.*

V–VI. **Comparison of redemption of second tithe, delivery of divorce documents, delivery of gifts, all accomplished by agents; M. Giṭ. 6:1; T. Giṭ. 4:1**

viii. *Coins are spent at the current value they have at the time of sale (cf. M. M.S. 4:8).*

Y. M.S. 4:5

I–II. *Value of an* issar *and of* $.\overline{09}$ *of an issar*

III. *This applies whether or not the coins have a doubtful status.*

IV. **One who follows the rules of second tithe is deemed trustworthy with regard to other**

tithes; T. M.S. 3:15–16, M. Bik. 3:10.

c. Produce and coins the status of which is in doubt (cf. M. M.S. 4:9–12)

i. Found coins are deemed unconsecrated unless there is specific evidence to the contrary (cf. M. M.S. 4:9).

Y. M.S. 4:6

I. *Rationale for this unconsecrated status*

ii. Found produce is deemed unconsecrated unless its container is marked in a specific way (cf. M. M.S. 4:10–11).

Y. M.S. 4:6 (cont.)

II. Examples of markings and attendant statuses; T. M.S. 5:1

iii. Found coins are deemed consecrated only if they are found in a place where consecrated coins are known to have been (cf M. M.S. 4:12).

Y. M.S. 4:6 (cont.)

III. Examples of items found in a locale in which consecrated items were stored; M. Beṣ. 1:4, T. M.S. 5:2

IV. Storage locations of second tithe revealed in a dream; T. M.S. 5:9

V. ***Dreams and their interpretations by sages***

III. Special Topics (cf. M. M.S. 5:1–15)

A. Produce of a planting's fourth year (cf. M. M.S. 5:1–5)

1. Produce of the fourth year must either be eaten in Jerusalem or sold, as is true of second tithe (cf. M. M.S. 5:1).

Y. M.S. 5:1

I. *Fourth-year vineyards and fourth-year produce contrasted*

II–V. **Explanation of field markers for first three years of growth, fourth year of growth, graveyards; T. M.S. 5:13, T. Shab. 7:15, M. Mid. 3:1, M. Dem. 3:5**

VI. **Scriptural basis for marking a graveyard; T. Sheq. 1:5**

VII. **One need not mark a field so as to protect deceivers; T. Peah 2:5, T. M.S. 5:19**

2. *Originally fourth-year produce was sold only if it grew farther than a three-day journey from Jerusalem. Nowadays, it is sold regardless of where it grows (cf. M. M.S. 5:2).*

Y. M.S. 5:2

I. **Use of extra fourth-year grapes as decorations in Jerusalem; T. M.S. 5:14**

II–III. *Definition and counter-examples of a one-day journey from Jerusalem*

IV. ***Scriptural basis that Temple's rebuilding will precede reestablishment of Davidic monarchy***

3. *Houses' dispute: Do other laws that apply to second tithe apply as well to produce of the fourth year (cf. M. M.S. 5:3).*

Y. M.S. 5:2 (cont.)

V. **Second tithe, fourth-year produce, and Sabbatical-year produce; T. M.S. 5:17, 19**

VI. *Scriptural basis of deconsecrating fourth-year produce*

VII. *Scriptural basis of added fifth for fourth-year produce*

VIII. **Does status of fourth-year produce apply to vines owned**

by gentiles; M. Ter. 3:9, T. Men. 6:20, T. Ḥal. 1:5

4. *How the price of such fruit is established in special cases (cf. M. M.S. 5:4–5)*

I. *Establishment of the price of an unharvested crop*

B. *The law of removal (cf. M. M.S. 5:6–15)*

1. *All agricultural gifts must be distributed by Passover of the fourth and seventh years or they must be destroyed (cf. M. M.S. 5:6).*

Y. M.S. 5:3

II. *Scriptural basis of removal at end of the fourth and seventh years*

III. *Scriptural basis: may tithe be given directly to priests, or only to Levites, who then designate a portion for the priests?*

2. *Houses' dispute: How is the removal carried out nowadays (cf. M. M.S. 5:7).*

Y. M.S. 5:3 (cont.)

IV. *Houses' dispute limited to cooked dishes flavored wth consecrated produce*

V. *Scriptural basis for the Houses' positions*

3. *Are crops still in the field liable to the law of removal (cf. M. M.S. 5:8)?*

Y. M.S. 5:4

I. *Scriptural basis for Aqiva's rule exempting unprocessed food*

II. **Gamaliel's letters warning of approaching season of Removal; T. Sanh. 2:6**

4. *Produce may be distributed through an oral declaration (cf. M. M.S. 5:9).*

Y. M.S. 5:4 (cont.)

III. *Analogy: may tithe be given directly to priests or poor offerings to a wealthy person who will distribute them; M. Giṭ. 1:5, 6:1; Y. Peah 4:6*

5. *The text of the confession (Deut. 26:13–15) is the subject of a midrashic interpretation, which finds in it reference to the rabbinic laws of agricultural gifts (cf. M. M.S. 5:10–14).*

Y. M.S. 5:5

I. *Confession should be made on late afternoon of last day of Passover.*

II. *Rabbi and R. Simeon dispute: are first fruits subject to removal; M. Bik. 2:2.*

III–IV. *Cases in which one may not recite the Confession*

V. *Heave offering and dough offering may not be an entire crop, but only a portion thereof; Y. Ḥal. 1:6.*

VI. *Scriptural basis that anointing with second-tithe oil is a transgression of a positive commandment*

VII–VIII. *Israel's prayers and God's blessings are in an immediate relationship.*

IX. *The status of the Levitical cities of refuge and the recitation of the Confession; M. Mak. 7:8*

6. *A catalog of five legal actions of Yoḥanan the High Priest. The first of these is his abolition of the recitation of the Confession (cf. M. M.S. 5:15).*

Y. M.S. 5:5 (cont.)

X. *Abolition of the Confession attempts to prevent Israelite perjury; M. Yev. 9:4.*

XI–XIV. *Origin of Yoḥanan the High Priest's enactments*
XV–XVI. *Some of Yoḥanan the High Priest's enactments were praiseworthy, others not.*

It should be evident that the Talmud's Tractate Maaser Sheni relies directly upon the Mishnah for its outline and basic issues (cf. material in italics). More than two-thirds of the units carry forward the inquiry begun in that earlier work of rabbinic law. Another quarter, represented by boldface in the outline, cites and comments upon the Tosefta or the Sifra, two fourth-century rabbinic treatises closely aligned with the Mishnah. So the Talmud's content is, to a very large extent, determined not by the interests of its own authors, but by the books they considered normative. In the bulk of the tractate, these thinkers and legislators rarely innovated, except within the categories laid out in the tradition they received.

The Talmud's Agenda in Context

Only a few passages in Tractate Maaser Sheni depart from the agenda of the antecedent legal tradition and take up truly talmudic issues (boldface italics). In only three places the authors of Tractate Maaser Sheni, perhaps touched off by a mere phrase or word, presented a collection of materials entirely unrelated to the overall theme of this tractate:

1. Y. M.S. 3:1.II–IV treated the theme of contrived legal distinctions, those that have no real basis in fact, but only preserve some rabbinic principle, such as ease of day-to-day living;
2. Y. M.S. 4:6.V presented a series of dream-visions and the interpretations given by famous sages. The underlying point was that whatever explanation a sage gave for a dream inevitably would come to pass;
3. Y. M.S. 5:2.IV, in what appears to be a brief anti-Christian allusion, interpreted Deut. 32:14 to mean that the Temple building would be rebuilt before Davidic rule over the people of Israel was reestablished.

The relative paucity of such materials—however interesting—returns us to the rabbis' conservatism. While the world around them went on at rapid pace, still these sages found value in returning to the classics of the tradition, explaining to new generations the wisdom of ages gone by.

Goals and Methods of Translation

In my translation of Tractate Maaser Sheni, I attempt to render into English the meaning conveyed by the Talmud's mixture of Hebrew and Aramaic. As I have explained elsewhere,[6] translating the Talmud turns out to be a twofold job: first, one must render the Talmud into clear ideas; second, one attempts to convey those ideas in English. In order to understand the Talmud, whether in English or in Aramaic, the reader first must ferret out each of the many unexpressed concerns and then call to mind the relevant bits of the Mishnah. He or she must form a mental image of the case at hand, then attempt to see how the Talmud's brief statement of the law relates to the many issues latent in the passage. The student of the Talmud must translate the terse wording of each such rule into a longer, more explicit philosophic discussion, with premises, arguments, and conclusions. In translating the Talmud into English, it is this larger, broader understanding that I attempt to place into intelligible English sentences. Whenever possible, therefore, I avoid a literalistic, word-for-word rendition in favor of capturing the larger meaning of an entire passage.

This translation is based, in the main, upon four textual witnesses: the Leiden Codex Scal. 3 of 1334; Codex Vaticanus 133; the first printed edition, Daniel Bomberg, ed., Venice, 1523–24; and the current vulgate, published in Vilna in 1922.[7] In establishing the text and meaning of any given passage, I rest upon the foundational commentaries of Moses Margoliot (PM), Elijah, Gaon of Vilna (GRA), and a preliminary draft of Tractate Maaser Sheni prepared by Peter Haas of Vanderbilt University (Haas).

My translation itself attempts to show the structure of each

6. See Brooks, *Talmud of the Land of Israel: Tractate Peah*, pp. 23–27.
7. See Bokser, "Annotated Bibliography," pp. 141–59.

passage by identifying quotations from the Mishnah, Tosefta, and other early rabbinic works by use of various typefaces. Throughout the translation that follows, quotations from Scripture and passages of the Mishnah are cited in *oblique type;* Tosefta, Sifre, and Sifra are cited in **boldface**. In addition, my own inserted explanations and expansions are contained within square brackets, so the reader may differentiate my attempts to understand the Talmud from its own words. Cross references to the Hebrew Bible and other texts are found in parentheses.

I Yerushalmi Maaser Sheni Chapter One

Y. M.S. 1:1 (M. M.S. 1:1–2)

M. M.S. 1:1

[A] *[As regards produce designated as] second tithe—*

[B] *(1) they may not sell it, (2) they may not take it as a pledge, (3) they may not give it in exchange [for other produce to be eaten as second tithe], and (4) they may not reckon weight with it.*

[C] *Even within Jerusalem, [where such produce may be eaten by its owner], a person may not say to another, "Take some of this wine and give me oil."*

[D] *[This prohibition against simple, everyday use applies] likewise to all other [consecrated] produce.*

[E] *But people may give [such produce] to one another as a gift.*[1]

M. M.S. 1:2

[A] *[As to] the tithe of cattle, [the fat and blood of which are offered in the Temple, while the meat must be eaten by the farmer in the precincts of Jerusalem, under restrictions similar to those that apply to second tithe] (see Lev. 27:32)—*

[B] *(1) they may not sell it [if the animal is] unblemished [and] live, (2) nor [may they sell it if the animal is] blemished, [whether it is] live or slaughtered, and (3) they may not give [such an animal] to a woman as a betrothal gift.*

[C] *[But as to] a firstling [i.e., an animal's first calf]—*

[D] *(1) [the priests to whom the animal is given] may sell it [if the*

1. Cf. Haas, *Maaser Sheni,* p. 15.

animal is] unblemished [and] live, (2) [they may sell it if the animal is] blemished, [whether it is] live or slaughtered, and (3) they may give [such an animal] to a woman as a betrothal gift.

[E] *They may deconsecrate [produce designated as] second tithe neither with (1) a poorly minted coin, nor with (2) a coin that is out of circulation, nor with (3) money that is not in one's possession.*[2]

[I.A] *[As regards produce designated as] second tithe—(1) they may not sell it* (M. M.S. 1:1B1):

[B] *"They may not sell it"*—[Scripture] describes it as holy: [*"All the tithes from the land, whether seed from the ground or fruit from trees, are the* LORD*'s; they are holy to the* LORD*"* (Lev. 27:30). Since sanctified produce belongs to God, the farmer has no right to sell it.]

[C] *"They do not give it as a pledge"* (M. M.S. 1:1B2)—because [Scripture] describes it as blessed: [*"Should the distance be too great for you, should you be unable to transport the (tithes) because the place where the* LORD *your God has chosen to establish His name is far from you and because the* LORD *has blessed you (with abundant crops), you may convert them to money"* (Deut. 14:24–25). Since all produce the farmer grows is a blessing directly from God, the tithes separated may not be utilized in pledging simple debts.]

[D] **How [are we to understand], *"They may not sell it?"* One person should not say to another, "Take this *maneh*'s [worth of] second-tithe [produce] and give me in exchange fifty *zuz* [one-half *maneh*] in unconsecrated [coin]"** (T. M.S. 1:1G–H).

[II.A] Who is the Tannaitic authority [behind the opinion cited in M. M.S. 1:1B1]: *"They do not sell it"?* It is Rabbi Meir.

[B] But in R. Judah's [opinion], the logical conclusion of [an argument] *a minori ad majus* would be that it is permissible to sell [second-tithe produce, together with the responsibility for transporting the food to, and eating it within, Jerusalem]: After all, one is permitted to sell [produce in the status of] heave offering, even though [consumption of such food] is prohibited to nonpriests. Since second-tithe [produce] may [be consumed] by nonpriests, should it not logically follow that one is permitted to sell [it]?

2. Cf. ibid., p. 18.

[C] [Taking R. Meir's position, one might respond as follows]: "No! For even if you rule that [produce in the status of] heave offering may be sold, that is only because it need not [be eaten in] the precinct [of Jerusalem]. But how can you rule that [produce in the status of] second tithe, which must [be eaten in] the precinct [of Jerusalem, may also be sold, and possibly transported in and out of Jerusalem]?" [The upshot is that, according to this reasoning, the farmer may not freely sell second-tithe produce, *contra* Judah above.]

[D] [The rules governing the use of] first fruits might prove [R. Judah's point that second-tithe produce may be sold, notwithstanding its consecrated status]. For [first fruits, like second tithe], must [be eaten] in the precinct [of Jerusalem], yet one is permitted to sell them. [By analogy, should it not be permitted to sell second-tithe fruit?]

[E] [Again in support of R. Meir's position that one may not sell second-tithe produce, one could respond as follows]: "No! For even if you rule that first fruits [may be sold], that is only because their [consecrated status] does not adhere[3] to coins [for which they are exchanged]. But how can you rule that [produce in the status of] second tithe, the consecrated status of which is always transferred to such coins, [may be sold]?"

[F] [The rules governing the use of produce grown during] the Sabbatical year might prove [R. Judah's point that produce in the status of second tithe may be sold]. For [the consecrated status of Sabbatical-year fruit] does adhere to coins [for which the produce is sold], yet it is permitted to sell [such food]! [Once again, it follows that produce in the status of second tithe also may be sold despite its consecrated status].

[G] Said R. Yudan, "[The case of Sabbatical-year produce proves nothing of the sort]! [Rather, we must] infer that selling produce of the Sabbatical year is [the appropriate means of] deconsecrating it. [But we may not conclude that this produce—or any other—may be sold in its consecrated status.]"

[III.A] Said R. Jeremiah, "Who is the Tannaitic authority [behind the opinion cited at M. M.S. 1:1B1]: *'They do not sell it'?* It is Rabbi Meir."

[B] But in R. Yudan's [opinion], the logical conclusion of [an argu-

3. Romm edition, 1b.

ment] *a minori ad majus* would be that it is permissible to sell [second-tithe produce, together with the responsibility for transporting the food to, and eating it within, Jerusalem]: After all, one is permitted to sell Sabbatical-year [produce], even though it is forbidden to utilize money [derived from its sale] to repay a debt. Since money [derived from the sale of] second-tithe [produce] may be used to repay a debt, should it not logically follow that one is permitted to sell it? (cf. Y. M.S. 1:1.II.A–B).

[C] Furthermore, [this must be the correct inference], because we find that people may pay debts with money [in the status of second tithe], in accord with the following, which we recite in another context on Tannaitic authority: *[Consider a case in which a purchaser bargained to redeem some second]-tithe produce for one* selaᶜ, *and took over possession [of the produce] from [the farmer]. [If the buyer] had not yet paid [the redemption price one* selaᶜ, *and the produce's market value went up and] now stands at two* selaᶜs, *[what should the buyer do]?*[4] *[He should pay (the farmer one* selaᶜ *and earn a profit of one* selaᶜ *(for he now owns produce worth double the purchase price fixed when he took possession of it). But (one-half of the produce he acquires, that is, the one* selaᶜ's *worth for which he never paid any cash whatsoever, and which therefore never actually was deconsecrated, retains the status of) second tithe, and he now owns (it and must dispose of it properly).*[5] *(Now consider a case in which a purchaser bargained to redeem some second)-tithe produce for two* selaᶜs, *and took over possession (of the produce) from (the farmer). (If the buyer) had not yet paid (the redemption price of two* selaᶜs, *and the produce's market value went down and) now stands at one* selaᶜ, *what should the buyer do)? (So as to avoid confusion regarding the status of the coins paid), he should pay (the farmer) one* selaᶜ *in unconsecrated coin (which then becomes consecrated in place of the second tithe); (he should also pay) one* selaᶜ *from his own coins (that already have the status of) second tithe. (In this way, the farmer knows that all of the coins he receives have the special status and restrictions of second tithe)]* (M. M.S. 4:6). [In the end, the buyer pays his bill with coins in the status of second tithe, as Yudan allows at B above.]

[D] Said R. Yose, "[M. M.S. 4:6, just cited], deals with a different situation [and does not show that ordinary debts may be paid

4. The remainder of the quote of M. M.S. 4:6 is supplied by the translator for clarity.

5. See Haas, *Maaser Sheni*, p. 213, n. 26

with consecrated coin]. For [in that case], even initially [the purchaser] owed [the merchant money in the status of] second tithe. [All of the produce being sold had that consecrated status. When the produce's value fell, the buyer still owed the original amount in consecrated coin. He therefore pays for the produce in unconsecrated coin, which becomes consecrated on account of the sale, and pays the rest of what he owes with other, already consecrated money. In this way, the seller merely receives what he bargained for, a full price in consecrated coin. Now, had you cited a case in which] one had an [ordinary] debt and repaid it with coins [in the status of second] tithe, [your argument] would be sound."

[E] Said R. Yudan, "Our Tannaitic teaching[6] [implicitly] rules that it is prohibited to sell [produce in the status of second tithe without at the same time transferring its status to the money used to purchase it]. For in another context we have recited on Tannaitic authority: *['One who attempts to betroth a woman by giving her produce in the status of the second tithe as her bride price, whether by mistake or on purpose, has not validly betrothed her,' the words of R. Meir]. [R. Judah says], 'If he did so on purpose, he has not validly betrothed her, but if he did so by mistake, he has validly betrothed her'* (M. Qid. 2:8). Now, if you rule that one may sell [second-tithe produce], then [by analogy you must rule that] one may effect betrothals with it. But any item that one is forbidden to sell [cannot be used as legal tender and so] is forbidden for use in effecting betrothals. [Since Meir in M. Qid. 1:8 declares that one may not use second-tithe produce to effect a betrothal, it follows likewise that one may not sell such food.]"

[F] [As further support of the notion that one may not effect a betrothal with consecrated money], have we not recited on Tannaitic authority: ***They may not buy (1) slaves, (2) real estate, (3) or unclean beasts with money [in the status of] Sabbatical-year produce. And if one did buy [items in this status], one must eat in their place [the money's value in acceptable produce]*** **(M. Shevi. 8:8). Said R. Yose, "This proves that it is prohibited to betroth a wife through [payment of] money [in the**

6. Hebrew: *matnîtîn*. The more common rendering, "our passage of the Mishnah," presupposes that "The Mishnah" already served as the title to a specific document. But see the usage below, Y. M.S. 5:3.III.B, which makes clear that the phrase sometimes refers simply to Tannaitic teaching in general. See also Albeck, *Studies*, pp. 1–3, and Bokser, "Annotated Bibliography," pp. 171–75.

status of] Sabbatical-year produce. For indeed what is the difference between acquiring a wife and acquiring a handmaid?" (Y. Shevi. 8:5).

[G] R. Yose in the name of R. Zeira; R. Yudan in the name of R. Illa: "On the strength of this argument, everyone agrees [that one may not sell produce in the status of second tithe, but may only transfer its status to coins]."

[H] R. Yose in the name of R. Aḥa, "Everyone agrees [that one may not sell second-tithe produce, but may only transfer its status to coins]. This assures that each individual remains responsible [for bringing his own second tithe] to the precinct [of Jerusalem]."

[IV.A] **What [case illustrates M. M.S. 1:1B]: *They do not take it as a pledge?* One who enters his associate's home to extract a pledge [so as to secure a loan] may not[7] take [produce that his associate has designated as] second tithe** (T. M.S. 1:1, with slight variations).

[B] It is repeated on Tannaitic authority: **They may not give it as a pledge** (T. M.S. 1:1)—[that is to say,] one may not give [a coin in the status of second tithe] to a shopkeeper [and then, bit by bit], eat its worth [in food purchased from the shop].[8]

[C] One who transgressed and took a pledge [consisting of consecrated money or produce] or one who transgressed and gave a pledge [consisting of consecrated money or produce], must comport his actions with the following: **"One who eats [food] he [previously had declared to be] second tithe [as he might eat any unconsecrated food, e.g., without bringing it to Jerusalem], whether by mistake or on purpose, should appeal to heaven [for forgiveness]," the opinion of Rabban Simeon b. Gamaliel. Rabbi says, "[One who transgresses in this way] by mistake should appeal to heaven; [but if he transgressed] on purpose, he must replace [the consecrated goods] with [food of] equal value." "And if [he misused consecrated] money, [what is the law]? [If he transgressed] by mistake, he should appeal to heaven; [but if he transgressed] on purpose, he must replace [the consecrated money] with [coins of] equal value," the opinion of Rabban Simeon b. Gamaliel. Rabbi says, "Whether [he transgressed] by mistake or on purpose, he**

7. Bomberg edition: 52c.
8. Romm edition: 2a.

must replace [the consecrated money] with [coins of equal value]" (T. M.S. 3:9–10).

[D] R. Zeriqa in the name of Ḥezekiah: "The applied law (*halākhâh*) accords with Rabbi in [the case of one who misuses consecrated] coins, [i.e., one must replace them with other money of equal value]; and [the applied law] accords with Rabban Simeon b. Gamaliel in [the case of one who misuses consecrated] produce, [i.e., one need only appeal to heaven for forgiveness]." [In support of this decision regarding the law's application], said R. Illa, "One time such a [transgression] in fact occurred with regard to the use of consecrated money, and [the rabbis] ruled in accord with Rabbi [that the transgressor had to replace the money with other coins of equal value]."

[E] [As an] alternative [to the rulings at C–D, one who transgresses by taking or giving a pledge consisting of consecrated money or produce] should comport his actions with the following: ***They may not (1) plant [a tree], (2) sink [a vine into the ground so that it emerges nearby as an independent plant], or (3) graft [one branch to another] during the year preceding the Sabbatical within thirty days of the New Year. [Since these plants would take root after the beginning of the Sabbatical year, this would constitute forbidden cultivation of the Land.] And if, [in violation of the rule], one (1) planted [a tree], (2) sank [a vine into the ground], or (3) grafted [one branch to another, within thirty days of the Sabbatical year,] one must uproot [that which was planted, sunk, or grafted, so as to rectify his transgression]*** **(M. Shevi. 2:6).**[9] **If one did not uproot [the plant as specified], what is the law regarding its produce? R. Ba and R. Illa**[10] **were holding session in Tyre. This case came before them, and R. Illa ruled that [the transgressor] must discard all the produce. Said R. Ba, "Having never been appointed to the upper chamber, [I cannot render an authoritative decision]." [Since they had but one opinion], they went out and followed [common wisdom on the matter]. R. Jonah and R. Isaac b. Ṭavlai in the name of R. Eleazar, "[Rabbinic authorities] should not innovate as regards a rabbinical ban. [The authorities cannot, therefore, force the farmer to destroy the fruit in question, since the planting was prohibited**

9. See Newman, *Sanctity of the Seventh Year,* p. 60.

10. So Y. Shevi. 2:7, which reads, "R. Illa," consistent with the next clause of the passage. Tractate Maaser Sheni reads, "R. Ami."

only by rabbinical ordinance.]" Said R. Yose, R. Isaac b. Ṭavlai in the name of R. Eleazar, "[Rabbinic authorities] should not add restrictions to the applied law [derived from Scripture]" (Y. Shevi. 2:6).

[F] R. Jacob b. Aḥa in the name of R. Zeira: "[Neither procedure (C–D or E) adequately rectifies matters]. [But the appropriate course of action may be derived] from that which is recited on Tannaitic authority: **They do not take [second tithe] as a pledge, and they do not give it as a pledge** (T. M.S. 1:1)—this proves that if one transgressed and took [consecrated produce or money] as a pledge, or transgressed and gave [consecrated produce or money] as a pledge, we impose a fine on him."

[**V**.A] *They may not reckon weight with it* (M. M.S. 1:1B4). . . .

[B] [The prohibition is against using consecrated] coins [as weights for secular purposes].

[C] [And this prohibition applies] even [if such secular use will eventually lead to proper deconsecration of the coins, as, for example, if one were to use the consecrated coins to weigh] an unconsecrated *selaᶜ* [that one intends to] consecrate as second tithe.[11]

[D] [If] one had a *selaᶜ* [in the status of] second tithe, and knows its [exact weight], what is the law as to using it [not for secular purposes, but] to weigh a second *selaᶜ* [in the status of] second tithe, so that [the exact weight of this second coin] will be known? [No answer is provided to this question.]

[E] [If two] brothers divided up [consecrated coins that had come into their possession], what is the law as to one brother weighing [his consecrated coins] against [the consecrated coins of] the other? [Again, no answer is provided.]

[**VI**.A] We recited on Tannaitic authority: *Even within Jerusalem, [where second-tithe produce may be eaten by its owner], a person may not say to another, "Take some of this wine and give me oil"* (M. M.S. 1:1C). [Similarly, of course, one may not say,] "Take some of this oil and give me wine."

[B] But one may [give second-tithe produce as a gift, by] saying to another, "Take this wine because you have none"; "Take this oil because you have none."

11. See T. M.S. 1:1; B. Shab. 22b.

[C] [And in a case in which one says,] **"Take this wine, because I have no oil"** (T. M.S. 1:2)—they wished to rule that [such exchanges are] prohibited.

[D] One finds, however, that it has been recited on Tannaitic authority [that such exchanges are] permitted! In fact, the arrangement is not prohibited under the rubric of trade, because the [first party, who gave away the wine], cannot legally force the [second party to give him oil in exchange]. Logically, therefore, the two are not engaged in the trade [of consecrated produce].

[E] [But] to what end would one say, **"Take this wine, because I have no oil?"** [Doesn't this statement imply that he does in fact wish to trade the wine illegally for consecrated goods? No! His intent rather is this]: "If I had any anointing oil, I would give you some; [since I have none, however, I give you wine]."

[VII.A] *But people may give [second-tithe produce] to one another as a gift* (M M.S. 1:1E). **This Tannaitic teaching represents the opinion of R. Meir, for R. Meir ruled that a gift is not [legally equivalent to] a sale** (Y. Maas. 2:1).[12]

[B] Said R. Yose, "It is the opinion of all that [gifts of consecrated produce are allowed, so this ruling does not exclusively represent the opinion of R. Meir]." This [universal opinion is found in] the following, which is repeated on Tannaitic authority: "One person said to another, 'What did you eat today?' If the answer comes back, 'Summer [fruits],' the [questioner] would know that he ate a firstborn [male of a cow, given to priests who either eat it themselves or sell it cheaply], for just as summer fruit is sold cheaply, so too firstlings are sold cheaply. If the answer comes back, 'Manna,' the [questioner] would know that he ate second-tithe [produce], for just as manna was given as a gift [by God], so too second tithe may be given as a gift."[13]

[C] They [further] rejected [the original attribution of this ruling to R. Meir (A), as follows]: "Everyone agrees that [an animal designated as] tithe of cattle may not be sold, and yet you must agree that it may be given away (cf. M. Bekh. 5:1). Similarly, [even though second tithe may not be sold, everyone agrees that it] may be given away."

[D] R. Mana did not accede [to this attribution to the entire rabbinic

12. See B. Bekh. 52b.
13. So PM.

consistory]. [In his opinion], rather, [the ruling represents the view of] R. Judah, for R. Judah[14] declared, "[Second-tithe produce] is [the farmer's personal] property, [to be disposed of freely]."

[E] They rejected [this exclusive attribution to R. Judah, as follows]: "Everyone agrees that [an animal designated as] tithe of cattle is not [the farmer's personal] property, and yet you must agree that it may be given away (cf. M. Bekh. 5:1). Similarly, [even though second-tithe produce is not the farmer's personal property, everyone agrees that it] may be given away."

[VIII.A] [The[15] various cases explicitly mentioned at M. M.S. 1:2B imply that if] one slaughters [an unblemished animal in the status of tithe of cattle, its meat] is permitted for sale! [On the analogy of second-tithe produce, however, this should be forbidden.]

[B] The Tannaitic authorities of R. Yannai's circle [recited]: "It makes no difference whether [the consecrated animal] is live or slaughtered, unblemished or blemished, [in all events, tithe of cattle may never be sold]."

[C] To what end, then, do we formulate [M. M.S. 1:1B1's rule as, *"They may not sell (the tithe of cattle if the animal is) unblemished (and)] live,"* without including "slaughtered"? [The implied distinction is not substantive, but only a formal parallel with the law governing firstlings], which is recited immediately after the law in question: *[But as to] a firstling—(1) [the priests to whom the animal is given] may sell it [if the animal is] unblemished [and] live; (2) and [they may sell it if the animal is] blemished, [whether it is] live or slaughtered* (M. M.S. 1:2C–D). [The distinction between a live and a slaughtered animal, while operative in connection with firstlings, nonetheless plays no part in the laws governing the tithe of cattle, which under no circumstances may be sold.]

[D] R. Abba b. Jacob in the name of R. Yoḥanan[16] [offered further proof that the tithe of cattle must not be sold]: "It is stated in the current legal context, *'[All tithes of the herd or flock—of all that passes under the shepherd's staff, every tenth one—shall be holy to the Lord]; . . . it cannot be redeemed'* (Lev. 27:32–33),

14. See B. Qid. 52b.
15. In the Bomberg edition, this passage is numbered Y. M.S. 1:2.
16. See B. Bekh. 32a.

and it is stated in the context of items dedicated for use by the priesthood, *'Nothing [that he has proscribed for the LORD] may be sold or redeemed'* (Lev. 27:28). Just as 'it cannot be redeemed' stated in the context of dedicated items precludes both the sale and the redemption of the item, so too the phrase *'it cannot be redeemed'* used in the current legal context [of the tithe of cattle] precludes both their sale and redemption."

[E] R. Jacob the Southerner argued before R. Yose, "[The distinction between the laws governing sale of firstlings and the tithe of cattle in fact emerges from Scripture itself]. [For] nowhere is it written [in Scripture] concerning firstlings, 'You shall not redeem a blemished animal'; [since firstlings therefore may be sold in some cases, we may rightly infer that they may be sold in all cases]. [But in the laws governing] the tithe of cattle, the Torah does not distinguish whatsoever between those that are live or slaughtered, those that are unblemished or blemished." [Since the sale of the tithe of animals is prohibited in a general manner, then, we rightly assume that such sale is prohibited in all cases.]

[IX.A] *They may not give [an animal designated as the tithe of cattle] to a woman as a betrothal gift* (M. 1:2C).[17] But [since it is the meat of the animal that is consecrated], they may give its sinews, bones, horns,[18] and hoofs.

[B] Said R. Eleazar, "[In betrothing a woman, people may give the nonmeat portion of the tithe of cattle] because it is written [in Scripture that all tithes are] a blessing (cf. Deut. 14:22–26), [hence the nonedible portions may be used in any way to benefit the farmer]."

[C] [R. Eleazar's statement may be rejected as involving a direct contradiction of the Tannaitic ruling at hand. For on the basis of Deut. 14:22–26, which makes no distinction between the edible and nonedible parts of all tithes], the [farmer] may use even its meat [as a betrothal gift]! [Yet since this would be in clear violation of M. M.S. 1:2C, the proper ruling must be that one cannot give any part of the tithe of cattle—edible or nonedible—as a betrothal gift.]

17. Romm edition: 3a.

18. So Codex Vaticanus, the Romm edition, and the parallel at E (Hebrew: *qarnāv*); the Leiden Codex and Bomberg editions read "its entrails" (*qirvāv*), an apparent scribal error.

[D] [Further proof that no part of the tithe of cattle may be used as a betrothal gift is available from the following]: Said R. Yose, "The [sages] derived [the laws governing] tithes exclusively from [the laws governing] items dedicated for use by the priesthood: just as people may not use an item dedicated for use by the priesthood as a betrothal gift, so too they may not use any consecrated item as a betrothal gift."

[E] On this basis, [with regard to the tithe of cattle], people surely may not give its sinews, bones, horns, or hoofs as betrothal gifts.

[F] [To reject this overly stringent ruling, therefore], there is a need for the ruling of R. Eleazar: [People may give the nonmeat portion of the tithe of cattle] because it is written [in Scripture that all tithes are] a blessing.

[G] [Proof that one may in fact use the nonedible parts as betrothal gifts is found in the following unanswered question:][19] R. Yudan inquired: "A man said to a woman, 'Lead that [animal designated as] tithe of cattle over to me, and be betrothed to me thereby, after is has been [properly] slaughtered.' Given that he can slaughter it [whenever he desires], does the betrothal take effect immediately or only after the slaughter?" [Clearly, after the slaughter he intends to give her the leftover pieces—the hide and sinews and the like. The only question is when that gift takes legal effect. Although the issue goes unresolved, the Talmud has made its desired point, in support of R. Eleazar.]

[**X**.A] R. Zeira in the name of R. Ba bar Memel: "[In the case of] a person who steals [an animal designated as] tithe of cattle from another—if the animal is live, we require him to return it; but if [the thief slaughtered and] ate [part of the animal], that which he has eaten has been eaten!" [The thief cannot be required to pay for the loss suffered, for this would amount to a sale of consecrated goods, clearly prohibited by M. M.S. 1:2A–B.]

[B] R. Eleazar in the name of R. Mana: "[In all cases], do we not require the thief to pay the loss? Or, do we not require him to pay if [the loss] was less than a *peruṭah*?" [The question is whether ordinary rules governing thefts apply—in which case

19. So RiDVaZ. PM disagrees, seeing this as a separate unit demonstrating the distinction between live and slaughtered animals. Since the legal conundrum never is settled, however, it seems more likely to me that the point of including the ruling is its simple statement that one may use parts of an animal designated as the tithe of cattle as a betrothal gift.

losses less than a *peruṭah* in value are unrecoverable—or whether any loss, however large, is unrecoverable, lest the thief in effect purchase the consecrated flesh.]

[C] Said R. Ḥinena: "[The ordinary rules governing thefts apply]. [The thief repays nothing] only in cases in which [the animal] was worth less than a *peruṭah* at the time of the theft; but if it was worth more than a *peruṭah* at the time of the theft, we require him to pay [its value to the owner]."

[**XI.**A] *[(As to) a firstling—(1) (the priests to whom the animal is given) may sell it (if the animal is) unblemished (and) live, (2) and (they may sell it if the animal is) blemished, (whether it is) live or slaughtered, but (3) they may not give (such an animal) to a woman as a betrothal gift* (M. M.S. 1:2C–D).][20] R. Judah b. Pazzi in the name of R. Joshua b. Levi: "[If a priest wishes to use a firstling as a betrothal gift], it must be alive, not slaughtered; [at the moment of slaughter, a portion of the animal must be offered on the altar, and the priest therefore may not indiscriminately dispose of the animal]."

[B] In another context,[21] we repeat on Tannaitic authority: *[A priest] who uses his share [of the priestly gifts] as a betrothal gift, whether they were Most Holy Things or Lesser Holy Things—[the woman] is not betrothed.*[22] *[(But if the priest used) second-tithe produce (as his betrothal gift, what is the law)? "Whether by mistake or on purpose—he has not effected a betrothal," the opinion of R. Meir. R. Judah says, "If he so used (second-tithe produce) by mistake, he has not effected a betrothal; if he did so on purpose, he has effected a betrothal." (If the priest used) a consecrated item (as his betrothal gift, what would be the law)? "If he so used (a consecrated item) on purpose, he has effected a betrothal; if he did so by mistake, he has not effected a betrothal," the opinion of R. Meir. R. Judah says, "Whether by mistake or on purpose—he has not (effected a betrothal)"]* (M. Qid. 2:8).

[C] Said R. Judah b. Pazzi: "R. Judah derived the rules governing all consecrated items from those governing firstlings: just as first-

20. This quote of the Mishnah is added by the translator for clarity.

21. The remainder of this unit appears also at Y. Qid. 7:7. See also B. B.Q. 12b and B. Qid. 52b.

22. The remainder of the quote from the Mishnah is added by the translator for clarity.

lings may be given as a betrothal gift, so too any consecrated item may be given as a betrothal gift. R. Meir derived the rules governing all consecrated items from those governing the tithe of cattle: just as the tithe of cattle may not be given as a betrothal gift, neither may any consecrated items be given as betrothal gifts."

[D] R. Judah b. Pazzi thus had contradicted himself! In the context [of his comment upon M. Qid. 2:8 (cf. C above)], he rules [that one may use a firstling as a betrothal gift], whether the firstling is alive or slaughtered; and in the other context [of his comment on M. M.S. 1:2 (cf. A above)] he rules [that one may do so only] if it is live, but not after it is slaughtered.

[E] [The two statements in fact are not contradictory.] In the one context he gives his own opinion, while in the other context he speaks in the name of R. Joshua b. Levi. [Accordingly, Judah b. Pazzi himself believes that firstlings may be used as betrothal gifts in any case, while it is actually Joshua b. Levi who rules that they may not be freely used after they have been slaughtered.]

[F] [In fact, there is no contradiction] even if you say that in both contexts [R. Judah b. Pazzi] gives his own opinion! [For Judah b. Pazzi's comments on M. Qid. 2:8 must be understood within the limits set there, particularly the priest's using *his own share* of the consecrated items; when he ruled that "a firstling may be given as a betrothal gift" (cf. C above), then, he referred only to] a live [firstling, and] one may give a betrothal gift from only those parts that will become his after the slaughter, [such as the hide, sinews, hooves, and bones]. [This in fact is the same distinction Judah b. Pazzi makes in his comment upon M. M.S. 1:2 (cf A above).][23]

[G] [Returning now to the notion that one statement represents Judah b. Pazzi's opinion, the other that of Joshua b. Levi, the Talmud asks:] What is the [scriptural] reasoning behind R. Joshua b. Levi's [opinion that a slaughtered firstling may not be used as a betrothal gift]? [Scripture states:] *"But the meat [of the firstling] shall be yours: it shall be yours like the breast of the elevation offering"* (Num. 18:18). [The breast of the elevation offering is burned on the altar and is to be eaten only by priests. Based

23. Romm edition: 3b.

on Scripture's comparison, Joshua therefore argues that the meat of a firstling, once slaughtered, is forbidden to nonpriests, including a prospective bride.]

[H] And what is the [scriptural] reasoning behind R. Judah b. Pazzi's[24] [opinion]? [Num. 18:18 utilizes the phrase] *"shall be yours"* [twice, the repetition serving to indicate that the meat of the firstling belongs fully to the priest, who therefore may use it for whatever purpose he wants], even after the slaughter.

[I] How does R. Joshua b. Levy explain [the repetition of] *"shall be yours"*? The repetition alludes to a different *"shall be yours,"* [namely, that the meat *"shall be"* available *"to you"* two times, that is], over [a period of] two days and [an intervening] night [as is the case for communion-meal sacrifices; cf. Lev. 7:17–18].

[**XII**.A] The Tannaitic teaching at hand, [*"They may not deconsecrate (produce designated as) second tithe with a poorly minted coin"*] (M. M.S. 1:2F), does not accord with the opinion of R. Dosa.[25] For it has been repeated on Tannaitic authority: *"They may deconsecrate [produce designated as] second tithe with a poorly minted coin," the opinion of R. Dosa. But the sages prohibit [such use of poorly minted coins]*[26] (M. Ed. 3:2; cf. T. M.S. 1:4).

[B] What [scriptural verse provides a] rationale for R. Dosa? *"[Should the distance be too great for you, should you be unable to transport (the consecrated produce), because the place where the LORD your God has chosen to establish His name is far from you and because the LORD your God has blessed you, you may convert (the produce) to money]; wrap up the money (*ve-ṣartā ha-kesef*) [and take it with you]"* (Deut. 14:24–25). [This implies that the second-tithe produce may be deconsecrated with] any coin that may be wrapped (*niṣrar*) separately from other [unconsecrated coins].

[C] What [scriptural verse provides a] rationale for the rabbis? *"Wrap up the money,"* (ve-ṣartā ha-kesef) (Deut. 14:25)—this implies that the second-tithe produce may be deconsecrated with

24. The Romm edition here has a variation on the name: R. Yudan b. Pazzi.

25. So the Romm edition, consistent with the quote from M. Ed. 3:2. Other versions read "Yose."

26. M. Ed. 3:2 reads, "But sages rule, 'They may not deconsecrate [such produce].'"

any coin[27] that bears a stamping (*yesh lô ṣôreh*), and because of that stamping circulates [as legal tender].

[D] R. Yose in the name of R. Yoḥanan: "The opinion of R. Dosa [thus implies that] people may deconsecrate [second]-tithe [produce] with [something that is not a coin at all, namely,] a *litra*-weight made of silver (*lîṭrāʾ shel kesef*), [for this too may readily be wrapped separately from other bits of precious metal]."

[E] [Why does R. Yose, quoting R. Yoḥanan, refer to a "*litra*-weight made of silver"?] If he had specified only "*litra*-weight,"[28] we might reason that [Scripture's command to "wrap up the money"] implies [that one may use any precious metal, including] gold. And if he had said only "silver," we might[29] reason that it thus excludes the use of scraps of metal from pans or kettles. [Thus in formulating Dosa's position, one has to state that only] a "*litra*-weight made of silver" [may be used] in place of a poorly minted coin.

[F] **Everyone agrees that they may not deconsecrate [second-tithe produce] with the tokens given to attendants in the bath house** (T. M.S. 1:4 with slight variations).

[G] That which you have ruled applies in cases where the bathhouse tokens are valuable for payment of the attendant, [in which case they in fact serve as prepayment but are not equivalent to cash]. But in cases where the bathhouse tokens are valuable for payment of the entrance fee, [in which case the tokens in fact are equivalent to cash], they may be used to deconsecrate [second-tithe produce].

[H] [As regards] a damaged coin that the government accepts [as currency]—R. Yose in the name of R. Jonathan: "It is like a poorly minted coin, [which may not be used to deconsecrate second-tithe produce]" (cf. M. M.S. 1:2). R. Ḥiyya in the

27. The Talmud here lacks from the beginning of C to "deconsecrated with any coin." I follow GRA and PM in supplying the first half of C for two reasons. First, the Talmud's usual rhetorical pattern would provide a balanced inquiry into the scriptural roots of both opinions in the dispute. Second, if the latter half of C were added to the explanation of R. Dosa's opinion (B), it would appear that he required the coins used to deconsecrate the second-tithe produce to be well minted and therefore circulating regularly, so attributing to him the same position as held by the rabbis.

28. So the emedation of GRA and RiDVaZ. The Talmud itself erroneously reads "silver" in both halves of the inquiry.

29. Bomberg edition: 52d.

name of R. Jonathan: "It is like coins issued by previous rulers" (cf. T. M.S. 1:6).[30] Thus we rule, "If the old coin continues to circulate at its face value, one may deconsecrate [second-tithe produce with it]; but if it no longer [circulates], one may not deconsecrate [second-tithe produce with it]."

[I] [As regards] coins [issued by the leaders] of a revolt, such as Ben Koziva (= Bar Kokhba)—one may not use them to deconsecrate [second-tithe produce, since such coins can no longer circulate under the current authorities] (cf. T. M.S. 1:5).

[J] [In violation of the foregoing rule, a person once deconsecrated some second tithe with illegal currency and so] possessed [and could not discard] some coins that placed him in danger [as a possible revolutionary partisan]. The case came before R. Imi, who ruled, "He must throw the proceeds [of the deconsecration, i.e., the illegal coins], into the Dead Sea." [Although the transfer of consecrated status was illegal in the first place, it is de facto valid; the second-tithe coins must therefore be removed from the person forthwith, but may not be recirculated as ordinary, unconsecrated currency.]

[K] [A person once deconsecrated some second tithe with a large number of copper pieces, and so] possessed consecrated small change[31]—R. Jacob bar Zevadi in the name of R. Abbahu: "He must deconsecrate them as he would tokens valuable for entrance to a bathhouse (cf. F above). Hence when he wishes to spend them [in Jerusalem to purchase food to be eaten as second tithe], he must use them at the same value at which he [originally] deconsecrated [the second-tithe produce]."

[L] It is taught on Tannaitic authority, **"They may not deconsecrate [second-tithe produce] using coins from here[32] [i.e., the Land of Israel] in Babylonia; nor using coins from Babylonia here [i.e., in the Land of Israel] (T. M.S. 1:6).**[33] [In explanation of this ruling]: **"not using coins from here [i.e., the Land of Israel] in Babylonia"**—that is, if one is present in Babylonia [and the money remains in the Land of Israel]; **"nor using coins**

30. Romm edition: 4a.

31. See Jastrow, vol. 1, pp. 302–3, s.v. *dîsqans*.

32. So Codex Vaticanus, reading *she-kaʿan,* in accord with the glosses that follow. The Leiden Codex, and the Bomberg and Romm editions read *she-hen*.

33. GRA lacks this opening quote of T. M.S. 1:6 and simply supplies the glossed version that completes K.

from Babylonia here [i.e., in the Land of Israel]"—that is, if one is present here [in the Land of Israel, and the money remains in Babylonia].

[M] [A person] possessed some Babylonian coins in Babylonia, while he was present here [in the Land of Israel][34]—let us rule that if he can make the journey [to Babylonia], he may deconsecrate [second tithe with those coins]. But if he cannot [journey to Babylonia], he may not deconsecrate [second tithe with those coins].

[N] They approved of this ruling.[35] Said R. Avin, "For this reason, all coins [from whatever country] circulated [as legal tender] in Jerusalem."

[O] In accord with [Ps. 48:1–2], *"[The LORD is great and much acclaimed in the city of our God, His holy mountain]—fair-crested, joy of all the earth,"* may we infer that if one possesses coins [anywhere in *"all the earth,"* even in an inaccessible locale such as] **the royal hill country or a Roman camp**[36] (T. M.S. 1:6), he may use them to deconsecrate [second tithe]? [To avoid this misinterpretation], Scripture states, *"Wrap up the money in your hand"*[37] (Deut. 14:25). What is the meaning of "in your hand"? "Under your control." [The implication is that a person may deconsecrate second tithe with only money over which one has immediate control, but not with coins that are, at least for the time being, inaccessible.]

[P] [In opposition to the rule that one must have immediate control over the money], R. Jonah inquired [about the following case in which the coins are temporarily out of a person's control]: **A person's wallet fell into a cistern** (T. M.S. 1:6)—imagine there were one million [*dinars*] in it. If the person has the wherewithal to spend one-half million *dinars* to retrieve [the wallet], then the other one-half million *dinars,* which he surely will recover, is as if already in his possession, [and may be used to deconsecrate second-tithe produce]. [Contrary to Avin's ruling, by analogy, one may use coins in temporarily inaccessible locations such as the royal hill country to deconsecrate second tithe.]

34. Romm edition: 4b.

35. So PM, vocalizing *ṭîvevû kêyn,* and connecting the phrase to R. Avin's lemma.

36. See Haas, *Maaser Sheni*, p. 196, nn. 14–15, and Jastrow, vol. 2, p. 1408, s.v. *qaṣrâ*ʾ III.

37. NJPST omits "in your hand," a necessary phrase for the interpretation offered here.

Y. M.S. 1:2 (M. M.S. 1:3–4)[38]

M. M.S. 1:3

[A] *(1) [As regards] one who purchases [in Jerusalem] a domesticated animal [with money derived from the sale of second tithe] for [use as] a communion-meal sacrifice, or a wild animal for [use as] ordinary meat—[since his intention is to purchase only the meat], the hide is deemed to be unconsecrated, even if [the value of] the hide exceeds [the value of] the meat.*

[B] *(2) [As for] sealed jugs of wine [that are purchased in Jerusalem with money derived from the sale of second tithe]—in a place where [such jugs] normally are sold sealed [so that the jug simply comes along with the wine], the jar [itself] is deemed unconsecrated.*

[C] *(3) [And with regard to] nuts and almonds [that are purchased in Jerusalem with money derived from the sale of second tithe]—the shells are deemed unconsecrated.*

[D] *(4) [With regard to] mead [made from grape skins and stalks]—before it was fermented, [since it remains "water"], it may not be purchased with money [derived from the sale of second] tithe. After [the mead] has fermented, [since it now in fact is "wine"], it may be purchased with money [derived from the sale of second] tithe.*[39]

M. M.S. 1:4

[A] *(1) [As regards] one who purchases [in Jerusalem] a wild animal [with money derived from the sale of second tithe] for [use as] a communion-meal sacrifice, or a domesticated animal for [use as] ordinary meat [both of which purchases are improper]*[40]*—the hide is not to be treated as unconsecrated. [Rather, the entire animal, both flesh and hide, is accorded the status of second tithe, must be resold, and the proceeds used to buy food.]*

[B] *(2) [As for] open or sealed jugs of wine [that are purchased in Jerusalem with money derived from the sale of second tithe]—[in] a place where they normally are sold open [and the purchased wine ladled into a container belonging to the buyer], the*

38. In the Bomberg edition, this passage is numbered Y. M.S. 1:3.
39. Cf. Haas, *Maaser Sheni*, p. 23.
40. Cf. ibid., pp. 24–25.

jar [itself, if purchased along with the wine], is not to be treated as unconsecrated. [Rather, the jar has the status of second tithe, must be sold, and the proceeds used to buy food.]

[C] *(3) [And with regard to] baskets of olives or baskets of grapes [offered for sale] with their containers [and purchased with money derived from the sale of second tithe]—the value of the container is not to be treated as unconsecrated. [Again, since the buyer easily could have provided his own container, any basket he acquires together with the second tithe is accorded consecrated status, must be resold, and the proceeds used to buy food.]*[41]

[**I.**A] It has been recited on Tannaitic authority: The son of Bag Bag says, "[Support for the contention that packing items acquired together with produce to be consumed as second tithe generally remain unconsecrated may be found at Deut. 14:26]: *'Spend the [consecrated] money on anything you want—[cattle, sheep, wine, or other intoxicant, or anything you may desire].'* [The verse's reference to *'anything you may desire'* indicates that] a person may buy a cow for its hide, a sheep for its wool, or wine for its jug." [In all these cases, nonetheless, the container remains unconsecrated as a mere incidental to the sale.]

[B] Said R. Zeira, "The rule [that incidentals remain unconsecrated] applies so long as the seller is an ordinary person. But if the seller is a professional, then the case becomes one in which he sells the [food item] by itself and the [incidental] by itself." [Since professionals generally charge an added amount for hides, jugs, or wool, such a sale must be considered a transaction in its own right, with the result that the otherwise incidental items become consecrated as second tithe.]

[C] Said R. Zeira, "[Furthermore,] the Tannaitic teaching at hand states this [possible distinction between a food item and its incidentals]: *'[As for] sealed jugs of wine [that are purchased in Jerusalem with money derived from the sale of second tithe]—in a place where [such jugs] normally are sold sealed, the jar is deemed unconsecrated'* (M. M.S. 1:3B)." [The implication is that, if wine normally is sold in open jugs, so that the liquid easily may be purchased without the container, then the jug constitutes a separate sale and takes on consecrated status, as at M. M.S. 1:4B].

41. Romm edition: 5a. Cf. Haas, *Maaser Sheni*, p. 24.

[D] Said R. Mana, "[An extension can be made] on the basis of the foregoing [at B]: just as you rule that **'If the seller is a professional, then the case becomes one in which he sells the [food item] by itself and the [incidental] by itself'** (Y. M.S. 1:2.I.B), so too if the buyer is a professional, then the case becomes one in which he buys[42] the [food item] by itself and the [incidental] by itself."

[**II**.A] [In line with the general principle regarding the purchase of incidental packing material], the reed matting [wrapped around] dates and the material in which dates are packed remain unconsecrated [when the dates are purchased for consumption as second tithe]. [Such materials, used in the pressing process, are wholly incidental to the transaction, and so are not accorded the status of second tithe.]

[B] [But as for] baskets in which dates [are packed]—some Tannaim rule [that the basket itself remains] unconsecrated, and some Tannaim rule [that the basket itself becomes] consecrated [when the dates are purchased with consecrated money].

[C] Said Rav Ḥisda, "One who rules 'unconsecreated' [speaks of a case in which the dates] have been pressed [into the basket, so that the container is an integral part of the purchase]. One who rules 'consecrated' [speaks of a case in which the dates] were not pressed [directly into the basket, but only placed there for sale; clearly such a container constitutes a separate purchase and must be resold in order to purchase food]."

[**III**.A] [The present passage of Mishnah may be further extended, as found at M. Ḥul. 1:7]: *[With regard to] mead*[43] *[made from grape skins and stalks]—before it has fermented, [since it remains "water"], it may not be purchased with money [derived from the sale of second] tithe. [Furthermore], such ["dirty water"] invalidates a small immersion pool [into which more than three* logs *are poured] (cf. M. Miq. 7:2). After [the mead] has fermented, [since it now in fact is "wine"], it may be purchased with money [derived from the sale of second] tithe. [Furthermore], such ["wine"] does not invalidate an immersion pool [into which it is poured, unless it changes the appearance of the water] (cf. M. Miq. 7:2).*

42. Codex Vaticanus reads, "then the case becomes one in which he *does not* buy. . . ." Haas comments: "The logic of the argument requires that this reading be rejected."

43. See B. Ḥul. 25b.

[B] **The present Tannaitic teaching, [which claims that fermented mead in fact is a food substance (cf. M. M.S. 1:3D and the parallel at M. Ḥul. 1:7)], accords with the opinion of R. Judah. For in another context we recite on Tannaitic authority: *"[If] one who steeps [grape skins and stems in order] to make mead, adds a fixed measure of water, then finds the same measure [of liquid after the steeping]—[the liquid is] exempt [from the separation of tithes, for apparently none of the grape-skin juice is present in the mead]. But R. Judah declares the liquid subject [to the separation of tithes even if no additional juice is present, since the water is flavored by the skins and stems]"* (M. Maas. 5:6).[44] Said R. Abbahu, sometimes quoting R. Eleazar and sometimes quoting R. Yose in the name of R. Ḥanina, "This [dispute between the rabbis and Judah refers to a case in which the mead] has already fermented." Said R. Yose, "[The present Tannaitic teaching in fact represents] the opinion of all [sages, and it in fact makes no difference whether the mead has fermented or not; for there is general agreement that] one may even [utilize money derived from the sale of] second tithe to purchase salt-brine"** (Y. Maas. 5:3). [R. Yose's opinion notwithstanding, in the circumstances adduced by Abbahu at Y. Maas 5:3, only Judah's position—that the fermented mead in fact is a food substance and so subject to the separation of tithes—is consistent with the rule cited at A.]

[**IV**.A] [*(As regards) one who purchases (in Jerusalem) a wild animal (with money derived from the sale of second tithe) for (use as) a communion-meal sacrifice, or a domesticated animal for (use as) ordinary meat (both of which purchases are improper)—the hide is not to be treated as unconsecrated. (Rather, the entire animal, both flesh and hide, is accorded the status of second tithe, must be resold, and the proceeds used to buy food)* (M. M.S. 1:4A).][45] [In opposition to this rule], said R. Eleazar, "[Since his purchases are improper altogether], he in no way transfers (*qānâh*) [the consecrated status of] tithe [to the animal]. [Accordingly, neither the meat nor the hide is deemed consecrated; the money paid, however, remains in the status of second tithe and must be properly spent on food for consumption in Jerusalem.]"

[B] Said R. Yose, "Early on, we used to rule: *'One who purchases [with second-tithe funds in Jerusalem] . . . a domesticated ani-*

44. See Jaffee, *Theology of Tithing*, pp. 158–59.
45. This quote of M. M.S. 1:4A is supplied by the translator for clarity.

mal for [use as] ordinary meat' (M. M.S. 1:4A)—[given the improper nature of the sale],[46] the designation [of the animal] is switched to that of communion-meal sacrifice (*nitpas ha-shem li-shelāmîm*), even against his will. [That is, the meat would have to be offered and consumed in accord with the rules of the communion-meal sacrifice; the hide, similarly, would have to be sold and the proceeds used to buy a further communion-meal sacrifice. Later, a new version of the rule was propounded, as now is found at M. M.S. 1:4A, to the effect that the entire animal must be resold and the proceeds used to purchase second-tithe food.] But we never said anything approaching that which R. Eleazar ruled, 'He in no way transfers [the status of] second tithe [to the animal].'"

[C] R. Yose in the name of R. Yoḥanan: "[The argument about the proper status to be accorded to something incidental to the purchase of a domesticated animal may be illustrated as follows]:[47] [Consider the case of] a domesticated animal in Jerusalem, [purchased with money derived from the sale of] second tithe, [that gives birth to a firstborn calf]. [Such a calf seems subject to two mutually exclusive consecrated statuses: as a firstling, the calf should be consecrated for priestly use (Deut. 15:19–23); at the same time, on the analogy of a hide purchased together with meat as second tithe, the mother's second-tithe status should transfer to the calf. At issue is which status takes precedence.] According to R. Meir, [and following the argument advanced at M. M.S. 1:4A, the calf has the status of second tithe and so] is exempt from [the laws of] the firstling. According to R. Judah, [and following the argument advanced by R. Eleazar at A, the calf does not acquire its mother's status, and so] is subject to [the laws of] the firstling."

[D] R. Jeremiah, [representing Meir's side of the argument], inquired of R. Zeira, "If [the second-tithe animal] gives birth to a firstborn, what is the law as to the required portions being offered on the altar [in accord with the law of firstlings]? [Would we] not [reason that the status of] second tithe is accorded even to these required portions, [such that by burning them wholly on the altar] one prevents [second tithe] from being consumed [as required by its regulations]?" [The upshot is that the status of second tithe ought to take precedence in this case.]

46. Romm edition: 5b.

47. On the connection between the following material and the debated interpretation of M. M.S. 1:4, see RiDVaZ.

[E] [R. Zeira, taking up Judah's side], replied to [R. Jeremiah], "But consider [the following ruling reported by R. Yose], *'One who purchases [with second tithe funds in Jerusalem] . . . a domesticated animal for [use as] ordinary meat'* (M. M.S. 1:4A)[48]—[(given the improper nature of the sale), the designation (of the animal) is switched to that of communion-meal sacrifice, even against his will]. [Would you] not [agree that, even though the status of] second tithe ought to be accorded to the required sacrificial portions, still it does not turn out to be a case of preventing [second tithe] from being consumed [as required by its regulations]?" [If, in the case cited by Yose at B, one may offer an animal purchased with second-tithe money upon the altar, then by analogy, one ought to be able to offer a firstling born into the status of second tithe on the altar, just as Judah rules (C).]

[F] [R. Jeremiah] said to him [R. Zeira], "In [the case cited by Yose], it is on account of the [improper] act of buying [a domesticated animal for use as ordinary food] that the status of [second] tithe was taken away [and replaced by the consecrated status of communion-meal sacrifice, the only permissible use of domesticated animals in Jerusalem]. [This fact, however, has no bearing on the case currently under discussion, regarding a calf born into the status of second tithe; since such an animal already is consecrated as second tithe, the laws governing firstlings simply cannot apply.]"

[G] Said R. Yose [in support of Jeremiah], "[In the case I adduced, concerning a domesticated animal purchased with second-tithe funds], we could not have ruled as we did, [that the animal takes on the status of a communion-meal sacrifice], but for the fact that the Torah has permitted spending [second]-tithe funds only for the purposes of buying communion-meal sacrifices." [The ruling has no further consequences, just as Jeremiah stated.]

[H] What [case] illustrates [the practical difference] between [R. Jeremiah and R. Zeira]? [Consider again the situation in which a domesticated animal in Jerusalem, purchased with money derived from the sale of second tithe], and therefore consecrated as a communion-meal sacrifice, gives birth to a firstborn calf (cf. C above). One who says that the Torah has permitted spending [second]-tithe funds only for the purposes of buying communion-

48. The concluding phrase here is added by the translator for clarity on the basis of the parallel at B.

meal sacrifices will go ahead and offer [the required portions on the altar, in keeping with its status as a communion-meal sacrifice]. But one who says that, on account of the [improper] act of buying [a domesticated animal for use as ordinary food], the status of [second] tithe ought to be taken away, will not go ahead and offer [the required portion on the altar]. [Since this firstling never was 'bought,' its status as second tithe never was removed. Accordingly, the laws governing firstlings cannot take effect.][49]

[I] Said R. Yose, "We may advance all the arguments we like, but a Tannaitic teaching directly supports R. Zeira, [who says (E–F) that the purchase of a domesticated animal sets aside its status of second tithe and imposes a new status, that of a communion-meal sacrifice]: *'[(If one vows to make a thank offering on condition that)*[50] *it and the bread (which accompanies it are to be derived) from food in the status of (second) tithe, one may do so]; only one may not offer [bread made from] wheat [in the status of second] tithe, but must use money in the status of second tithe [in order to purchase the loaf]'* (M. Men. 7:5). Now the only difference between [offering bread made from] wheat [in the status of second tithe] and [using second-tithe] money [to buy the loaf] is that the act of purchase causes a foodstuff's status as [second] tithe to be taken away [and replaced by another consecrated status, in this case, that of thank offering]."

[J] Said R. Ḥinanah before R. Mana, "[Let us assume that the householder *did* in fact] offer [bread made] from wheat [in the status of second tithe]. [Now the portion of the wheat separated as] heave offering [will be given to and consumed by] a priest; the remainder, [after designation as a thank offering], belongs to its owners [and is eaten by them]. [Since all of this wheat will therefore eventually be consumed as required by the laws governing second tithe], what reasoning prohibits offering [the wheat in this manner]?"

[K] [R. Mana] said to him [R. Ḥinanah], "Imagine that the blood [of a thank offering is accidentally] spilled [on the bread that accompanies it, the bread deriving from second-tithe wheat]. Would this not render [such bread, by virtue of the sacrificial blood on it], invalid? [Given its invalid status, the bread would

49. See *Gilyonei Ephraim* for textual emendations that render the passage coherent.

50. See B. Men. 81b.

be forbidden for consumption, in obvious violation of the rules concerning second tithe. On the other hand, if such bread were *purchased* with money in the status of second tithe, this disqualification would make no difference, since the purchase would have served to remove the consecrated status of second tithe.]"

[V.A.] [M. M.S. 1:4A states: *(As regards) one who purchases (in Jerusalem) . . . a domesticated animal for (use as) ordinary meat (such a purchase having been declared improper). . . .*][51]

[B] [In explanation of this prohibition], said R. Yoḥanan, "[The purchase of a domesticated animal with second-tithe money should give that animal the consecrated status of a communion-meal sacrifice (see above, Y. M.S. 1:2IVB)]. [In extension of this rule], they prohibited [using second-tithe money in the purchase] of a blemished female animal—[which in any case would be unsuitable for the altar and therefore remain in the Israelite's pasture]—[lest the new owner breed it and profit] from its offspring; [since the offspring would inherit its mother's consecrated status, the Israelite owner is forbidden from selling it]. [The ban on purchasing the mother prevents this situation from arising altogether.] [Furthermore], they prohibited [using second-tithe money in the purchase] of a blemished male animal so as [to make males subject to the same rule as] a blemished female."

[C] They [further] say in the name of R. Yoḥanan, "The ban [on using second-tithe money to purchase female domesticated animals extends] even to unblemished animals, [as in the following]:[52] At first they ruled, 'People may [use money in the status of second tithe] in the purchase of domesticated animal for [slaughter and] use as ordinary meat.' But since this reduced [the number of sacrifices made] at the altar, [because people preferred to buy meat strictly for personal use as second tithe instead of sharing the meat with the priests if purchased as communion-meal sacrifices], they changed the ruling: 'People may not [use consecrated money] to buy [a live animal strictly for personal use as second tithe, whether they intend to purchase a domesticated animal or]

51. Romm edition: 6a. This quote from the Mishnah is added by the translator for clarity.

52. So GRA, who supplies the phrase "as in the following" (*de-*), which ties the extension of R. Yohanan's lemma to the quote that follows. The Talmud itself lacks the connection provided by the single particle *de-*.

even a wild animal or fowl [which ordinarily are unsuitable for use as communion-meal sacrifices]."[53]

[D] [The ban on using second-tithe money in the purchase of any sort of female animal] accords with [sages' opinion in] the following passage recited on Tannaitic authority: **Produce**[54] **of the Sabbatical year and produce in the status of second tithe are the same [with respect to the following rule]: "They deconsecrate it [through exchange] for**[55] **an animal or fowl, or for a beast that is blemished; this applies whether these are alive or slaughtered," the words of Rabbi Meir.**[56] **But sages say, "They referred only to a case in which they [already] are slaughtered"** (T. Shevi. 7:8).

[E] R. Jeremiah in the name of R. Samuel bar Rav Isaac: "The [sages quoted in T. Shevi. 7:8] prohibited [using consecrated money in all such purchases of live animals] lest [the buyers] breed these animals and raise entire flocks, [for this would allow an improper profit to be made from consecrated animals]."

[F] R. Zeira took issue with R. Jeremiah.[57] [R. Zeira] said to him, "R. Samuel bar Rav Isaac remains alive, yet you dress him in your own coarse garments[58] [i.e., you cloak your own opinions in his name, even though the proper explanation is already at hand]! For do we not rule in R. Yohanan's name (see C above) that even unblemished domesticated animals are under the ban [against purchase for use as second tithe, lest meat suitable for the altar be appropriated for private use]? [How can you place a completely different explanation in R. Samuel's mouth?]"

53. PM proposes an alternative in which the mention of wild animals and fowl is intended as a question—"Does the ban on purchasing animals with second-tithe money extend even to wild animals and to fowl?"—to which D forms an answer. The substance of the matter, namely, that the prohibition clearly includes *all* purchases of ordinary meat with second-tithe money, is unaffected by this alternate rhetoric.

54. See B. Suk. 40b and B. B.Q. 97b.

55. So the Tosefta's version. The Talmud here inserts, "a blemished female or any kind of wild," but lacks, "or for a beast that is blemished." The Talmud's version seems to be based on similar language at C.

56. Tosefta itself reads, "Rabbi."

57. So the Leiden Codex and Codex Vaticanus. The Bomberg and Romm editions reverse the order of the names, but this renders the debate unintelligible.

58. So Jastrow, vol. 2, p. 842, s.v. *marṭûṭ*, who follows the Bomberg edition and reads *marṭûṭêkhôn* ("your coarse garments"), not *marṭûṭêvān*, as in the Leiden Codex and the Romm edition.

[G] It may rather be that [Samuel's opinion, that we must prevent improper profits from the breeding of animals purchased with consecrated money], was voiced only with regard to sales of produce of the Sabbatical year; [accordingly, Jeremiah's quote is not intended to contradict R. Yoḥanan, but to supplement the toseftan ruling alone]. Indeed, it turns out that it was explicitly taught regarding Sabbatical-year produce.

Y. M.S. 1:3 (M. M.S. 1:5–7)[59]

M. M.S. 1:5

[A] *One who buys [with money derived from the sale of second tithe] (1) water, (2) salt, (3) unharvested produce, or (4) [perishable] produce that cannot withstand the trip to Jerusalem, has not acquired [items with the status of second] tithe. [Rather, these items retain their ordinary status, even though the money, by virtue of the transaction, becomes deconsecrated.]*[60]

[B] *[As regards] one who buys [perishable] produce [with money derived from the sale of second tithe]—(1) [if this erroneous use of the money was] unintentional, the money should be refunded to its [former] possessor [and to its former status; i.e., the money is returned to the purchaser, who now must use the cash to purchase proper food].*

[C] *(2) [But if this erroneous use of the money was] purposive—[the produce] must be brought to, and eaten in, the [holy] place [i.e., Jerusalem]. And if the Temple does not [stand], [the pieces of fruit] must be allowed to rot.*[61]

M. M.S. 1:6

[A] *[As regards] one who buys a domesticated animal [with money derived from the sale of second tithe]—(1) [if this erroneous use of the money was] unintentional, the money should be refunded to its [former] possessor [and to its former status; i.e., the money is returned to the purchaser, who now must use the cash to purchase proper food].*

59. Romm edition: 6b. In the Bomberg edition, this passage is numbered Y. M.S. 1:4.
60. See Maimonides, *Commentary*, p. 214.
61. Cf. Haas, *Maaser Sheni*, p. 29.

[B] *(2) [But if this erroneous use of the money was] purposive—[the animal] must be brought to and eaten in the [holy] place [i.e., Jerusalem]. And if the Temple does not [stand], [the animal] must be buried together with its hide.*[62]

M. M.S. 1:7

[A] *People may not purchase (1) slaves, (2) real estate, or (3) an unclean animal with money [derived from the sale of] second tithe.*

[B] *If someone purchased [one of the above, the purchase stands, but, in accord with the normal procedure for second tithe], he must eat [food worth the same value] in its place.*

[C] *People may not offer (1) sacrificial birds [required] of men [who have] a discharge (see Lev. 15:1–15), (2) sacrificial birds [required] of women [who have] a discharge, (3) sacrificial birds [required of women] after childbirth (see Lev. 12:1–8), (4) sin offerings, or (5) guilt offerings,*[63] *if these are purchased with money [derived from the sale of] second tithe.*

[D] *If someone offered [one of the above, the sacrifice is valid, but, in accord with the normal procedure for second tithe], he must eat [other food worth the same value] in its place.*

[E] *This is the general rule: [in the case of] any substance unsuitable for eating, drinking, or anointing that was [purchased] with money [derived from the sale of] second tithe—[the purchaser] must eat [food worth the same value] in its place.*[64]

[**I.**A[65]] In one context, we repeat on Tannaitic authority, "*People may not purchase (1) slaves, (2) real estate, or (3) an unclean animal with money [derived from the sale of] second tithe.*[66] *If someone purchased [one of the above, the purchase stands, but, in accord with the normal procedure for second tithe], he must eat [other food worth the same value] in its place*" (M. M.S. 1:7). Yet in another context, [immediately preceding this rule, at M. M.S. 1:6], you make a different ruling, [namely, that an unblemished

62. Cf. ibid., p. 30.

63. So the text of Mishnah itself. The Bomberg and Romm editions lack C4–5.

64. Cf. Haas, *Maaser Sheni*, p. 35.

65. See PM, who suggests reordering units I and II for greater clarity.

66. So the emedation of GRA and PM. The Talmud itself, however, reads, "Sabbatical-year produce," as if quoting M. Shevi. 8:8. This reading, however, renders the debate that follows at B–E meaningless.

animal purchased in violation of the regulations regarding second-tithe money does in fact become consecrated and itself must be transported to Jerusalem and consumed there]. [Why are these two Tannaitic teachings inconsistent?]

[B] R. Jonah says, "R. Ḥiyya bar Rav Joseph and Samuel disputed [the explanation of this inconsistency, although both agree it can be explained by showing how the divergent rulings in fact correspond to different circumstances].

[C] "One said that the one passage [M. M.S. 1:7] refers to [an out-and-out] purchase [of the slaves, real estate, or unclean animal; the buyer still must, therefore, consecrate as second tithe the appropriate value in proper food]. The other [passage, M. M.S. 1:6], refers to [a case in which the holder of the second-tithe money explicitly attempts to] deconsecrate [his money when he buys the domesticated animal; although such a transaction is prohibited, it does create a legal effect, and so the animal itself must be eaten within Jerusalem, as befits all second tithe].[67]

[D] "The other said that the one [passage, M. M.S. 1:6, in which the money paid is returned to the original holder of the second tithe for proper deconsecration, refers to a case in which] the seller remains available, [and so can be forced to help undo the misuse of the consecrated money]. The other [passage, M. M.S. 1:7, refers to a case in which] the seller has gone his way, [and so the second-tithe money paid to him cannot be retrieved; in such a case, the animal purchased must be consumed as second tithe, even though its purchase was, strictly speaking, prohibited]."

[E] We do not know [which of these rabbis] expressed which opinion. [But] based on what R. Yose said in the name of Samuel (see below, Y. M.S. 1:3. IV. A), "[Such] purchases [of slaves, real estate, or unclean animals, although prohibited], are in fact valid purchases; it seems obvious that [Samuel] was the one who ruled that the one passage [M. M.S. 1:7] refers to [an out-and-out] purchase [of the slaves, real estate, or unclean animal, while] the other [passage, M. M.S. 1:6], refers to a case in which the holder of the second-tithe money explicitly attempts to] deconsecrate [his money when he buys the domesticated animal] (see C above).

67. Romm edition: 7a.

[II.A] The current Tannaitic text (M. M.S. 1:5) accords with [the opinion of] R. Aqiva, but not that of R. Ishmael.

[B] R. Ishmael interpreted [the relevant verses of Scripture, Deut. 14:24–26, according to the well-established rule of "general-specific-general," as follows]:[68] *"[Should the distance be too great for you, . . . you may convert (the tithes) into money, . . . take it with you to the place that the* LORD *your God has chosen] and spend the money on anything you want. . . ."*—this is a general rule;[69] *". . . on cattle, sheep, wine, or other intoxicant . . ."*—these are specific instances; *". . . or anything you may desire"*—this again is a general rule. And in a case of a general rule, [followed by] specific instances, [followed again by] a general rule, you are to apply the overall regulation only to cases in the same category as the specific instances. [In the case at hand, the verse] teaches you that just as these specific instances are [items that are] products of the produce of the earth, so too I [am permitted to spend consecrated money] only on [items that are] products of the produce of the earth.

[C] R. Aqiva applied [the general-specific-general pattern as follows]: Just as these specific instances explicitly refer to foodstuffs that grow from the produce [of the land, as for example, the cattle referred to by the verse], or to that which is a complement to the produce [of the land, as for example, the wine mentioned by Scripture], so too I [apply the law] only to those foodstuffs that grow from the produce [of the land], or to that which is a complement to the produce [of the land].

[D] What illustrates the difference between these [two opinions]? In R. Aqiva's opinion, fish, locusts, morels,[70] and mushrooms may be purchased with second-tithe money, [because they are eaten as complements to the produce of the earth]. [R. Ishmael, by contrast, prohibits such purchases, because the items do not grow directly from the earth.][71]

[III.A] Said R. Ḥaggai, "[Consider the ruling that, if one attempted to deconsecrate second-tithe money outside of Jerusalem, the money

68. See B. Eruv. 27b, B. Naz. 35b, and B. B.Q. 54b.
69. Bomberg edition: 53a.
70. So Jastrow, vol. 1, p. 646, s.v. *kemêhîm*.
71. See PM for an explanation of the growth of each foodstuff mentioned here.

in fact remains consecrated and should be returned to its original holder for proper disposal (M. M.S. 1:5, as interpreted by Samuel at Y. M.S. 1:3. I.B–E)]: This Tannaitic teaching clearly implies that people may not deconsecrate money by exchanging it for produce when [they are] at a distance from the [holy] place [i.e., Jerusalem]."

[B] He told this to R. Avina, who praised him.

[C] He told this to R. Jeremiah, who rebuked him, [as follows]: "Have we not recited on Tannaitic authority, *'If [the consecrated] coins were in Jerusalem and [the unconsecrated] produce was in the provinces,*[72] *[(the farmer) may say, "These coins are hereby deconsecrated in exchange for that produce, (so long as the produce is transported to Jerusalem and eaten there)]"'* (M. M.S. 3:4)."

[D] [R. Ḥaggai responded]: "The case you cite is exceptional, in that one [of the items, namely, the money, in fact] is in the [holy] place."[73]

[E] When R. Ḥaggai departed [from his teachers], he found a teaching [to the effect that the deconsecration is valid whether] the coins and produce both are in Jerusalem or the coins and produce both are in the provinces. He said, "If R. Jeremiah knows this ruling, his rebuke of me is well founded." [Ḥaggai] then wished to reverse himself [and rule that all deconsecrations are valid de facto, no matter where the coins and produce are].[74]

[F] Said to him R. Zeira, "Do not reverse yourself, for R. Eleazar said, '[The debate between] R. Meir and our rabbis, [in which Meir rules, **"They may deconsecrate (second-tithe money outside of Jerusalem through exchange) for an animal or fowl, or for a beast that is blemished; this applies whether these are alive or slaughtered,"** and the rabbis rule, **"Only in a case in which they (already) are slaughtered"**] (see T. Shevi. 7:8, cited above at Y. M.S. 1:2.V.D)—this [debate refers only to using

72. The remainder of the quote from the Mishnah is added by the translator for clarity.

73. So the emedation of GRA and PM: "one is in place" (*she-hāyâh ʾeḥād be-māqôm*). Some support for this reading is found in Codex Vaticanus, which reads "in one place" (*be-māqôm ʾeḥād*). The Leiden Codex, Bomberg edition, and Romm edition all read "another place" (*ʾaḥar māqôm*).

74. Romm edition: 7b.

the money with a] doubtful [status as second tithe]; but [if the money in question has] certain [status as second tithe], one may not [deconsecrate it outside of Jerusalem].'"

[G] [R. Ḥaggai responded to R. Zeira]:[75] "Now on the basis of what R. Eleazar said, [the ruling I found, that deconsecration of second-tithe money in all events is valid (cf. E above)]—this must be R. Meir's ruling [as at T. Shevi. 7:8]! This proves, [by contrast, that the rabbis decisively rule that], whether [the money has] doubtful [status as second tithe] or whether [it has] certain [status as second tithe, the deconsecration must take place inside Jerusalem]." [As a consistory, therefore, the rabbis offer a precedent for Ḥaggai's opinion that second-tithe money must be deconsecrated within Jerusalem itself; just as Zeira urged, accordingly, Ḥaggai should maintain his view.]

[H] R. Zeveda was in session teaching his son [the following passage]: **"In the present era, [when the Temple no longer stands, and with regard to] a person who wishes to deconsecrate [second-tithe] coins [in exchange for] produce—'[As a consequence of his action], both the [coins] and the [produce] are consecrated,' according to the opinion of the [members of the] House of Shammai. The [members of the] House of Hillel say, '[The intention has no effect, so] the coins remain [consecrated], as they were, and the fruit remains [unconsecrated], as it was'"** (T. M.S. 3:14).

[I] R. Qrispa passed by and said to [R. Zeveda], "This Tannaitic ruling has been taught only in the case of deconsecrating produce with coins [so as to enable an easier trip to Jerusalem]. But [in the case of later] deconsecrating [those] coins with produce [in order to eat the food in Jerusalem as required of second tithe], everyone agrees [that the produce] does not take on consecrated [status, owing to the Temple's destruction]."

[J] But have we not recited [the following] Tannaitic teaching: *[(As regards) one who buys (perishable) produce (with money derived from the sale of second tithe)— . . . (if this erroneous use of the money was) purposive—(the produce) must be brought to, and eaten in, the (holy) place (i.e., Jerusalem)]. And if the Temple does not [stand], [the pieces of fruit] must be allowed to*

75. So PM.

rot (M. M.S. 1:5A, C)? [This implies that the holder of second-tithe coins may use them to consecrate foodstuffs, even after the Temple's destruction.]

[K] This [apparent contradiction] can be explained [by holding that the Mishnah's ruling applies only] when one had consecrated [the produce] while the Temple still stood, [surely a valid transaction], but [then, before he consumed the food], the Temple was destroyed. [It is only in this narrow circumstance, then, that he should allow the food to rot; in all other cases, the produce would never acquire the status of second tithe, and his coins would remain sanctified.]

[L] The son of Bibi taught, "[Scripture's own formulation allows us to differentiate the cases of redeeming second-tithe produce for coins to transport to Jerusalem—which clearly may be done only outside of Jerusalem's limits—and later deconsecrating those coins in exchange for produce—which of course should be accomplished only inside the city.] *'[Should the distance be too great for you] . . . you may convert [the tithes] into money'* (*ve-nātatâh ba-kāsef;*[76] Deut. 14:24–25)—[this implies that] you may redeem [produce for coins] only at a distance from the [holy] place; [it further implies that] you may not redeem [produce for coins] near the [holy] place. *'[Wrap up the money and take it with you to the place that the LORD your God has chosen], and spend the money'* (*ve-nātatâh ha-kesef;* Deut. 14:25–26)—[this implies that] you may deconsecrate [the coins for food to eat] near the [holy] place; [it further implies that] you may not deconsecrate [the coins for food to eat] at a distance from the [holy] place.

[IV.A] R. Yose[77] in the name of Samuel, "The purchases [of slaves, real estate, or unclean animals with consecrated coins, although prohibited by M. M.S. 1:7], are in fact valid purchases." [While the buyer does acquire ownership of the items, however, the goods themselves do not become consecrated; rather, the buyer must still procure other food and eat it as second tithe.]

76. So the emendation of PM, in accord with Scripture itself. The Talmud here reads *ve-nātatâh et-ha-kesef*, an apparent scribal confusion based on the following phrase.

77. Codex Vaticanus attributes to "R. Jonah" consistently throughout this unit.

[B] R. Yose b. Ḥanina [disputes this interpretation of M. M.S. 1:7A–B, because even though M. M.S. 1:7C states, *"People may not offer (1) sacrifical birds . . . , if these are purchased with money [derived from the sale of] second tithe,"* nonetheless, all agree that the birds] do effect atonement,[78] [and so must have acquired consecrated status de facto, even though their purchase with second-tithe money is forbidden].

[C] Said R. Hila, "[Derive the proper ruling, which supports Yose b. Ḥanina], from that which we repeat [at the conclusion of] the Tannaitic teaching, *'[This is the general rule: (in the case of) any substance unsuitable for eating, drinking, or anointing that was (purchased) with money (derived from the sale of) second tithe]—[the purchaser] must eat [food worth the same value] in its place'* (M. M.S. 1:7E), we can prove [that all such items] are indeed consecrated, [despite their purchase with second-tithe money being forbidden]. [If they did not have consecrated status, we could rectify the situation more fully through the return of the consecrated coins and the invalidation of the entire transaction.]"[79]

[D] Said R. Yose, "[Again in support of Yose b. Ḥanina], from the moment one draws [an item toward oneself], the purchase is a fully valid transaction. From that point on, [the transfer of money is to be seen] as an independent transaction. [Taking possession transfers ownership of the item; payment goes a step farther and transfers the consecrated status of the coins to the item.]"

[E] Said R. Yudan, [endorsing the distinction between acquiring and sanctifying a purchase with second-tithe money], "[After taking possession of the foodstuff, the buyer] must separately reiterate [the intention] to consecrate it." [This is] because he reasoned, "Lest he [believe] it consecrated, but it was not consecrated." [The oral declaration removes any doubt as to the householder's intention regarding the disposition of the second-tithe money, which now clearly is used to deconsecrate appropriate foodstuffs.]

78. So PM, based on Codex Vaticanus (*kî-pôrâh;* cf. the Leiden Codex, which reads *bî-pôrâh*). The Bomberg and Romm editions read *kî-pôdeh,* meaningless in context.

79. Romm edition: 8a.

2 Yerushalmi Maaser Sheni Chapter Two

Y. M.S. 2:1

M. M.S. 2:1

[A] *[Produce designated as] second tithe is permitted for eating, drinking, and anointing; for eating that which normally is suitable for eating, for drinking that which normally is suitable for drinking,*[1] *and for anointing with that which normally is suitable for anointing.*

[B] *[In illustration of the foregoing]: One must not anoint with wine or vinegar, but may anoint with oil, [since oil ordinarily may be purchased for this purpose].*

[C] *People must not add spices to oil [purchased as a foodstuff with money derived from the sale of second tithe], nor may they buy spiced oil with money [in the status of] second tithe [for use as food]. [Since spices render oil fit only for anointing, this would violate the rule of eating what is suitable for eating.] But a person may add spices to wine [in the status of second tithe, because the spices enhance the flavor of the wine and do not render it unfit for drinking].*

[D] *[If some unconsecrated] honey or spices fell*[2] *into [a container of consecrated wine] and increased [its value], the increase is [divided] proportionately [between the consecrated wine and the unconsecrated honey or spices].*

1. So Sirillo, and presupposed below at Y. M.S. 2:1.III.A. The Talmud's citation of the Mishnah lacks: *"for drinking that which normally is suitable for drinking."*

2. So the Mishnah itself. The Talmud here reads: *"If he placed [some unconsecrated] honey or spices into [a container . . .]."*

[E] *[As regards] a fish that was cooked with leeks [in the status of] second tithe and [the leeks] increased [the fish's value]—the increase is [divided] proportionately [between the consecrated leeks and the unconsecrated fish].*

[F] *[As for] dough [in the status of] second tithe that a person baked into a loaf [over wood that was not purchased with second-tithe funds]*[3] *and [the baking] increased [the bread's value]—the increase is [accounted entirely] to the [loaf designated as] second [tithe].*

[G] *This is the general rule: [in the case of] any beneficial [ingredient] whose presence [in the resulting mixture] is perceptible—any increase [in value] is [divided] proportionately [between the second tithe and the unconsecrated ingredient].*

[H] *But [in the case of] any beneficial [ingredient] whose presence [in the resulting mixture] is not perceptible—any increase [in value] is [accounted] to the second [tithe].*[4]

[**I**.A] *[Produce designated as] second tithe is permitted for eating, drinking, and anointing . . .* (M. M.S. 2:1A).

[B] It is permitted for eating because [the word] "eating" is written concerning it: [*"You shall eat*[5] *the tithes of your new grain . . . in the presence of the* LORD *your God"* (Deut. 14:23)]. And [it is permitted] for drinking, since drinking falls under the general rubric of eating.

[C] How do we know that drinking falls under the general rubric of eating?[6]

[D] (1) R. Jonah derived this from the following [verse of Scripture]: *"Therefore I say to the Israelite people: No person among you shall eat blood"* (Lev. 17:12). To what sort of case do we apply [the word "eat"]? If [we rule about eating] congealed blood, has it not been repeated on Tannaitic authority: **"Congealed blood is neither a food nor a drink"** (T. Toh. 2:5)? Rather, we must

3. So Maimonides, *Commentary*, p. 216.

4. Romm edition: 8b. Bomberg edition: 53b. Cf. Haas, *Maaser Sheni*, pp. 39–40.

5. Throughout this proof that drinking falls under the general rubric of eating, NJPST uses a variety of terms to translate the Hebrew root ʾ*ākhal:* "consume," "partake."

6. See Y. Shevu. 3:1 and Y. Yoma 8:3.

be referring to [blood in] its usual, [liquid] state, and Scripture calls [drinking such blood] "eating."

[E] But has it not been repeated on Tannaitic authority:[7] **"One who melts fat and sips it; one who scalds blood and eats [the curdled skimmings] — this one is liable"** (T. Ker. 2:20). [Since congealed blood here is referred to as "eaten," R. Jonah must be mistaken that Lev. 17:12 necessarily speaks of "eating" blood that is liquid; perhaps in that case too the blood is congealed. The upshot, at any rate, is to deny that the cited verse can prove that drinking falls under the general rubric of "eating."]

[F] How did R. Jonah deal [with this apparent contradiction? He reinterpreted T. Toh. 2:5 as follows]: **"[Congealed blood] is neither a food"**—so as to pass along food-uncleanness; **"nor a drink"**—so as to pass along drink-uncleanness. [He conceded, then, that the verse and Toseftan ruling do not prove that the word "eat" may refer to drinking liquids.]

[G] (2) R. Jonah [then] retracted and derived [that drinking is included in the general rubric of "eating"] from this [verse of Scripture]: *"Spend the [second-tithe] money on anything you want—[cattle, sheep, wine, or other intoxicant. . . . And you shall eat there, in the presence of the* L*ORD your God, and rejoice with your household]"* (Deut. 14:26). [Obviously, "eat" here is used for drinking wine and other liquor.]

[H] What case do we presuppose? If one adds wine to a cooked dish so as to impart flavor [to the food], wouldn't that flavor diminish [as the wine cooks off]? ["Eating" such a stew does not prove that drinking wine falls under the general rubric of "eating."][8]

[I] The rabbis of Caesarea say, "One must resolve [the uncertain status of wine added as a flavoring] by considering cooked dishes of rice and figs.[9] [The wine added to these dishes]—in fact any ingredient added to the food—becomes part of the food. [Contra Jonah at G–H, 'eating' these dishes in no way should be construed as including drinking the wine or liquid.]"

7. See B. Ḥul. 120a and B. Men. 21a.

8. As PM notes, the parallel passages continue: "Hence, we must deal with [a case in which the wine is in] its usual, [liquid] state, and Scripture explicitly refers [to imbibing this wine] as 'eating'."

9. So Jastrow, vol. 1, p. 33, s.v. *ʾûrzānayāʾ*; p. 252, s.v., *gamzûzînayâh*.

[J] (3) R. Yose [continuing the attempt to prove that the rubric of "eating" includes imbibing liquids], derives [the point] from this [Tannaitic teaching]: *"[A person who took] an oath not to eat, but then ate and drank, is liable for only one*[10] *[infraction]"* (M. Shevu. 3:1). [Hence, we may infer that the two acts are governed by the single rubric "eating."]

[K] The associates said [to R. Yose], "The Tannaitic teaching continues: *'[A person who took]*[11] *an oath not to eat and not to drink, but then ate and drank, is liable for two [infractions]'* (M. Shevu. 3:1). [This shows that eating and drinking are separate actions; for if drinking were already prohibited by the oath not to eat, the second oath would be meaningless, since an oath covering another oath has no legal effect. Here the person is liable for two infractions, and this can only be because both oaths are in force because they govern separate acts.]"

[L] [R. Yose responded], "These [oaths and infractions are parallel to the situation if] one has two loaves of bread and first says, 'I swear not to eat this loaf,' and then says, 'I swear not to eat this [other] loaf.' [If he ate the two loaves], would he not be liable for two [infractions, one for each separate oath]? [In the same way, the second clause cited from M. Shevu. 3:1 presupposes that the person has made two separate oaths; its conclusions therefore are irrelevant to the present inquiry, and so the proof at J stands: drinking indeed is subsumed under the rubric of 'eating.']"

[M] (4) R. Ḥanania in the name of R. Pinḥas derives [the law] from this [Tannaitic teaching]: " *'[A person who took] an oath not to eat, but then ate food that is not really edible or drinks a liquid that is not really potable, is exempt from [liability for breaking his oath]'* (M. Shevu. 3:4). [The implication is that], had he

10. So M. Shevuot itself, and the parallels at Y. Yoma 8:3, which I follow, as do GRA and RiDVaz. Tractate Maaser Sheni itself has a slightly corrupted version of J–L:

> J. R. Yose derives [the point] from this [Tannaitic teaching]: *"[A person who took] an oath not to eat, but then ate and drank, is liable for two [infractions]"* (a variation on M. Shevu. 3:1). [Each activity is thus a separate instance of "eating."]
> K. The associates said, "He is liable for only one [infraction] (again, cf. M. Shevu. 3:1). [Since drinking here constitutes no infraction, it must not fall under the rubric of 'eating'.]"
> L. Said to them R. Yose, "What they said at the end [must be compared to the following]: one has two loaves of bread. . . ."

11. See B. Shevu. 21a–23a.

drank a liquid that *was* potable, he would be liable! And did he not make his oath *not to eat?* [So 'eating' does in fact subsume drinking.]"

[N] [This conclusion] fits this Tannaitic teaching [i.e., M. Shevu. 3–4], for we stipulated [that the person took] an oath not to eat. But in the case of the rabbis [i.e., the associates of M. Shevu. 3:1, cited above at K], who stipulated [that the person took] an oath not to eat and not to drink, [this conclusion does not follow, and the proof that drinking is a form of "eating" is not in hand].

[O] (5) R. Ḥinana derived [the law] from this [Tannaitic teaching]: *"[On the Day of Atonement],*[12] *one who eats and drinks in a single act of inadvertent transgression is liable for only one [infraction of the law against eating on that day]"* (M. Yoma 8:3). [Since both acts together compromise but one infraction, it must be the case that drinking is under the general rubric of "eating."]

[P] (6) R. Abba Mari derives [the law] from this [verse of Scripture, recited upon removing tithe produce in the third year of each Sabbatical cycle]: *"[I have cleared out the consecrated portion from the house]; . . . I have not eaten of it while in mourning,"* (Deut. 26:14). [Shall we imagine that, by forswearing having "eaten of it," the farmer means, "[I did, however], drink [of it]"? [Obviously not! "Eating" clearly subsumes drinking.]

[Q] [This conclusion] fits [the case stipulated by] one who says, "[A person took] an oath not to eat, but then drank." [In this situation, clearly, drinking is deemed a form of eating.] But [in the case stipulated by] one who says, "[A person took] an oath not to drink, but then ate," [no penalty would seem to apply, because] drinking is under the general rubric of "eating," but eating is not under the general rubric of "drinking."[13]

[R] (7) [Finally], there are those who attempt to derive [that drinking is a form of "eating"] from this [verse of Scripture]: *"You may not eat, within your gates, the tithe of your grain, or of your grape juice, or of your oil"*[14] (Deut. 12:17). "Grape juice"

12. See B. Yoma 81a and B. Ker. 18b.

13. Romm edition: 9a.

14. NJPST: *"You may not eat in your settlements of the tithes of your new grain or wine or oil";* throughout this entire section, I translate more literally to reflect the Talmud's concern for the terminology used by Scripture.

refers to [drinking] wine; "oil" refers to anointing, and yet Scripture calls it "eating." [This shows first that drinking is under the general rubric of "eating," but second that anointing with oil also is subsumed under this general rubric.]

[S] [The remainder of this unit turns toward a new, but related, problem: how to establish that anointing, like drinking, is under the general rubric of "eating."] The [verse of Scripture adduced at R] is not clear [proof that anointing is subsumed under "eating"]. If you hold that it is clear [proof, you would need to reverse prevailing opinion and hold that one who anoints with second-tithe oil] outside the city walls [of Jerusalem] should be flogged. [Since such floggings are specified only for those who in fact consume the consecrated food, it follows that anointing with consecrated oil is not legally equivalent to eating it, but is a misuse of a lower status.]

[T] Said R. Yose b. Ḥanina, "[The conclusion just reached,[15] that Deut. 12:17 is not clear proof that 'eating' includes anointing, rests on a fallacious assumption that all those who consume second-tithe produce outside Jerusalem should be flogged]. [In fact], the [rabbis specify a penalty of] flogging [for one who eats consecrated produce] outside the city walls [of Jerusalem] only when ritually clean [produce in the status of] second tithe has been brought into Jerusalem [fully in accord with the law to eat it there], and then [in violation of the law] has been taken out." [Only in this case of deliberate violation does one incur flogging; hence the lack of this punishment in the case of anointing with oil does *not* mean that "eating" does not include anointing, and Deut. 12:17 remains a likely scriptural source for this ruling.]

[U] [Continuing the line of reasoning at S–T], from what [source may we show that Deut. 12:17] is not a clear [proof that anointing is under the general rubric of "eating"]? From this passage, which is repeated on Tannaitic authority:[16] **"On the Sabbath, anointing is permitted, whether or not it is for personal pleasure; on the Day of Atonement, anointing is forbidden, whether or not for personal pleasure; on the Ninth of Av and on public fasts, however, anointing for personal pleasure is prohibited, while anointing for other reasons is permitted"** (Y. Shab. 9:4). [Since eating clearly is prohibited on these last two

15. See B. Mak. 19b.
16. See Y. Yoma 8:1 and Y. Taʿan. 1:6.

fast days, we have shown a disanalogy between eating and anointing, now calling into question the strength of the scriptural basis cited above.]

[V] And furthermore, has it not been repeated on Tannaitic authority: "Anointing and drinking [consecrated liquids] are equivalent with respect to prohibitions and restitution [for wrongful use], but not with respect to the punishment [for transgressing such prohibitions]. On the Day of Atonement, [anointing and drinking consecrated liquids] are equivalent with respect to prohibitions [for wrongful use], but not with respect to the [attendant] punishment." [These differences in punishment can only stem from the fact that Deut. 12:17 explicitly forbids eating and drinking, while anointing is forbidden only on the basis of rabbinic analogy. At any rate, the point stands: Deut. 12:17 does not provide clear scriptural proof that anointing, like drinking, is under the general rubric of "eating."]

[W] [In direct opposition to this conclusion], is it not recited on Tannaitic authority: **"[Scripture states],[17] *'[No lay person shall eat of the sacred donations. . . . (The priests)] must not allow [the Israelites] to profane [the sacred donations that they set aside for the LORD, or to incur guilt requiring a penalty payment, by eating such sacred donations: for it is I the LORD who make them sacred]'* (Lev. 22:10, 15–16). [The verse's reference to 'profaning' the consecrated materials appears] to include one who anoints [with consecrated stuff] or who drinks [them]"** (Sifra Emor 6:8).

[X] Said R. Yoḥanan, "[We] have no mention of anointing here! [Since the verse does not explicitly refer to anointing, but only to profaning the consecrated materials, this passage cannot be adduced as clear scriptural proof that anointing falls under the general rubric of 'eating.']"

[Y] Said R. Abba Mari, "Now if anointing is not mentioned [in this passage], then neither is drinking! [But that is absurd], for [if Lev. 22:10–16] did not[18] [prohibit both eating and drinking, then how could the] two separate scriptural prohibitions combine [to form a single infraction]? [The conclusion is that this reference to eating and then more broadly to 'profaning' sacred

17. See B. Nid. 32b.

18. So PM; printed texts appear to contract the words *de-lōʾ kên* into *de-lekhên*.

tithes must mean to prohibit drinking, and, by extension, other misuses of the second-tithe oil, such as anointing.]"

[Z] On what clear [scriptural basis can we derive] that [one who anoints with second-tithe oil outside of Jerusalem has transgressed] the positive commandment [to consume the second tithe within the city limits]? R. Eleazar in the name of R. Simai: "[Scripture states], '*[When you have set aside in full the tenth part of your yield . . . you shall declare before the LORD your God: "I have cleared out the consecrated portion from the house; . . . I have not cleared out any of it while I was unclean], and I have not deposited any of it with the dead*'" (Deut. 26:12–14). How shall we understand this? If [the verse means only] to exclude procuring a casket or shrouds for [the deceased]—items prohibited [for purchase with consecrated funds, since they cannot be eaten] by the living—[the phrase turns out to be superfluous]. For if [utilizing second-tithe money to buy] something is prohibited to the living, then [the same purchase] surely is prohibited for the dead, [and so there must be a different meaning for the verse]! What then in fact might be permitted for the living, but prohibited for the dead? I would say: this [verse must mean] anointing [with oil in the status of second tithe]." [By extension, we know that anointing outside the city walls of Jerusalem would be a violation of the positive commandment to consume the second tithe] (cf. Y. M.S. 5:5.VI.B).

[**II**.A] How [might we illustrate the rule that *"[(Produce designated as) second tithe is permitted for eating, drinking, and anointing]; for eating that which normally is suitable for eating"* [M. M.S. 2:1A]?

[B] We do not require a person [to consume distasteful items such as the following, despite their status as second tithe]: bread that became moldy, vegetable peelings, or a cooked dish that [has decayed and] lost its [appetizing] appearance.

[C] The same rule applies if the grower wished to eat raw beets [in the status of second tithe] or a bowl of raw wheat [in the status of second tithe]: we pay no attention to him, [because the foods in question are deemed inedible in this form].

[**III**.A] How [might we illustrate the rule that][19] *"[(Produce designated as) second tithe is permitted for eating, drinking, and anoint-*

19. See Y. Shevi. 8:2.

ing . . .], for drinking that which normally is suitable for drinking" [M. M.S. 2:1A]?

[B] We do not require [a person] to drink[20] [distasteful items such as the following, despite their status as second tithe]: [preservative or medicinal] mixtures of oil and brine or of vinegar and brine,[21] or wine with heavy sediment.

[C] One who is concerned about a toothache should not swish [consecrated] vinegar [through his teeth] and then spit it out, [since this would not constitute "drinking" second tithe]. But he may wish [the vinegar through] them and swallow it, effectively soaking [his teeth in the vinegar] to whatever extent necessary, without hesitation.

[D] One who is concerned about a sore throat should not gargle with [consecrated] oil [and then spit it out, since this, too, would not constitute "drinking" the second tithe]. But he may pour a large quantity of oil into a [medicinal] mixture of oil and brine and sip it. [Since he *is* "drinking" the oil, the secondary, healing effect of the mixture is inconsequential.]

[**IV**.A] *[(Produce designated as) second tithe is permitted for eating, drinking, and anointing . . . ; for anointing with that which normally is suitable for anointing. (In illustration of the foregoing)]: One must not anoint with wine or vinegar, but may anoint with oil, [since oil ordinarily may be purchased for this purpose]* [M. M.S. 2:1A–B]—

[B] One who is concerned about [a skin irritation on] his head or who has scalp eczema may anoint [the affected parts] with [consecrated] oil, but not with wine or vinegar, [since that is not their ordinary use].

[C] Wine in the status of second tithe to which spices have been added—one is forbidden to anoint with it. Oil in the status of second tithe to which spices have been added—one is permitted to anoint with it. What is the difference between [wine and oil]? The latter [spiced oil] is characteristically used [as an unguent], but [spiced wine] is not ordinarily used for [anointing; second-

20. Romm edition: 9b.

21. So Jastrow, vol. 1, p. 84, s.v. *ʾenîgārôn,* a corruption of Greek *ἐλαιόγαρον*.

tithe produce, as M. M.S. 2:1A specifies, must be consumed in its characteristic fashion].

[D] R. Yudan inquired, "As to second-tithe oil that turned rancid—[what is its status]?" Said R. Mana, "Since it went rancid, it loses its consecrated status, [and so need not be consumed but may be discarded]." Why is it necessary [to state this obvious point]? [Mana's rule prevents a misanalogy with] Sabbatical-year [produce], for even if [such produce] spoils, it retains its consecrated status, [and so may not be freely discarded].

[E] [The remainder of this unit investigates another possible analogy, namely, that between activities permitted on the Sabbath in general, and those permitted with regard to second-tithe produce at any time.][22] Simeon bar Ba in the name of R. Ḥanina: "[On the Sabbath], one who [heals a wound by] whispering [an incantation over it] may apply oil to the head [of the patient] and then whisper [the incantation], provided that he [pours the oil directly upon the patient's head] and does not apply the oil by hand or with a swab (*kelî*); [the departure from ordinary procedure is required to prevent 'working' on the Sabbath]." [But] R. Jacob bar Idi, R. Yoḥanan in the name of R. Yannai: "He should apply [the oil to his patient's head] either by hand or with a swab."

[F] What [is the practical difference] between these [two opinions]?

[G] [One possible difference has to do with whether or not the practitioner finds the medicated oil] repulsive.[23] Those who rule that he should apply it either by hand or with a swab must also hold that [medicated oil] is repulsive; [by use of the hand or swab,

22. See Y. Shab. 14:3 for a parallel to the remainder of this unit.

23. So *Qorban HaEidah* at Y. Shab. 14:3, followed by Neusner, *Talmud of the Land of Israel: Shabbat*, p. 388. I follow this interpretation because it reflects the underlying Hebrew *me'îsâh* (see Jastrow, vol. 2, pp. 723–24, s.v. *mā'as*, "to loathe"); yet most interpreters of Tractate Maaser Sheni follow PM and derive *me'îsâh* from the verb *nāmês* (see Jastrow, vol. 2, p. 808, s.v. *mismês* II, "to press or squeeze," and p. 809, s.v. *māsas*, "to melt away"), and render: "[One possible difference has to do with whether or not the practitioner] may massage [the medicated oil]: Those who rule that he should apply it either by hand or with a swab must also hold that he may massage [the medicated oil; since the oil in fact constitutes an unguent, and not a required part of the 'healing,' rubbing it into the skin does not constitute forbidden work on the Sabbath]. But those who rule that he should pour [the oil directly on the patient's] head and then whisper [the incantation] must hold that he may not massage [such oil into the patient's skin; here the application of oil is deemed a necessary part of the 'healing,' and so cannot be allowed under the rules of avoiding 'work']."

then, the application is made differently from the work-a-day fashion]. But those who rule that he should pour [the oil directly on the patient's] head and then whisper [the incantation] must hold that [such oil] is not repulsive; [by requiring this direct application, then, one achieves the required change in normal procedure].

[H] [A second possible difference between the two opinions]: Said R. Jonah, "The practical difference is [whether or not on Sabbath the practitioner may anoint the patient's head with] second-tithe [oil]. Those who rule that he should apply [the medicated oil] either by hand or with a swab [do so in order to make the point that] second-tithe [oil] is altogether forbidden [for use in healing; since some of the oil would necessarily adhere to the practitioner's hand or to the swab, and so go to waste, the requirement makes it clear that second-tithe oil cannot be so used at all]. But those who rule that he should pour [the oil directly on the patient's] head and then whisper [the incantation, do so in order to make the point that even] second-tithe [oil] is permitted [for such use, although the practitioner must take pains to prevent any waste of the consecrated oil]."

[I] Said R. Yose, "Is it not the case that any activity that is permitted on the Sabbath is likewise permitted [at all times with regard to] second-tithe [produce]; and any activity that is prohibited on the Sabbath is likewise prohibited [at all times with regard to produce in the status of] second tithe? And is it not furthermore recited on Tannaitic authority: **A woman may sponge her child with wine [on the Sabbath] in order to reduce a fever, [through the cooling of the evaporating alcohol]** (T. Shab. 12:13). [Yet sponging with wine in the status of] heave offering is forbidden, and what holds for heave offering also holds for second tithe! [The upshot is that heave offering and—by clear implication—second-tithe oil are forbidden for use as medicinal lotions on the Sabbath; this means that the prohibition for second-tithe produce must hold true at all times, so that medicinal uses are not permitted at all, contra one opinion expressed throughout the foregoing, at E–H.]

[J] How do we account, then, [for that other opinion, that a practitioner may anoint the patient's head even on Sabbath, and so, presumably, with second-tithe oil at any time]? [This use on the Sabbath alone, with no implication for treatment of second-tithe oil whatsoever, may be acceptable] provided that he does it differently on the Sabbath than he would on a weekday.

[V.A] *[As regards]*[24] *[a fish that was cooked with leeks [in the status of] second tithe and [the leeks] increased [the fish's value]—the increase is [divided] proportionately [between the consecrated leeks and the unconsecrated fish]* (M. M.S. 2:1E).

[B] Said R. Hoshaia, "This [Tannaitic teaching cannot[25] represent the view] of R. Judah, for we have recited on Tannaitic authority: *'R. Judah permits [nonpriests to consume] pickled fish* (ṣaḥanah) *[cooked with onions in the status of heave offering], for [the onions] are used only to absorb the stench [of the fish, but not to flavor the brine]'* (M. Ter. 10:1)."[26] [M. M.S. 2:1 clearly states that, without regard to the purpose for which one adds the second-tithe leeks, the resulting mixture takes on some of their special status, and upon the sale of the cooked dish, any increase in value due to the leeks must be split proportionately; Judah, by contrast, seems to hold that the consecrated status of an ingredient passes to the main mixture only if the intention was to flavor that mixture.]

[C] The rabbis of Caesarea inquired: "[What about] this, which R. Abbahu said[27] in the name of R. Yoḥanan, 'In all cases of [mixtures potentially] forbidden [because one minor ingredient is consecrated], they assess whether a like amount of onions or leeks [would impart flavor to the mixture; if so, the dish takes on the consecrated status of the minor ingredient, even if, in fact, it imparted no taste whatsoever].' [This ruling clearly] does not accord with R. Judah, [whose rule about eliminating the odor of pickled fish seems to be idiosyncratic and to establish no precedent at law].[28] [Thus] R. Judah concedes about onions [that were dedicated as a direct gift] to the Temple; R. Judah concedes about onions [that had been grown and presumably blessed] by an idolater—[owing to the intensity of their consecration or forbidden quality—they may not be added even to absorb the odor of pickled fish]."[29]

24. See Y. Ter. 10:1.
25. So GRA, RiDVaZ, and PM, as well as the parallel found at Y. Ter. 10:1.
26. Cf. Avery-Peck, *Talmud of the Land of Israel: Tractate Terumot*, p. 448.
27. See B. Ḥul. 97b.
28. So PM.
29. Romm edition: 10a.

[VI.A] *[This is the general rule: (in the case of) any beneficial (ingredient) whose presence (in the resulting mixture) is perceptible—any increase (in value) is (divided) proportionately (between the second tithe and the unconsecrated ingredient). But (in the case of) any beneficial (ingredient) whose presence (in the resulting mixture) is not perceptible—any increase (in value) is (accounted) to the second (tithe)]* (M. M.S. 2:1G–H).[30]

[B] Said R. Yoḥanan, "[By 'perceptible,' M. M.S. 2:1 means that] whenever [an unconsecrated, minor ingredient causes] an overall increase in volume, *any increase [in value] is [divided] proportionately [between the second tithe and the unconsecrated ingredient].* But whenever [an unconsecrated, minor ingredient causes] no overall increase in volume, *any increase [in value] is [accounted] to the second [tithe].*"

[C] [Providing a different interpretation of the current Tannaitic ruling], R. Simeon b. Laqish said, "[By 'perceptible,' M. M.S. 2:1 means that] whenever [an unconsecrated, minor ingredient causes] a definitive improvement in flavor, *any increase [in value] is [divided] proportionately [between the second tithe and the unconsecrated ingredient].* But whenever [an unconsecrated, minor ingredient causes] no definitive improvement in flavor, *any increase [in value] is [accounted] to the second [tithe].*"

[D] A Tannaitic teaching itself disputes [the interpretation given by] R. Yoḥanan [above at B]: *[As for] dough [in the status of] second tithe that a person baked [over wood that was not purchased with second-tithe funds] and [the baking] increased [the bread's value]—the increase*[31] *is [accounted entirely] to the [dough designated as] second [tithe]* (M. M.S. 2:1F). [R. Yoḥanan, by contrast, would rule that the heat from the unconsecrated wood enlarged the bread's volume, and so any increase in its value should be accounted proportionately to the loaf and to the cost of fuel.]

[E] One may resolve [this apparent contradiction by endorsing R. Simeon b. Laqish's interpretation and noting] that [the cooking caused] no definitive improvement in flavor. [Following this interpretation—which therefore should be preferred to R. Yoḥanan's—the ruling makes perfect sense and the increase in value is accounted only to the second tithe.]

30. This quote of the Mishnah is added by the translator for clarity.
31. Bomberg edition: 53c.

[F] [Again], the Mishnah-passage itself disputes [the interpretation given by] R. Yoḥanan [above at B]: *[As regards] a fish that was cooked with leeks [in the status of] second tithe and [the leeks] increased [the fish's value]—the increase is [divided] proportionately [between the consecrated leeks and the unconsecrated fish].* [R. Yoḥanan, by contrast, would rule that adding the leeks as flavoring would not swell the fish itself and enlarge its volume, and so any increase in its value should be accounted to the unconsecrated fish alone.]

[G] R. Yose in the name of R. Hoshaia, "You may resolve [this apparent contradiction by assuming] that he cooked the two [ingredients until they became] one mass. [Under this assumption, the volume of the fish has in fact been enlarged by adding the leeks, and even Yoḥanan would agree that any increase in value is to be divided proportionately.]

[H] R. Jonah in the name of Rav Hoshaia inquired [about the preceding interpretation]: "Imagine one cooked [the fish] by itself and [the leeks] by themselves [in separate pots] and then [after cooking] mixed them together. Would the fish absorb anything other than the flavor of the leeks, or would the leeks absorb anything other than the flavor of the fish? [In such a case, the fish itself would not have swelled and increased in volume; the ruling that the added value be divided proportionately therefore is contrary to Yoḥanan's stated view.]"[32]

[I] [Once more], a Tannaitic teaching disputes [the interpretation given by] R. Yoḥanan [above at B]: *[On a holiday],*[33] *a woman who borrows spices, water, and salt from a friend [in order to*[34] *mix them with her own flour and make] dough—these [ingredients, all mixed together], are governed by the holiday [restrictions that apply] to both [women, and therefore may be transported only to those locations where the women are permitted to walk on the holiday]* (M. Beṣ. 5:4). [Although these borrowed items will not affect the volume of the dough, but only its flavor, this passage nonetheless rules that the entire mixture must be governed by the holiday rules that apply to the minor ingredients, still owned by the second woman; this obviously contradicts Yo-

32. Romm edition: 10b.
33. See B. Beṣ. 37b.
34. Bertinoro interpolates here: "to spice a cooked dish or"; the difference in meaning—apparently prompted by the recognition that spices are usually not added to dough, but to stews—does not affect the Talmud's overall argument.

ḥanan, who would rule that the whole—since there was no increase in volume—remains the exclusive property of the first woman.]

[J] Said R. Ba, "[The cited Tannaitic teaching has no bearing on the larger issues addressed by R. Yoḥanan, concerning mixtures of foodstuffs with two separate statuses]. [For the rabbis] established [the rules governing] holiday limits [and the transport of the dough in question only to make a point about] commercial law. [By asserting that the women in fact have simply constituted a partnership, each still 'owning' her ingredients, we assure that no purchase or sale took place, for this would be a clear violation of the holiday.]" You may confirm this [motivation on the basis of a teaching] spoken in Babylonia in the name of Rav Ḥisda—although we do not know whether it was an [Amoraic] tradition (*shemûʿaʾ*) or recited on Tannaitic authority (*matnîtāʾ*): Even [if the woman baking the bread borrowed] wood [for fuel, still the bread may be transported only to those locations permitted to both the baker and the woman who loaned her the fuel]. [This is the ruling even though] we reason that the wood [adds] nothing substantial [to the baked product; it follows that the basic issue here is different from that taken up by—and cannot contradict—Yoḥanan.]"

[K] A Tannaitic teaching disputes [the interpretation given by] R. Simeon b. Laqish [above at C]: **"A cooked dish [of produce in the status] of second tithe that was seasoned with unconsecrated spices—the increase is [accounted entirely] to the [produce with the status of] second [tithe]"** (cf. T. M.S. 1:16).[35]

[L] One may resolve [this apparent contradiction by asserting] that [the spices were insufficient and caused] no definitive improvement in flavor. [Accordingly, even on Simeon b. Laqish's view, the Toseftan rule is correct and any increase in value should be accounted to the consecrated food alone.]

35. So the Talmud's version of the Toseftan passage. T. M.S. 1:16 itself reads, **"the increase is [divided] proportionately [between the consecrated produce and the unconsecrated spices]."** As PM notes, the Tosefta's own version does not contradict Simeon b. Laqish's view; PM therefore accords it the status of a scribal error. One speculative explanation of the Tosefta's reading is that this ruling was brought into conformity with its continuation (cited by the Talmud two paragraphs later, at M), which otherwise appears contradictory.

[M] [The preceding rule sets up an apparent contradiction, for] is it not recited on Tannaitic authority [in the continuation of T. M.S. 1:16]: **"A cooked dish of unconsecrated [produce] that was seasoned with spices [in the status of] second tithe—its second-tithe [ingredients] remain consecrated and so] are not released from the requirement of redemption"** (T. M.S. 1:16)? [Here, as above at K, we ought to assume that the spices will entirely dissolve in the cooking broth, losing their separate identities and consecrated status; nonetheless, they retain their status as second tithe, in apparent contradiction to the foregoing Toseftan quote.]

[N] [The second half of T. M.S. 1:16 does not contradict the first, but addresses a different circumstance, as follows]: According to R. Yoḥanan [the second Toseftan ruling addresses a situation in which] there is an increase in the volume of the dish; [hence, the minor, consecrated ingredients retain their status as contributors to the cooked food]. According to R. Simeon b. Laqish, [the second Toseftan ruling addresses a situation in which] the [spices cause] a definitive improvement in flavor, [so that, once again, the minor, consecrated ingredients do in fact contribute to the overall dish].

Y. M.S. 2:2 (M. M.S. 2:2–4)

M. M.S. 2:2

[A] *R. Simeon says, "People in Jerusalem may not anoint [one another] with oil designated as second tithe, [lest some of the oil remain on one's friend's hands and benefit the friend, in violation of the rule that each farmer must use all of his second tithe personally]."* [36]

36. So Maimonides, *Commentary*, p. 216: "R. Simeon does not dispute M. M.S. 2:1's ruling that second tithe may be utilized as an ointment, as a person who does not understand R. Simeon or this dispute might think. . . . Rather, R. Simeon's opinion is as I shall explain: he rules that it is forbidden for a person to ask an acquaintance in Jerusalem—to which place one must bring second tithe—to massage him with oil in the status of second tithe. This is forbidden because the hand of the masseur who anoints him itself becomes anointed, and it might appear that this anointing is a payment for the massage. That would be forbidden in the same vein as paying one's associate with money in the status of second tithe."

[B] *But the sages permit [them to anoint with oil declared second tithe].*

[C] *The [sages] said to R. Simeon, "It is a fact that we rule leniently in [the case of anointing with oil in the status of] heave offering (see T. Ter. 10:10), [even though heave offering in general] is [subject to] stringent [rules]. Shouldn't we therefore also rule leniently in [the case of anointing with oil in the status of] second tithe, which [in general] is [subject to] lenient [rules]?"*

[D] *[R. Simeon] said to them, "Granted that we rule leniently in the case of anointing with [oil in the status of] heave offering, which in general is subject to] strict [rules, but we do so because heave offering] is subject to leniency in the case of vetches and fenugreek (see M. Ter. 8:8–12, 10:5–6). But must we really be lenient in the case of anointing with [oil in the status of] second tithe, [which although generally subject to] lenient [rules, nonetheless is] subject to strict rules in the case of vetches and fenugreek [as exemplified by the next two passages of Mishnah]?"* [37]

M. M.S. 2:3

[A] *Fenugreek that [has the status of] second tithe must be [picked and] eaten [when] sprouting, [while it is suitable for human consumption, but may not be allowed to dry on the vine for animal fodder].* [38]

[B] *As for [fenugreek that was separated as] heave offering—*

[C] *The [members of the] House of Shammai say, "Anything done with it must be [completed] in [a state] of cleanness, [lest the heave offering become unclean, requiring that it be destroyed instead of consumed (see M. Ter. 8:8–12, 10:5–6)]. [The rule that fenugreek must be dealt with only in a state of cleanness applies in all cases] except using it as shampoo. [Since in this case the fenugreek already has dried up and so no longer is useful as food, one need not scruple about its state of cleanness.]"*

[D] *But the [members of the] House of Hillel say, "Anything done with it may be [completed] in [a state of] uncleanness, [even though the fenugreek itself will no longer be useful as a foodstuff]. [Since fenugreek's main use is not as a food, even though it is edible, the priest to whom it is given as heave offering may*

37. Cf. Haas, *Maaser Sheni*, p. 46.
38. So Maimonides, *Commentary*, p. 217.

use it as he pleases, without scrupling about its suitability for consumption. This leniency with respect to cleanness applies in all cases] except for steeping it [in water]. [This is forbidden if the fenugreek is in a state of uncleanness because the water placed upon it would allow the uncleanness to spread directly to the priest's hands.]"[39]

M. M.S. 2:4

[A] *Vetches that [have the status of] second tithe must be [picked and] eaten [when] sprouting, [while suitable for human consumption, but may not be allowed to dry on the vine for animal fodder].*[40]

[B] *But [since vetches are not always used for human food, like simple coins in the status of second tithe] they [may be brought] into Jerusalem and out again (see M. M.S. 3:5).*

[C] *[If] the vetches become unclean—*

[D] *R. Ṭarfon says, "They should be divided up among [pieces of] dough, [such that no loaf of bread contains more than an egg's bulk of the unclean vetches]. [Since one is liable only for eating more than this measure, this procedure assures that none of the produce in the status of second tithe is wasted, and that the laws of cleanness are upheld (see M. Ter. 5:2).]"*

[E] *But sages say, "The [unclean vetches] should be deconsecrated."*

[F] *As for [vetches that were separated as] heave offering—*

[G] *The [members of the] House of Shammai say, "[If the vetches are to be prepared as food for humans], people must soak and crush [them] in [a state of] cleanness. But people may feed [the vetches to cattle] in [a state of] uncleanness. [Since the vetches clearly are not intended for human consumption, the rules of cleanness need not be scrupulously maintained.]"*

[H] *But the [members of the] House of Hillel say, "People must soak [them] in [a state of] cleanness. But people crush [the vetches in order to] feed [them to cattle, and this of course may be completed] in [a state of] uncleanness."*

[I] *Shammai says, "[In order to avoid the problem of uncleanness*

39. Cf. Haas, *Maaser Sheni*, p. 46.
40. So Maimonides, *Commentary*, p. 217.

altogether], vetches should be eaten dry. [Since no water is put upon them, they remain insusceptible to uncleanness.]"

[J] *Rabbi Aqiva says, "[Since vetches are generally used only for cattle fodder, even though they are edible], anything done with them may be [completed] in a [state of] uncleanness."*[41]

[**I**.A] What leniency applies to [produce in the status of] heave offering (cf. M. M.S. 2:2C)?

[B] [The leniency is found in] this ruling, recited on Tannaitic authority: **A priest who anointed [himself] with oil [in the status of] heave offering may later give his grandson—[whose father was] an Israelite—a piggyback ride,**[42] **[even though the child will absorb some of the oil]. [The priest] need not scruple [that the rubbed-off oil, which benefited a mere Israelite, has been used improperly]** (T. Ter. 10:10).

[C] Said R. Yoḥanan, "Here, [in responding to the *a minori ad majus* argument of the sages, R. Simeon] answers with a scribal ruling—[which subjects second-tithe vetches and fenugreek to strict laws (M. M.S. 2:2D)]—in explaining a ruling of Torah—[specifically, what types of anointing are permitted by Deut. 26:12–14 (see above Y. M.S. 2:1.I.Z)].[43]

[**II**.A] The Tannaitic teaching [(M. M.S. 2:3A) must be interpreted in] this fashion:[44] [Fenugreek in the status of second tithe] is permitted for consumption [only during its] sprouting phase; [at later moments, as it dries and is unsuitable for human consumption, it would have to be sold and the proceeds used to buy suitable food].

[B] [With regard to the Houses' dispute over the treatment of fenugreek designated as heave offering (M. M.S. 2:3B–D)], what [case illustrates the difference] between their [rulings]?

[C] Said R. Jonah, "[This dispute] between [the Houses is best illustrated by the case of] one who draws [dried fenugreek out of water in which it has been soaking]. [Such soaking would render any food susceptible to cultic uncleanness (see Lev. 11:34–38).

41. Cf. Haas, *Maaser Sheni*, pp. 46–47.

42. So the Tosefta itself, which reads: *mêvîʾ ʿal gabāv;* the Talmud's version reads: *maʿagalô ʿal gabêi mêʿāv*.

43. So GRA and PM. Romm edition: 11a.

44. In the Bomberg edition, this unit is numbered Y. M.S. 2:3.

Since food to be consumed as heave offering must be protected in a state of ritual cleanness, at issue is whether such reconstituted produce is in fact edible.] The [members of the] House of Shammai say, 'One must draw [the refreshed fenugreek out of the water] with clean hands; [since the plants are once again soft enough to eat, one must take pains not to transfer uncleanness to them].' But the [members of the] House of Hillel say, 'One may draw [the fenugreek out of the soaking water] with unclean hands; [once dried, the fenugreek is no longer a foodstuff, and even if softened, cannot contract food-uncleanness].'"

[D] It has been recited on Tannaitic authority: **[*(Fenugreek that was separated as) heave offering* (M. M.S. 2:3B)—the (members of the) House of Shammai say, "Anything done with it must be (completed) in (a state) of cleanness)." But the (members of the) House of Hillel say, "Anything done with it may be (completed) in (a state) of uncleanness, except using it as shampoo."]**[45] **This [version of the Houses' dispute] is the formulation of R. Meir. But the formulation of R. Judah [is that represented at M. M.S. 2:2C–D, namely]: *The [members of the] House of Shammai say, "Anything done with [the fenugreek] must be [completed] in [a state] of cleanness, [lest the heave offering become unclean, requiring that it be destroyed instead of consumed (see M. Ter. 8:8–12, 10:5–6)]. [The rule that fenugreek must be dealt with only in a state of cleanness applies in all cases] except using it as shampoo. [Since in this case the fenugreek already has dried up and so no longer is useful as food, one need not scruple about its state of cleanness.]" But the [members of the] House of Hillel say, "Anything done with it may be [completed] in [a state of] uncleanness, [even though the fenugreek itself will no longer be useful as a foodstuff]. [Since fenugreek's main use is not as a food, even though it is edible, the priest to whom it is given as heave offering may use it as he pleases, without scrupling about its suitability for consumption. This leniency with respect to cleanness applies in all cases] except for steeping it [in water]. [This is forbidden if the fenugreek is in a state of uncleanness because the water placed upon it would allow the uncleanness to spread directly to the priest's hands]"*** (T. M.S. 2:1).

45. The opening portion of this passage of Tosefta is added by the translator for clarity.

[E] What is [the practical difference] between them? Said R. Matanaia, "The disagreement concerns softening [the fibers]. The [members of the] House of Shammai rule, 'One softens them with clean hands, [because the fibers may be eaten and so are susceptible to food-uncleanness]'; but the [members of the] House of Hillel rule, 'One may soften them with unclean hands, [since the fibers are not considered to be food].'"

[III.A] *[(Since vetches are not always used for human food, like simple coins in the status of second tithe) they (may be brought) into Jerusalem and out again]* (M. M.S. 2:4B)[46]—[Such permission to remove edible vetches from Jerusalem applies only if the removal] is for the purpose of preparing them into a dough and returning [the baked good for consumption]; for preparing them into a dough and returning [it].[47]

[B] This Tannaitic teaching [M. M.S. 2:4B][48] reflects the opinion of Rabban Simeon b. Gamaliel, for: *Rabban Simeon b. Gamaliel has ruled,*[49] *"[Like coins], produce [in the status of second tithe] may be brought into [Jerusalem] and then out again, [even though it might spoil before being eaten within the city limits]"* (M. M.S. 3:5C).[50]

[C] [M. M.S. 2:4B does not reflect the opinion of a single authority, but] is the view of the entire [rabbinic consistory]. For this is a leniency that [the sages] enacted with regard to vetches—more precisely, only with regard to a dough made of vetches; only with regard to a dough made of actual second-tithe produce. [These two conditions assure that the lenient ruling allowing the food to be taken out of Jerusalem applies only to a pseudo-food—vetch dough—and only to a pseudo-consecrated item—vetches in the status of second tithe, which usually are inedible altogether. The sages permit the transfer owing to the questionable nature of the consecration that applies in such a narrow case.][51]

46. In the Bomberg edition, this unit is numbered Y. M.S. 2:4. The quote of the Mishnah is added by the translator for clarity.

47. The duplication here, perhaps the result of scribal error, may also serve to emphasize the ruling.

48. In the Bomberg edition, this unit is numbered Y. M.S. 2:5.

49. The Bomberg edition lacks: "for: Rabban Simeon b. Gamaliel has ruled."

50. Romm edition: 11b.

51. So PM.

[IV.A] *[(If) the vetches become unclean—R. Ṭarfon says, "They should be divided up among (pieces of) dough, (such that no loaf of bread contains more than an egg's bulk of the unclean vetches). (Since one is liable only for eating more than this measure, this procedure assures that none of the produce in the status of second tithe is wasted, and that the laws of cleanness are upheld)]* (M. M.S. 2:4C–D)[52]—

[B] R. Gorion in the name of Yose b. Ḥanina, "The opinion of R. Ṭarfon: 'People[53] may not redeem holy things [that have become unclean] so as to [use them in the only way permitted by their unclean status], by feeding [the now deconsecrated food] to dogs, [for this would be a denigration of the consecrated foodstuffs].'"

[C] Said R. Jonah, "[In light of sages' ruling that one may deconsecrate unclean second-tithe vetches (M. M.S. 2:4E)], it would appear that people may not redeem [unclean, consecrated] food suitable for human consumption so as to feed [that food] to animals. But people *may* redeem [unclean, consecrated] foodstuffs that are *not* suitable for human consumption, [such as vetches]. [Such use cannot constitute a denigration of consecrated status, because this food ordinarily would be used as animal fodder, not human food.]"

[D] R. Isaac bar Elishav inquired, "[If this same consecrated food] had been rendered unclean in the provinces, [before its transport to Jerusalem, wouldn't R. Ṭarfon still rule that] it may not be redeemed, since 'People may not redeem holy things [that have become unclean] so as to [use them in the only way permitted by their unclean status], by feeding [the now deconsecrated food] to dogs, [for this would be a denigration of the consecrated foodstuffs]' (cf. B, above)?"

[E] Said R. Jonah, "Is everything that is rendered unclean rendered unclean to the same extent?[54] [Of course not! Ṭarfon would be

52. This quote of the Mishnah is added by the translator for clarity.

53. See B. Pes. 29a.

54. So PM, who reads *ve-hen de-niṭmeʾû niṭmeʾû;* the Romm edition reads *ve-hen nôṭêi niṭāmêi*. I cannot improve on Haas's comment: "The text here is clearly corrupt. . . . There have been several attempts to rewrite the text. PM reads Jonah's response to be, 'Is everything that is rendered unfit rendered unfit in the same way?' The argument is that unclean human food is subject to more restrictions than are unclean plants that are not generally deemed to be human food. Schwab, in his French translation, has R. Jonah respond that getting around

wrong to insist that his rule applies in all cases, regardless of circumstance, location, or edibility of the consecrated produce.]"

Y. M.S. 2:3 (M. M.S. 2:5–7)

M. M.S. 2:5

[A] *[Consider a case in which] unconsecrated coins and coins [in the status of] second tithe [fell to the ground] and scattered [over the same area, so that it was unclear which coins were consecrated and which were unconsecrated].*

[B] *[In such a case] each [coin the farmer] picks up is counted as second tithe, until he has restored [the value of the second tithe in the mixture], and the remaining [coins he picks up are deemed unconsecrated]. [This assures that, even if he misses a few coins, the value of the second tithe will be preserved.]*

[C] *But if he mixed [consecrated and unconsecrated coins together in an undifferentiated heap], he scoops them up [by the handful and must deem the coins to be consecrated or unconsecrated] by proportion, [even if he misses a few coins and so fails to preserve the full value of the second tithe].*

[D] *This is the general rule [governing mixtures of second tithe and unconsecrated produce]: That which the householder collects one by one [is counted] as second tithe [until he has restored the value of the consecrated produce in the mixture]. That which has become an intermingled heap [is scooped up by the handful and deemed consecrated or unconsecrated] by proportion.*[55]

M. M.S. 2:6

[A] *[Consider a case in which] a [silver]* selaʿ *[coin that had the status of] second tithe and an unconsecrated* [selaʿ] *were confused [so that the consecrated coin could not be identified]. [In order to rectify this unacceptable situation, the householder fol-*

Isaac's objection is like a ship's pilot who has trouble sailing. He derives *nôṭêi* from *ναύτης*, the Greek word for sailor (cf. Schwab, p. 215). Jastrow (vol. 2, p. 886, s.v. *nôṭûmêi*) claims that the text should read: *ve-hûʾ she-lîqēṭ mî-kan û-mî-kan*, 'and if he collects them from here and there.' This phrase is attributed to R. Jonah below in Halakha 3. I do not see how he fits it into the context of the discussion here."

55. Cf. Haas, *Maaser Sheni*, p. 52.

lows this procedure]: he produces a selaᶜ*'s worth of [copper] coins and says, "The [silver]* selaᶜ *[in the status of] second tithe, whichever one it is, hereby is deconsecrated with these [copper] coins." [Immediately after transferring the consecrated status to the copper coins], he selects the finer of the two [silver* selaᶜ*s] and deconsecrates [the copper coins] with it.*

[B] *For they ruled, "They may deconsecrate silver [coins] with copper [coins] out of necessity. [But they may] not [do so with the intention of] allowing [this situation] to stand. Rather, [the householder in question] must immediately thereafter deconsecrate [the copper coins] with the silver [coins]."*[56]

M. M.S. 2:7

[A] *The [members of the] House of Shammai say, "One should not exchange [and thereby deconsecrate silver]* selaᶜ *[coins in the status of second tithe] for gold* dinars*." [Such an exchange might delay the householder's trip to Jerusalem because of later difficulty in making change for the gold coins.]*[57]

[B] *But the [members of the] House of Hillel permit [deconsecrating silver coins with gold coins, since one is always allowed to exchange items in the status of second tithe for even more precious commodities].*

[C] *Said R. Aqiva, "Once, on behalf of Rabban Gamaliel and R. Joshua, I exchanged silver [coins] for gold dinars, [and they did not protest].*[58]

[**I**.A] Said R. Zeira,[59] "[The ruling at M. M.S. 2:5A–B, that each coin a person picks up from a mixture of ordinary and second-tithe money is to be counted toward the second tithe, applies] up to the value of the second [tithe lost in the mixture], lest the remaining [coins] are lost; [in all events], those [coins] in the person's hand will thus replace the second [tithe]."

[B] Said R. Zeira, "Furthermore, the person must stipulate, 'If those [coins remaining on the ground] below are [in fact the] second [tithe], then these [coins] in my hand hereby replace them.'"

56. Cf. ibid., pp. 52–53.
57. So Maimonides, *Commentary*, p. 218.
58. Cf. Haas, *Maaser Sheni*, p. 60.
59. In the Bomberg edition, this unit is numbered Y. M.S. 2:6.

[C] Said R. Jonah, "This rule [that the first coins picked up are all to be counted toward the second tithe] applies if the person collects [the coins][60] from here and there, [so that it is possible that he has gathered all of the scattered second tithe]. But if he collects the coins [as if the mixture were divided] by a straight line, it is as if he had made a heap [of the two types of coins] and picked them up by the fistful. [Since it is implausible that he thereby might actually have selected all the second-tithe coins, he must assign the value of his fistful of money by proportion (cf. M. M.S. 2:5C).]"

[D] R. Yose in the name of R. Pedayah; R. Jonah in the name of R. Ḥezekiah: "Intermingling [such that one must assign value solely by proportion] occurs only with wine and oil. [In the case of coins, which always may be valued one by one, however, there can be no need to assign value by proportion.]"

[E] R. Yoḥanan said, "[The general rule allowing one to scoop up a mixture of consecrated and unconsecrated produce and to assign value by proportion applies only if the items are smaller] than olives that intermingle [into a homogeneous batch]."

[F] The current Tannaitic teaching disputes the opinion of R. Yoḥanan: *But if he mixed [consecrated and unconsecrated coins together in an undifferentiated heap], he scoops them up [by the handful and must deem the coins to be consecrated or unconsecrated] by proportion, [even if he misses a few coins and so fails to preserve the full value of the second tithe]* (M. M.S. 2:5C).

[G] One may resolve this [objection by claiming that this ruling speaks of coins that are] smaller than olives.

[H] *That which [the householder] collects one by one [is counted] as second tithe [until he has restored the value of the consecrated produce in the mixture]. That which has become an intermingled heap [is scooped up by the handful and deemed consecrated or unconsecrated] by proportion* (M. M.S. 2:5D)—

[I] R. Yose b. R. Bun in the name of R. Ḥuna: "This Tannaitic teaching in fact specifies [that only those coins that] were intermingled and then in fact scooped up by the fistful [are to have their value assigned] by proportion. [If, as at M. M.S. 2:5A–B,

60. Romm edition: 12a.

the coins are picked up one by one, no matter how they were mixed, the first coins selected are counted toward the value of the second tithe lost in the mixture.]"

[II.] It has been taught on Tannaitic authority:[61] ***[(Consider a case in which) a (silver)* selaᶜ *(coin that had the status of) second tithe and an unconsecrated* (selaᶜ) *were confused (so that the consecrated coin could not be identified). (In order to rectify this unacceptable situation, the householder follows this procedure): he produces a* selaᶜ's *worth of (copper) coins and says, "The (silver)* selaᶜ *(in the status of) second tithe, whichever one it is, hereby is deconsecrated with these (copper) coins." (Immediately after transferring the consecrated status to the copper coins), he selects the finer of the two (silver* selaᶜs*) and deconsecrates (the copper coins) with it]* (M. M.S. 2:6).**[62] **The son of Azzai says, "[In order to effect this deconsecration properly, the householder must use] two [*selaᶜs* of copper coins, and must deconsecrate both silver coins]"** (T. M.S. 2:5).

[B] R. Zeira said, "In a dream, I saw Ulla bar Ishmael eat a well-marbled piece of meat, [indicating that he knew the reason for the son of Azzai's stringent ruling].[63] The next morning, I went and inquired of him, 'Why [must one use] two [copper *selaᶜs* when redeeming a second-tithe coin that became confused with an ordinary coin]?' He said to me, 'If you so instruct him, he will at least hurry to redeem the one [silver, second-tithe *selaᶜ*].'" [The son of Azzai's stringency, in other words, is intended to urge compliance with the more minimal procedure spelled out at M. M.S. 2:6 and by Zeira himself at Y. M.S. 2:3.I.A–B.]

[C] **Ḥezekiah said,[64] "[When implementing the double procedure at M. M.S. 2:6A, first deconsecrating one of the two silver *selaᶜs* with copper coins, then reconsecrating one of them in exchange for the copper coins, the householder may act in his own best interests]. [Hence], when he deconsecrates one [of the silver coins, he may choose the finer coin], but give it a low valuation; and when he redeems [the copper coins] with**

61. In the Bomberg edition, this unit is numbered Y. M.S. 2:7.
62. This quotation of the Mishnah is added by the translator for clarity.
63. So PM.
64. See B. B.M. 52a–b.

[one of the now deconsecrated silver *sela*ᶜ*s*, he may choose the inferior coin], but give it a high valuation. [The upshot is that the householder can minimize the amount of produce he eventually will have to eat under the restrictions applicable to consecrated second tithe]" (Y. B.M. 4:5).[65]

[D] But have we not recited on Tannaitic authority: *[Immediately after transferring the consecrated status to the copper coins], he selects the finer of the two [silver* selaᶜs*] and deconsecrates [the copper coins] with it* (M. M.S. 2:6A)? Yet [according to Ḥezekiah], one chooses the inferior coin and gives it a high valuation! [Doesn't Ḥezekiah contradict a clear Tannaitic ruling?]

[E] Said R. Jonah, "I would say that [there is no real contradiction; this Tannaitic rule simply presumed that] this [finer silver coin] was in fact the second-tithe [coin lost in the mix-up]. [In other, less certain circumstances, by contrast, the householder would be free to select and reconsecrate the inferior coin, in accordance with Ḥezekiah's opinion.]"[66]

[F] At any rate, [the silver *sela*ᶜ chosen for redemption by the copper coins, whatever its condition, fine or inferior], does not finally become deconsecrated, [since one of the silver coins is immediately used to redeem those of copper]. [The result, then, is no net change, but only a recovery of the lost, consecrated item.]

[G] Said R. Jonah, "[In carrying out the process of redeeming one of the silver coins for copper, then, the householder] must not intend to deconsecrate it permanently. You may know that this is the case from that which we recite on Tannaitic authority: *[For they ruled, 'They may deconsecrate silver (coins) with copper (coins) out of necessity]. [But they may] not [do so with the intention of] allowing [this situation] to stand. Rather, [the householder in question] must immediately thereafter deconsecrate [the copper coins] with the silver [coins]'* (M. M.S. 2:6B)."

[H] R. Ḥaggai said before R. Zeira; Menaḥem in the name of R. Yoḥanan: "That which they ruled regarding *'[Second tithe of a] doubtful status . . . people may redeem [it silver for silver, copper for copper, (or even with a baser metal, hence) silver for copper, or copper for produce]'* (M. Dem. 1:2), [holds true also

65. For an alternative application of Ḥezekiah's ruling in the context of Y. B.M. 4:5, see PM, *Mareh Ha-Panim,* and GRA.

66. Romm edition: 12b.

of second tithe of] an assured status, when the necessity [of such a redemption arises, as for example in the case of the mix-up under discussion here]."

[I] But do we not recite on Tannaitic authority: *They may deconsecrate silver [coins] with copper [coins] out of necessity* (M. M.S. 2:6B). Does this not exclude [redeeming the coins] silver for silver, [a direct contradiction of M. Dem. 1:2]?

[J] R. Ba bar Cohen said before R. Jonah; R. Aḥa in the name of R. Yoḥanan: "[The proper formulation is this]: As for that which they ruled regarding *'[Second tithe of a] doubtful status . . . people may redeem [it silver for silver, copper for copper, (or even with a baser metal, hence) silver for copper, or copper for produce]'* (M. Dem. 1:2)—if one transgressed, and made such a redemption [of coins] with an assured status [as second tithe, notwithstanding the wrongful nature of this action, the coins] are in fact deconsecrated."

[K] R. Yudan b. Pazzi, R. Simeon bar Ba in the name of R. Yoḥanan: "[We agree that the proper formulation is this]: As for that which they ruled regarding *'[Second tithe of a] doubtful status . . . people may redeem [it silver for silver, copper for copper, (or even with a baser metal, hence) silver for copper, or copper for produce]'* (M. Dem. 1:2)—if one transgressed, and made such a redemption [of coins] with an assured status [as second tithe, notwithstanding the wrongful nature of this action, the coins] are in fact deconsecrated."

[L] It is recited on Tannaitic authority: **[*They may deconsecrate silver (coins) with copper (coins) out of necessity* (M. M.S. 2:6B), but not gold (coins) with silver (coins)]. R. Eleazar b. R. Simeon says, "Just as [in a case of necessity] people may deconsecrate silver [coins] with those of copper, so too [in a case of necessity] they may deconsecrate gold [coins] with silver." Rabbi said to him, "Why may people deconsecrate silver [coins] for those of copper? Because [a precedent has been set allowing silver to be redeemed for other metals], namely, they deconsecrate silver coins for those of gold. But may people deconsecrate gold [coins] for those of silver, seeing that they clearly may not deconsecrate gold [coins] for copper [coins]?" R. Eleazar b. R. Simeon said to him, "[The redemption of gold coins for silver may be allowed in cases of necessity], in as much as, in Jerusalem, [in order to allow the**

householder to purchase food to eat], people may deconsecrate their gold [coins] for any simple coins, [even copper]. [Since this exchange of copper for gold is allowed under clear necessity, the less radical exchange—silver for gold—ought to be allowed in usual circumstances] (T. M.S. 2:7).

[M] Based on the opinion of the two of them, [R. Eleazar b. Simeon and Rabbi], one may deconsecrate silver [coins] with those of gold,[67] but one may not deconsecrate silver [coins] with copper, [except out of necessity].

[**III**.A] *[The (members of the) House of Shammai say, "One should not exchange (and thereby deconsecrate silver)* selaᶜ *(coins in the status of second tithe) for gold* dinars.*" (Such an exchange might delay the householder's trip to Jerusalem because of later difficulty in making change for the gold coins)]* (M. M.S. 2:7A).[68] Said R. Yoḥanan,[69] "The [members of the] House of Shammai ruled only [that one may not use gold coins to deconsecrate second-tithe money] after [that consecrated status had once been transferred to other coins]. But in the initial [deconsecration of second-tithe produce], even the [members of the] House of Shammai concede [that one may use gold coins].

[B] What [scriptural verse provides] the rationale for the [members of the] House of Shammai? [Deut. 14:25 states]: *"[You may convert them (the tithes) into] silver."*[70] [But Scripture does] not [specify] gold [as a permitted metal to carry out the transfer to Jerusalem]. [Once one has acquired silver in exchange for the second tithe, then, one must transport it forthwith.]

[C] [If that explanation of the Shammaite position were correct, would one not also] say [that Scripture specifies] silver, but not copper? Yet have we not recited on Tannaitic authority: *[As regards a person outside Jerusalem] who breaks a [silver]* selaᶜ *in the status of second tithe [for smaller coins, hence deconsecrating the silver]—[the (members of the) House of Shammai say, "The entire* selaᶜ*('s worth of coins used to break the silver may consist) of (copper) coins"]* (M. M.S. 2:8A–B)?

67. So PM, GRA, and RiDVaZ, a reading that reflects the Toseftan passage quoted at L. The Romm edition, however, reads: "one may deconsecrate silver [coins] with [other] silver [coins], but one may not deconsecrate silver [coins] with copper, [except out of necessity]."

68. The quote from the Mishnah is added by the translator for clarity.

69. In the Bomberg edition, this unit is numbered Y. M.S. 2:8.

70. Hebrew: *kesef*. NJPST renders: "money."

[D] We may reason [that the Shammaites would] say: "Thus must this Tannaitic teaching [be interpreted]—*[As regards a person outside Jerusalem] who exchanges [small, common coins] in the status of second tithe [collectively worth]* a selaᶜ *[for a larger, silver coin, hence deconsecrating the small common coins]—[the (members of the) House of Shammai say, 'The entire* selaᶜ*('s worth of coins so used may consist) of (copper) coins']*." [On this reading of M. M.S. 2:8, of course, the Shammaite position as explained by Yoḥanan at A holds: one is permitted to deconsecrate second-tithe produce with any type of coin, including copper. But once that status has been transferred to silver coins, in keeping with Scripture's explicit reference, one is forbidden to transfer the consecrated status further.][71]

[E] Where do we now stand? What rationale [could we supply] for the [members of the] House of Shammai [who seem to allow a transfer to consecrated status from copper to silver, but not from silver to gold]? [Apparently, they reason that] silver and copper are [in a single category, for both are common currency[72] and may be referred to as *kesef* (lit., "silver," but more generally, "money")]. [Gold, however, owing to its preciousness, is in reality a commodity, not common coinage.]

[F] [Disputing Yoḥanan at A above], R. Simeon b. Laqish said, "Whether with regard to the initial [deconsecration of produce] or with regard to a later [transfer of consecrated status from one type of coin to another], the [members of the] House of Shammai dispute [with the Hillelites, and they do not permit use of gold coins at all]."

[G] What [scriptural][73] rationale underlies the [members of the] House of Shammai [in this case]? [Deut. 14:25's statement—*"You may convert them (the tithes) into silver; wrap up the silver and take it with you to the place that the* Lord *your God has chosen"*—implies that one must bring to Jerusalem] the silver (*kesef*) [to which the status of second tithe] was initially transferred, but one may not transport other coins (*kesef*).

[H] Do we not recite on Tannaitic authority: *[As regards a person outside Jerusalem]*[74] *who breaks a [silver]* selaᶜ *in the status of*

71. Romm edition: 13a.
72. So Haas.
73. See B. B.M. 45a.
74. See B. Bekh. 50b and B. Qid. 11b.

second tithe [for smaller coins, hence deconsecrating the silver]—[the (members of the) House of Shammai say, "The entire sela^c*('s worth of coins used to break the silver may consist) of (copper) coins"]* (M. M.S. 2:8A–B; M. Ed. 1:9).

[I] We may reason [that the Shammaites would] say: "Thus must this Tannaitic teaching [be interpreted]—*[As regards a person outside Jerusalem] who exchanges [small, common coins] in the status of second tithe [collectively worth]* a sela^c *[for a larger, silver coin, hence deconsecrating the small common coins]—[the (members of the) House of Shammai say, 'The entire* sela^c*('s worth of coins so used may consist) of (copper) coins']."* [Once again, on this reading, the Shammaite position, now as explained by Simeon b. Laqish, holds: outside Jerusalem, under no circumstances may one transfer the consecrated status of second tithe from silver coins to others, owing to Scripture's clear use of the phrase, *"Wrap up the silver and take it with you."* If one has other second-tithe coins, however, their status may legitimately be transferred to silver coins.]

[J] Where do we now stand? What rationale [could we supply] for the [members of the] House of Shammai [who seem to allow one to deconsecrate second-tithe produce for copper coins, even though Scripture explicitly refers to using silver coins]? [Apparently, they reason that] *"[You may convert them into] silver"* (Deut. 14:25) should be interpreted as *"[You may convert them] until you have silver."*[75]

Y. M.S. 2:4 (M. M.S. 2:8–10)[76]

M. M.S. 2:8

[A] *[As regards a person outside Jerusalem] who breaks a [silver]* sela^c *in the status of second tithe [for smaller coins, hence deconsecrating the silver]—*

[B] *The [members of the] House of Shammai say, "The entire* sela^c*['s worth of coins used to break the silver may consist] of*

75. For the meaning of this phrase, see GRA. He has a different order of stichs in this unit, apparently claiming that the Talmud here has been corrected to match the parallel in B. B.M. 44b–45a. He moves G–J after A, then concludes the unit with B–F.

76. Romm edition: 13b.

[copper] coins." [This assures that the householder will have coins of low denomination ready to spend when he reaches Jerusalem.]

[C] *But the [members of the] House of Hillel say, "[The* selaᶜ*'s worth of coins used to break the silver must consist] of one* sheqel *[= half* selaᶜ*] of silver [coins] and one* sheqel *of [copper] coins." [Since not all the money will be spent immediately upon the householder's arrival in Jerusalem, some money should be retained in silver coinage, lest the copper tarnish and lose some of its value.]*[77]

[D] *R. Meir says, "People may not deconsecrate silver coins and produce, [both in the status of second tithe] with other silver coins." [This is forbidden lest the householder transfer the consecrated status from one set of coins to another, which Meir holds is not permitted.]*

[E] *But the sages permit [this deconsecration, even though it involves transferring the sanctified status of second tithe from one set of coins to another].*[78]

M. M.S. 2:9

[A] *[In the case of a person] in Jerusalem who breaks a [silver]* selaᶜ *[in the status of] second tithe [for smaller coins]—*

[B] *The [members of the] House of Shammai say, "The entire* selaᶜ*['s [worth of coins used to break the silver may consist] of [copper] coins," [again assuring coinage of low denomination ready to spend].*

[C] *But the [members of the] House of Hillel say, "[The* selaᶜ*'s worth of coins used to break the silver must consist] of one* sheqel *of silver [coins] and one* sheqel *of [copper] coins." [As above, retaining some of the money in silver coinage avoids the possible loss of value when and if unspent copper coins tarnish.]*

[D] *Those who argued this point before the sages said, "[The coins used to break the* selaᶜ *of silver must consist] of three silver* dinars *[= three-quarters of a* selaᶜ*] and [one]* dinar *of [copper] coins." [Since the copper coins tarnish and lose some of their value so quickly, this proportion assures that not much of the second tithe is at risk of loss.]*

77. So PM.
78. Cf. Haas, *Maaser Sheni*, p. 64.

[E] *R. Aqiva says, "[The coins used to break the* sela^c *of silver may consist] of three [and three-quarter]* dinars *of silver [coins], while one-quarter [of the fourth* dinar *may consist of copper] coins." [This limits even further the amount of second tithe placed at a risk of loss.]*

[F] *R. Ṭarfon says, "[The first three* dinars *used to break the silver* sela^c *must be silver. As for the fourth, it must consist of] four* aspers *of silver coins [= four-fifths of a* dinar, *and the remaining* asper *(= one-fifth of a* dinar*) may be of copper]."*

[G] *Shammai says, "[Rather than breaking any portion of the silver for coins minted out of copper], he should deposit [the silver* sela^c *itself] in a shop and charge food against it."*[79]

M. M.S. 2:10

[A] *[Consider the case of a person who possesses some coins in the status of second tithe, and who wishes to provide drinks for his family, but] some of his dependents [are in a state of] uncleanness [and so not allowed to consume foodstuffs in the status of second tithe], while some of his [dependents are in a state of] cleanness [and so permitted to consume the drinks].*

[B] *[Such a person] lays down a [consecrated]* sela^c *and says, "This* sela^c *is deconsecrated with [the wine] that my [dependents in a state of] cleanness drink." [As a result, the* sela^c *is fully deconsecrated when they consume the drinks and no violation of purity laws is committed.]*

[C] *It turns out that the clean [dependents] and the unclean [dependents may] drink from [liquid contained in] the same jar, [so long as it is made out of clay, which does not impart uncleanness to its contents].*[80]

[**I.**A] R. Simeon b. Laqish said,[81] "What is the subject of the dispute between R. Meir and the sages (cf. M. M.S. 2:8D–E)? [They disagree over the procedure to follow in deconsecrating] produce valued at less than one silver [*sela^c*]. [Unlike Meir, sages here

79. Cf. ibid., pp. 64–65.

80. Cf. ibid., p. 69. My interpretative language here follows Maimonides, *Commentary*, p. 219. Note the suggested emendation of PM. He reads not "from the same jar" (*mi-kad ʾeḥād*) but "at the same time" (*be-vat ʾeḥād*). This emendation, while unsupported by manuscript evidence, nicely does away with problems concerning the type of jug and the transfer of uncleanness.

81. In the Bomberg edition, this unit is numbered Y. M.S. 2:9.

would permit the householder to combine his produce and some consecrated coins to bring the total value to one *sela*ᶜ, which then may be deconsecrated for silver, which is easy to transport to Jerusalem.]

[B] But with regard to produce valued at a full silver [*sela*ᶜ or more], even the sages concede [that the produce should be deconsecrated by itself, without involving an additional amount of second-tithe coins].

[C] [According to sages, then, if one possesses] a half *dinar* of silver [coins] and a half *dinar's* worth of produce, it is permitted [to combine them and deconsecrate the round sum of one *dinar* for transport to Jerusalem]. But [if one possesses a full] *dinar* of silver coins and a *dinar's* worth of produce, it is forbidden [to combine them, in as much as the produce itself may be sold for a single dinar, so that the other silver need not be deconsecrated secondarily]. How much more so is [such a transaction] forbidden [if one possesses] two *dinars* of silver and two *dinars* worth of produce!

[**II**.A] These are "Those who argued" [before the sages] (cf. M. M.S. 2:9D):[82] The son of Azzai and the son of Zoma.

[B] These are the students [who served as their clerks]: Ḥanina ben Ḥakinai and R. Eleazar b. Matia.

[C] This is the holy assembly [before whom they argued]: R. Yose b. Ha-Meshullam and R. Simeon b. Menasia.

[**III**.A] What rationale underlies Shammai's [ruling that the householder *"should deposit (the silver* sela*ᶜ *itself) in a shop and charge food against it]"* (M. M.S. 2:9G)?

[B] [This procedure protects the consecrated status of the money], lest the householder forget [that the money is second tithe] and spend it as if unconsecrated.

[**IV**.A] How are we to understand [the procedure to be followed when some family members are ritually unclean (cf. M. M.S. 2:10)]?[83]

[B] If [the householder] makes his declaration [that only the portion drunk by his clean dependents is consecrated] before [the

82. In the Bomberg edition, this unit is numbered Y. M.S. 2:10; see also B. Sanh. 17b.

83. In the Bomberg edition, this unit is numbered Y. M.S. 2:11.

entire family begins to drink from the jug], the drink would already be a mixture [of consecrated and unconsecrated liquid, and as a result, those in a state of uncleanness would be forbidden to drink].[84]

[C] And if [the householder] makes his declaration effective from the moment they have drunk, in retrospect, they will have imbibed unconsecrated [wine, since it becomes a second tithe only after they drink].

[D] Rather, we must address a situation in which one declares [that the wine is to be deemed consecrated from the moment] before [they drink of it, that consecration taking effect] upon their drinking it.

[E] [This declaration allowing the entire family to drink out of a single jar applies only if] those in a state of uncleanness had contracted corpse-uncleanness, for [the contents of] clay jugs do not become unclean [when touched] on the outside [by such persons]. But this does not apply if those in a state of uncleanness had flux-uncleanness, for one who suffers from flux-uncleanness renders a jug unclean merely by vibration, [and so would make all its contents unfit for consumption as second tithe through merely moving them].

[F] [This provision regarding those suffering flux-uncleanness] applies if no one else can pour [the wine into cups for each member of the family]. But if someone else can pour [the wine], even those suffering flux-uncleanness [may participate in this procedure].

84. Romm edition: 14a.

3 Yerushalmi Maaser Sheni Chapter Three

Y. M.S. 3:1

M. M.S. 3:1

[A] *One person may not say to another, "Take this [second-tithe] produce to Jerusalem [where we shall] divide [it between us]," [lest the portion set aside appear to be payment for transporting the food].*

[B] *But he may say to [his friend], "Take this [second-tithe produce] so that together we may eat and drink of it in Jerusalem," [since this merely constitutes an offer to share the food].*

[C] *[Alternatively]: but one person may give another [such second-tithe produce] as a free gift.*[1]

[I.A] *"One person may not say to another . . ."* (M. M.S. 3:1A)[2]—

[B] What is the difference between [the two circumstances spelled out at M. M.S. 3:1A, namely], a case in which one says, *"[Take this (second-tithe) produce to Jerusalem] so that together we may eat and drink of it,"* and a case in which one says, *"[Take this (second-tithe) produce to Jerusalem (where we shall)] divide [it between us]?"*

[C] R. Zeira in the name of R. Jonathan, "This is one of the laws based on a contrived distinction."[3]

1. Bomberg edition: 54a. Cf. Haas, *Maaser Sheni*, p. 73.
2. See Y. Shevi. 8:4 for this entire unit. See also B. A.Z. 62a–b.
3. Hebrew: *ʿîmʿûm*. Haas comments: "The literal meaning of *ʿîmʿûm* is to obscure, or to dim. I take the phrase 'a law of *ʿîmʿûm*' to mean a law that assumes a distinction where none is obvious, hence, 'a contrived distinction.' Jastrow (vol. 2, p. 1071) has 'irregular measure passed in an emergency.' I do not know why he assumes such laws must be the result of crisis."

[**II**.A] In another context, we recite on Tannaitic authority: *One who says to a worker, "Here is an* issar *for you [as a gift]," and "Gather vegetables [of the Sabbatical year] for me today"—his wage is permitted, [and exempt from restrictions of the Sabbatical year, since it was a gift]. [If, however, he said,] "In return for this* [issar], *gather vegetables for me today"—his wage is forbidden [and is subject to restrictions of the Sabbatical year, since the money was payment for the labor]. [As regards] one who took a loaf of bread worth a* dupondion *from the baker [and said], "When I gather [Sabbatical-year] vegetables from the field, I will bring you some [as a gift]"—[this exchange of produce] is permitted, [since the produce is a gift, not repayment of a debt]. [But if] he simply bought [the loaf of bread on credit, thereby incurring a debt to the baker], he may not [later] pay [the baker] with money [received from the sale of produce] of the Sabbatical year, for people may not discharge a debt with money [received from the sale of produce] of the Sabbatical year* (M. Shevi. 8:4).[4]

[B] What is the difference between [the two circumstances spelled out at M. Shevi. 8:4, namely], a case in which one says, *"Gather vegetables [of the Sabbatical year] for me today,"* and a case in which one says, *"In return for this* [issar], *gather vegetables for me today"*?

[C] R. Avin in the name of R. Yose b. Ḥanina, "This is one of the laws based on a contrived distinction."

[**III**.A] In another context, we recite on Tannaitic authority: *[On the Sabbath]*[5] *one person may borrow jugs of wine or oil, provided that he does not [explicitly] say, "Lend them to me [and I shall repay you later]"* (M. Shab. 23:1).

[B] What is the difference between a case in which one says, *"Lend them to me,"* and a case in which one says, *"Let me borrow them"*?

[C] R. Zeira in the name of R. Jonathan: "This is one of the laws based on a contrived distinction."

[**IV**.A] As for bread [baked by] gentiles—R. Jacob bar Aḥa in the name of R. Jonathan: "This too is one of the laws based on a contrived distinction."

4. Cf. Newman, *Sanctity of the Seventh Year,* pp. 163–64.
5. See B. Shab. 148a.

[B] R. Yose asked a question before R. Jacob bar Aḥa, "How is this one of the laws based on a contrived distinction?"[6]

[C] [R. Jacob replied], "Thus would I rule: 'In a locale where bread baked by an Israelite is available, logic dictates that bread baked by gentiles should be prohibited.' But the [sages] contrived a way to permit [purchase of this bread]. Or, 'In a locale where bread baked by an Israelite is not available, logic dictates that bread baked by gentiles should be permitted.' But the [sages] contrived a way to prohibit [such bread, even though none would be available whatsoever]."

[D] Said R. Mana, "Do we allow a contrived distinction to be used in prohibiting [that which logically is permitted]?" [On this reasoning, the second half of R. Jacob's rule, which would prohibit gentile-baked bread, must be inaccurate.]

[E] [R. Jacob responds]: "[In fact, we *can* prohibit based on a contrived distinction!] For isn't bread [baked by] gentiles like other gentile cooking? [And] thus have I ruled: 'In a locale where Israelite cooking is not available, logic dictates that gentile cooking should be permitted.' But the [sages] contrived a way to prohibit [foods cooked by gentiles]."

[F] [R. Mana, who persists in the belief that we do not prohibit based on a contrived distinction, would respond], "The correct formulation is only [this]: 'In a locale where bread baked by an Israelite is available, logic dictates that bread baked by gentiles should be prohibited.' But the [sages] contrived a way to permit [purchase of this bread], all in the interest of sustaining life."

[G] The rabbis of Caesarea in the name of R. Jacob bar Aḥa [ruled] in accord with those who permit [an Israelite to buy bread baked by gentiles], provided that [it is purchased at] a bakery. Nonetheless, we do not follow [this ruling].

[V.A] It has been recited on Tannaitic authority: [Even] in Jerusalem, one person may not say to another, "Bring this cask of wine from here to there, [where we shall] divide [it between us]." [As before, this division of the wine might constitute payment, even for the trivial task of transporting the wine within Jerusalem itself.]

6. The Leiden Codex lacks this stitch.

[B] Said R. Eleazar,[7] "This is the opinion of R. Judah and R. Neḥemiah."

[C] What circumstance do we envision such that [these two authorities prohibit this exchange]? If the case is one in which one says to the other, "Here, this [produce] is yours; now give me [that produce]"—all agree that this is prohibited, [because the householder in effect pays first to receive the other produce]. [Similarly, if the case is one in which one says to the other], "Give [that produce] to me, and I will give [this produce] to you," all agree that this is permitted, [because the order of the swap makes it clear that no payment, but only an exchange of gifts, has taken place].

[D] Rather, [since those positions are clearly held by the entire rabbinic consistory], we must envision a case in which one says to the other, "Give me [that produce]; I surely [promise] to give you [produce in exchange after I harvest it]."

[E] R. Judah and R. Neḥemiah prohibit [such an arrangement], because the crop of vegetables is not ready to hand [and so constitutes a promised payment, but not a gift]. But our rabbis permit [this arrangement], because the crop of vegetables in fact is ready to hand, [and so a potential gift, even if not yet harvested].

[VI.A] [Under the sharing arrangement permitted at M. M.S. 3:1B], once [the friend] has transported [the produce to Jerusalem], what is the law as to one saying to the other, "Take your portion; I will take mine"? What is the law if he says to the other, "You take this cask of wine and we—[my family and I]—will eat from the cask of oil I own over there"? Even: does the same apply to dividing the tithe of cattle [in this manner, after it has been transported to Jerusalem]?

[B] [In each of these cases] with regard to second tithe, since "selling" is explicitly [forbidden], you should rule that [such gifts] are permitted; with regard to the tithe of cattle, the sale of which is not explicitly forbidden, could you possibly rule that [such gifts] would be forbidden? Is it not obvious to you that this is permitted?

7. Romm edition: 14b.

[C] What is the law as to one who says to another, "Bring this [unconsecrated] domesticated or wild animal [to Jerusalem] and [together] we will eat[8] slaughtered meat [in the status of tithe of cattle] that I possess there?" [No answer is given. Still, by analogy to the cases above, if such an exchange could be viewed as payment of a labor bill, it would be forbidden; if viewed as an exchange of gifts, it would be permitted.]

Y. M.S. 3:2

M. M.S. 3:2

[A] *People may not purchase [produce in the status of] heave offering with money [derived from the sale of] second tithe, because [the regulations governing these two types of produce are incompatible and so would unduly] limit their consumption,*[9] *[for example, second tithe must be consumed within Jerusalem, while heave offering may only be eaten by priests and their dependants—neither limitation applies to the other consecrated food].*

[B] *But R. Simeon permits [the purchase of produce in the status of heave offering with money derived from the sale of second tithe].*

[C] *R. Simeon said to the [sages], "Given that we rule leniently in the case of a communion-meal offering, [by allowing its purchase with money derived from the sale of second tithe, even though the communion-meal offering may be rendered unfit for consumption under] the laws of refuse, remnant, and uncleanness, should we not likewise rule leniently in regard to [the purchase of] heave offering [which is not governed by these laws]?"*

[D] *They said to [R. Simeon], "Granted that we rule leniently in the case [of using money derived from the sale of second tithe to purchase] a communion-meal offering, [a type of offering that is] permitted for consumption by nonpriests. But should we rule*

8. Following the Romm edition. The Leiden Codex, Codex Vaticanus, and Bomberg edition all read: "and I will eat them."

9. So Maimonides, *Commentary*, p. 220, who follows the Talmud's second unit and notes that the limitation on proper consumption of these foodstuffs would apply to both offerings. The Mishnah, by contrast, seems here concerned more narrowly to spell out the restrictions that would be placed upon the consumption of the second tithe, here by members of the priestly caste alone.

leniently in the case of heave offering, which is forbidden for nonpriests [to eat, thus placing an undue restriction on its consumption as second tithe]?" [10]

[I.] [In regard to the Mishnah's view that *"People may not purchase (produce in the status of) heave offering with money (derived from the sale of) second tithe"* (M. M.S. 3:2A)—it has been recited on Tannaitic authority, "Lest the food become unfit."

[B] What is the meaning of "unfit"? Said R. Jonah, "[Second tithe with a dual status as heave offering] would become unfit if touched by a *ṭevul yom,* [an unclean person who has immersed but must now wait for sunset before becoming clean once again]. You would not be permitted to eat [such food], since [the touch of the person in the status of *ṭevul yom* renders heave offering] unclean, as a matter specified in Torah; [if in Jerusalem], you would not be permitted to deconsecrate [11] [it, since second-tithe produce remains] clean [even after being touched by a person in the status of *ṭevul yom*], as a matter specified in Torah. [The food thus may be neither eaten—owing to its status as unclean heave-offering—nor deconsecrated—owing to its status as clean second tithe.] Hence: "lest the food become unfit."

[II.A] What is the meaning of *"because [the regulations governing these two types of produce are incompatible, and so would unduly] limit their consumption"*? [Food in the status of] heave offering is forbidden [for consumption by] nonpriests, while second tithe [ordinarily] is permitted to nonpriests; [food in the status of] heave offering is forbidden [for consumption by] a person in the status of *ṭevul yom,* [an unclean person who has immersed but must now wait for sunset before becoming clean once again], while second tithe [ordinarily] is permitted to a person in the status of *ṭevul yom.* [Such additional regulations, due to the food's status as heave offering, mean that it is forbidden to some who might otherwise eat of it as second tithe.]

[B] Just as [the food's dual status] limits its consumption [as second tithe], so too [that dual status] limits its consumption [as heave offering]: [food in the status of] heave offering [ordinarily] is permitted [for consumption by] mourners before the burial of their dead (*le-ônān*), but second tithe is prohibited to such mour-

10. Romm edition: 15a. Cf. Haas, *Maaser Sheni*, pp. 74–75.
11. So the Romm edition; other versions lack this verb.

ners; [food in the status of] heave offering [ordinarily] does not need [to be eaten within] the city limits [of Jerusalem]; but second tithe does need [to be eaten within] the city limits. [Once again, the additional regulations governing second-tithe produce mean that the usual practices for eating heave offering might be forbidden.]

[C] One finds a Tannaitic teaching [that reflects this double limitation]: *[People may not purchase (produce in the status of) heave offering with money (derived from the sale of) second tithe], because [the regulations attendant upon the food's status as heave offering] limit its consumption [as second tithe], and [the rules governing the food's status as second tithe limit] its consumption [as heave offering].*

[III.A] It has been recited on Tannaitic authority: **People**[12] **may not purchase [produce grown during] the Sabbatical year with money [derived from the sale of] second tithe** (cf. T. Shevi. 7:1).[13] [Once again, the special rules governing the disposition of Sabbatical-year produce would unduly restrict the consumption of the food as second tithe, and vice versa.]

[B] Said R. Yose, "[Such purchase of Sabbatical-year produce with second-tithe money also is] under dispute [by R. Simeon and sages] (cf. M. M.S. 3:2A–B)." Said R. Jonah, "[This ruling regarding Sabbatical-year produce is] the opinion of all [authorities]. [R. Simeon's lenient ruling in his dispute with sages only concerns purchase of heave offering with second-tithe money, for he holds that] those who eat heave offering—[i.e., the priestly caste]—are scrupulous [about following the procedures applicable to the heave offering or any other consecrated item]."

[C] Responded R. Ḥunya before R. Mana, "Have we not recited on Tannaitic authority: *[If*[14] *an animal set aside for the Passover sacrifice] becomes confused with firstlings, [which may be eaten only by priests]—R. Simeon says, 'If [the animal had been designated for] a group of priests, they may eat [the meat and need not scruple about its dual status]* (M. Pes. 9:8). And in this re-

12. Y. Pes. 9:8.

13. T. Shevi. 7:1 itself reads: **"People may not deconsecrate [coins derived from the sale of second] tithe in exchange for produce of the Sabbatical year."** The Talmud's slight paraphrase seems not to affect the intended reference to this Toseftan unit.

14. See B. Pes. 98a.

gard, it is recited on Tannaitic authority: **[(If the animals had already been) slaughtered], they eat of them in accordance with the rules applicable to the most restricted animals [i.e., firstlings]" (T. Pes. 9:20).** [R. Simeon's dispute with sages obviously extends beyond the purchase of heave offering alone, contra R. Jonah's claim at B.]

[D] [R. Mana] replied to him, "[These citations extending the dispute to the disposition of a Passover sacrifice do not imply that Simeon and sages disputed about the purchase of Sabbatical-year produce with second-tithe money; rather you have shown only that] those who eat the Passover sacrifice in its prescribed time are as careful [to prepare and eat it properly] as are [the priests] consuming heave offering.

[E] "You may know that [the Passover sacrifice, like heave offering], is a special case [from the following juxtaposition]: we recite on Tannaitic authority: *'People*[15] *may not begin to roast meat, onions, or eggs [on Friday], unless they can finish roasting while daylight remains, [before the beginning of the Sabbath]* (M. Shab. 1:10). [By contrast], we recite [the following Tannaitic teaching with regard to the Passover sacrifice]: *'They*[16] *may lower the Passover sacrifice into the oven at dusk [on Friday afternoon, without worry that someone will tend the fire on the Sabbath]'* (M. Shab. 1:11). [The Passover sacrifice is significant enough that people will be careful to follow all rules that might apply to it, just as priests will follow all rules regarding the treatment of heave offering. In these cases alone, R. Simeon will allow the use of second-tithe money for these purchases, while sages refuse to permit the potential conflict of regulations.]"

[IV.A] R. Joshua b. Levi says,[17] "[When deconsecrating an offering], one pays the added fifth only when [the offering stems directly from] the initial consecration [at the harvest]. [Having paid this penalty once, one would not need to pay an additional fifth if later transferring the consecrated status to other food or coins.]"

[B] Said R. Eleazar: "And it has been recited so on Tannaitic authority: *'If [a firstling] is of unclean animals, it may be ransomed as its assessment, [with one-fifth added]'* (Lev. 27:27). Just as

15. See B. Shab. 19b.
16. See B. Eruv. 103a.
17. In the Bomberg edition, this unit is numbered Y. M.S. 3:3. See B. B.M. 54b and B. Tem. 9a.

such an unclean animal [in the status of a firstling] is special in that it [necessarily] stems from the initial consecration, [here owing to its birth], and [upon its redemption] a fifth is added [to its assessment], so any item that stems from the initial consecration [at harvest time] requires an added fifth [upon its redemption]."[18]

[C] R. Samuel bar Ḥiyya bar Judah in the name of R. Ḥanina: "[As regards] communion-meal offerings purchased with money [derived from the sale of second] tithe—[if such animals] become blemished and so are redeemed, the added fifth is paid, [since the communion-meal offering, until its redemption, stemmed from the initial consecration by the owner]."

[D] R. Samuel bar Ḥiyya bar Judah in the name of R. Ḥanina: "[As regards] communion-meal offerings purchased with money [set aside] for the Passover sacrifice—[if such animals] become blemished and so are redeemed, the added fifth is paid, [since the communion-meal offering, until its redemption, stemmed from the initial consecration by the owner]."

[E] Said R. Yudan, "One of these [rulings] is necessary and the other is merely redundant."

[F] Said R. Mana, "[The ruling about a communion-meal offering purchased with funds set aside for a] Passover [sacrifice (D above)] is necessary; the ruling about a communion-meal offering [purchased with money derived from the sale of second tithe (C above)] is redundant. [The 'Passover sacrifice' ruling is necessary] lest someone conclude that, since an animal set aside as a Passover sacrifice may be redesignated as a communion-meal offering, [the entire transaction would involve but] a single consecration, [that status merely being transferred from the Passover sacrifice to the communion-meal offering]. [This would mean that in reality no transaction would have taken place at all], such that one would not need to pay an added fifth. [To exclude such faulty reasoning, we require the ruling that explicitly demands payment of the added fifth in this case.]"

[G] Said R. Huna, "The rationale [behind equating the status of a Passover sacrifice and a communion-meal offering] is supplied by R. Samuel, who rules, 'An animal set aside as a Passover sac-

18. Romm edition: 15b.

rifice may not be substituted [for any other offering].' Yet he recites: 'If one did name a substitute for [an animal set aside as a Passover sacrifice before the holiday began, the first animal] retains its status as a Passover sacrifice [and must be put to pasture until it becomes blemished; it then may be redeemed according to the usual procedures and the proceeds used to purchase a communion-meal offering]. But if one names a substitute for it [after the holiday begins, the substitute] takes on the status of a communion-meal offering.' [This seems to imply that the two statuses are somewhat interchangeable.]"

[H] Said R. Mana to [R. Huna], "My master, [R. Samuel], never equated [the status of a paschal offering and that of a communion-meal offering]! [Even de facto, once the holiday began, the householder had no ability whatsoever to consecrate an animal as a Passover sacrifice, certainly not through an act of substitution; accordingly, if one makes such an attempt, the animal becomes consecrated in the most common status, that of a communion-meal offering.]"

[I] R. Ba, R. Ḥiyya in the name of R. Yoḥanan: "[Reverting to clarify the rule at C above]: **'[As regards] communion-meal offerings purchased with money [derived from the sale of] second tithe—[if such animals] become blemished and so are redeemed, [the added fifth is paid, (since the communion-meal offering, until its redemption, stemmed from the initial consecration by the owner)].'**"[19] In any case, neither the [now blemished animals nor the money used to redeem them] reverts to the status they had before, i.e., that of second tithe.

[V.A] R. Zeira and R. Hila, both in the name of R. Yose b. Ḥanina [transmit a dispute over the validity of Simeon's and sages' debate in M. 3:2D–E].[20] One side says: when communion-meal offerings are purchased with money [derived from the sale of second] tithe, the status of tithe is annulled, [since the single set of restrictions applicable to communion-meal offerings in fact encompasses all those of second tithe]. But when heave offering is purchased with money [derived from the sale of second] tithe, [the status of second] tithe[21] is not annulled, [because the two

19. Romm edition: 16a.
20. So Haas.
21. So the Romm edition. The Leiden Codex and the Bomberg edition read: "status of heave offering of the tithe," an apparent scribal error.

sets of restrictions are so different]. The argument (*mishnâh*) [from analogy between the two circumstances] thus breaks down, for they compare something from which [the status of] second tithe has been annulled, [namely, the communion-meal offering], with something from which [the status of] second tithe has not been annulled, [namely, the heave offering].

[B] The other side says that this proves nothing [about the analogies between the two circumstances]. [Rather, the argument is based precisely on how] something from which [the status of] second tithe has been annulled compares with something from which [the status of] second tithe has not been annulled.[22]

Y. M.S. 3:3 (M. M.S. 3:3–6)

M. M.S. 3:3

[A] *[Consider the case of a person] who possesses some coins [in the status of second tithe] in Jerusalem, and who needs them [for ordinary use, not just for purchasing food to eat], and whose friend owns [some unconsecrated] produce.*

[B] *[In order to use his money freely, such a person may] say to his friend, "These coins are deconsecrated in exchange for your produce."*

[C] *As a result, this [friend] must eat his produce in [a state of] cleanness, [because it now has the status of second tithe]. But the [other person] may freely use his coins for his needs [since they no longer have the sanctified status of second tithe].*

[D] *But one must not make this arrangement with a person who does not observe the laws of purity, unless [the coins were] of doubtful status.*[23]

M. M.S. 3:4

[A] *[If a person possesses some unconsecrated] produce in Jerusalem and [owns some] coins [in the status of second tithe, those coins being] in the provinces, [in order to satisfy the requirement to eat the value of the second tithe while in Jerusalem] he should*

22. The final line of this unit in the Romm edition belongs below at the beginning of Y. M.S. 3:3.I. It is erroneously printed here. See PM.
23. Cf. Haas, *Maaser Sheni*, p. 78.

declare, "Those coins are hereby deconsecrated [in exchange for] this produce."

[B] *[But if he possesses some] coins [in the status of second tithe] in Jerusalem and [owns some unconsecrated] produce, [the fruit being] in the provinces, he should declare, "These coins are hereby deconsecrated [in exchange for] that produce," provided that [forthwith] the produce is brought to Jerusalem and eaten [there in accord with the rules governing second tithe].*[24]

M. M.S. 3:5

[A] *Coins [in the status of second tithe] may be brought into Jerusalem and then out again [without their being spent for food to be eaten during the current visit to Jerusalem].*

[B] *But produce [in the status of second tithe], once brought into Jerusalem, [must be consumed during the current visit, lest it spoil], and so may not be taken out [of the city].*

[C] *Rabban Simeon b. Gamaliel says, "Also: produce [in the status of second tithe] may be brought into Jerusalem and then out again, [even though it might spoil before being eaten within the city limits]."*[25]

M. M.S. 3:6

[A] *[Consider a case in which] produce has been fully processed, [and so has become subject to the designation of tithes, but from which tithes—including second tithe—nonetheless have not yet been separated]. If such [untithed produce] is brought into Jerusalem and then out again, [that portion of the produce that eventually will be designated as] second tithe must be returned to Jerusalem and eaten there, [and may never be deconsecrated with money, for once brought into Jerusalem, that very fruit obtained the status of an offering placed upon the altar, which must never be removed].*[26]

[B] *[Now consider a case in which produce] has not been fully processed, [and so has not yet become subject to the designation of tithes]—such as baskets of grapes [being brought] to the wine-*

24. Cf. ibid., pp. 78–79.
25. Romm edition: 16b. Cf. Haas, *Maaser Sheni*, p. 80.
26. So Maimonides, *Commentary*, p. 221.

press or baskets of figs [being set aside] for storage. [What is the appropriate rule if such unprocessed produce is brought into Jerusalem and then out again?]

[C] *The [members of the] House of Shammai say, "[That portion of the produce that eventually will be designated as] second tithe must be returned to Jerusalem and eaten there, [and may never be deconsecrated with money, for once brought into Jerusalem, that very fruit obtained the status of an offering placed upon the altar, which must never be removed]."*

[D] *But the [members of the] House of Hillel say, "[Since, given its unprocessed state, the fruit was not yet subject to the separation of tithes], it may be redeemed and [then] eaten in any place, [even though it was brought into Jerusalem; the coins paid to redeem such food, of course, now must be brought to Jerusalem and spent there for food or drink]."*

[E] *R. Simeon b. Judah says on behalf of R. Yose, "[In fact], the [members of the] House of Shammai and the [members of the] House of Hillel never disputed concerning produce that had not been fully processed, [but had been brought into Jerusalem and then out again]. [Both Houses ruled] that [any portion later separated as] second tithe may be redeemed and [then] eaten in any place.*

[E] *"About what did they disagree?*

[F] *"[They disputed over the case in which] produce has been fully processed, [and while still untithed, the fruit is brought into Jerusalem and then out again].*

[G] *"For the [members of the] House of Shammai say, '[That portion of the produce that eventually will be designated as] second tithe must be returned to Jerusalem and eaten there, [and may never be deconsecrated with money, for once brought into Jerusalem, that very fruit obtained the status of an offering placed upon the altar, which must never be removed].'*

[H] *"But the [members of the] House of Hillel say, '[Such produce] may be redeemed and [then] eaten in any place, [even though it was brought into Jerusalem].'"*

[I] But *[if] produce has a doubtfully tithed status, [it is appropriate to be lenient, such that the food] may be brought into Jerusa-*

lem and then out again, and then redeemed [and eaten in any place].[27]

[**I**.A] [The procedure given at M. M.S. 3:3A–B, whereby one person's second-tithe money is deconsecrated in exchange for a friend's produce, is valid even if the friend is in a state of uncleanness, so long as that friend] says, "I have completed one immersion [and am waiting only for sundown to be in a state of cleanness]." [In such a case, the friend may be relied upon to follow the rules regarding consumption of consecrated food in a state of cleanness (cf. M. M.S. 3:3C).]

[B] *But one must not make this arrangement with a person who does not observe the laws of purity, unless [the coins were] of doubtful status* (M. M.S. 3:3D). Now if the money had an assured [status as second tithe, such a transfer may] not [be made], because people may not transfer any assuredly consecrated item to a person who does not observe the laws of purity.[28]

[**II**.A] *[Rabban Simeon b. Gamaliel says, "(Like coins), produce (in the status of second tithe) may be brought into Jerusalem and then out again, (even though it might spoil before being eaten within the city limits)]*[29] (M. M.S. 3:5C)—[but this is permitted only if his] intention is to make a dough and return [the baked good to Jerusalem for consumption]; to make a dough and return [the baked good to Jerusalem].[30]

[**III**.A] *[Consider a case in which) produce has been fully processed, (and so has become subject to the designation of tithes, but from which tithes—including second tithe—nonetheless have not yet been separated). If such (untithed produce) is brought into Jerusalem and then out again, (that portion of the produce that eventually will be designated as) second tithe must be returned to Jerusalem and eaten there, (and may never be deconsecrated with money)]* (M. M.S. 3:6A).[31]

[B] R. Simeon b. Levy said, "By this ruling, they have converted

27. Cf. Haas, *Maaser Sheni*, pp. 80–81.
28. The Romm edition erroneously places this stitch at the end of Y. M.S. 3:2. See PM.
29. The quote from the Mishnah is added by the translator for clarity.
30. Cf. Y. M.S. 2:4 for an exact parallel.
31. This quote of the Mishnah is added by the translator for clarity.

Jerusalem into a private courtyard.[32] Just as a private courtyard imposes liability for separating tithes [upon produce brought within it] (*ṭôvelet*), so too Jerusalem now imposes liability to separate tithes [from produce brought within the city limits]."

[C] Said R. Jonah, "Logically, even the [private] houses found [in Jerusalem] should not impose liability for separating tithes, in as much as all Israelites own [Jerusalem equally]. Rather: by this ruling they have converted Jerusalem into a private courtyard. Just as a private courtyard 'seizes' [anything brought within it, thereby indicating that the owner has taken possession of the item] (*tôfeset*), so too [the city limits of] Jerusalem 'seize' [the produce a householder brings into the city]. [While such ownership alone does not impose liability for separating tithes, it is one crucial component (cf. M. Maas. 1:1).]"

[D] Said Rabbi, "This ruling (M. M.S. 3:6A) implies: [As regards] a batch of produce that is subject to the separation of both first *and* second [tithes]—even if they permit [free consumption of the produce] from the standpoint of second tithe, [in as much as first tithe has not yet been separated and so second tithe has not really come due, still, since the untithed produce was brought within the city limits—which imposes liability for separating second tithe (cf. A–B above)—anyone who removes this produce from Jerusalem] should be flogged."

[E] R. Mana[33] responded, "But do we not recite on Tannaitic authority: *[(Now consider a case in which produce) has not been fully processed, (and so has not yet become subject to the designation of tithes)—such as baskets of grapes (being brought) to the winepress or baskets of figs (being set aside) for storage. (What is the appropriate rule if such unprocessed produce is brought into Jerusalem and then out again?)]*[34] *The [members of the] House of Shammai say, "[That portion of the produce that eventually will be designated as] second tithe must be returned to Jerusalem and eaten there, [and may never be deconsecrated*

32. Jastrow, vol. 2, p. 1596, s.v. *shemîrâh,* more literally translates "a well-guarded court." Of clearer importance here is the private nature of the courtyard, which thereby can indicate personal ownership of items brought within it.

33. Bomberg edition: 54b.

34. The first portion of the quote from the Mishnah is added by the translator for clarity.

with money, for once brought into Jerusalem, that very fruit obtained the status of an offering placed upon the altar, which must never be removed]" (M. M.S. 3:6B–C).

[F] "[In the Shammaites' opinion, apparently, whether or not the produce is fully processed makes no difference; the food is fully subject to second tithe by virtue of the fact that it was brought within the city limits.] Do you really rule that, by following [the viewpoint and instructions] of the [members of the] House of Shammai, [i.e., taking the produce out of Jerusalem and then later bringing it back, one will invariably deserve] to be flogged?

[G] "Rather, [the correct understanding of both the Shammaite position with regard to unprocessed produce and the general ruling with regard to fully processed produce extends only to the issue of the courtyard analogy, but not to punishment for *de facto* violation]. [And just as we] rule strictly about [Jerusalem's] boundaries [in fact constituting a private courtyard], so too [do the Shammaites] here rule stringently about the [city] boundaries [constituting a courtyard]."

[**IV**.A] R. Zeira inquired, "[Consider the case of a person who brings a batch of untithed, fully processed produce into Jerusalem], and [then] separates the appropriate second [tithe] for the batch from [other produce] in another locale—is [the first batch of produce] exempt [from the status of second tithe]? Or, have the [city] limits already seized [that very produce, such that the second tithe within it may never be removed from Jerusalem]?" [The question goes unanswered until below, Y. M.S. 3:3 VI.F.]

[B] [Similarly], R. Jonah inquired, "[In the same circumstances] if one set aside the entire batch [of untithed, fully processed produce] as second tithe for [other untithed produce] in another locale, has the entire [first batch of produce] been seized [by the city limits, so that it may never be removed from Jerusalem]? Or, [since this batch of produce is physically separate from the other food, does it constitute a distinct crop], no more than 10 percent of which could be seized [by the city limits and therefore be consecrated as second tithe on behalf of the crop in a different locale]?" [This question too goes unanswered.]

[**V**.A] *[(Now consider a case in which produce) has not been fully processed, (and so has not yet become subject to the designation of tithes)—such as baskets of grapes (being brought) to the wine-*

press or baskets of figs (being set aside) for storage][35] (M. M.S. 3:6B)—but if the baskets of dates or baskets of grapes are [brought to Jerusalem] to be eaten, [it is as if] they are fully processed, [and the rule at M. M.S. 3:6A applies to them].

[VI.A] **Said the [members of the] House of Hillel to the [members of the] House of Shammai,[36] "Given that you concede to us that [untithed] produce not yet fully processed [that was once brought into Jerusalem] may have the second tithe [that is eventually separated] from it redeemed and eaten in any locale (cf. M. M.S. 3:6E)—[should you not] likewise [concede to us in the case of a batch of] fully processed produce (cf. M. M.S. 3:6F—H)?"**

[B] **Said to them the [members of the] House of[37] Shammai, "No. For even if you rule [thusly] about produce not yet fully processed—in as much as one may declare such [food] ownerless and thereby avoid liability to tithing altogether—could you rule the same about fully processed produce—[especially since in this case] one may not avoid liability to tithing simply by declaring [the food] ownerless (cf. M. Peah 1:6C–D)"** (T. M.S. 2:11)?

[C] Said to them the [members of the] House of Hillel, "Even in the case of fully processed produce, one may declare it ownerless, and thereby avoid liability to tithing.[38] [This proves the point]: Is it really the case that one may not avoid liability to tithing by declaring baskets of dates or grapes ownerless that are ready to be eaten as is ownerless? [Of course not!] This [common-sense ruling] proves that baskets of dates or grapes that will be eaten as is are deemed fully processed (as at Y. M.S. 3:3.V.A), [yet if declared ownerless, are no longer subject to tithing]."

[D] Said to them the [members of the] House of Shammai, "No! [We remain opposed to your conclusion that the second tithe

35. The quote from the Mishnah is added by the translator for clarity.
36. In the Bomberg edition, this unit is numbered Y. M.S. 3:6.
37. Romm edition: 17a.
38. So *Mareh Ha-Panim*, which notes that the Hillelites here directly contradict the clear statement of M. Peah 1:6, given in the mouth of Aqiva, himself a Hillelite. T. M.S. 2:11, for its part, continues along a different line altogether, as follows: **"Said to them the House of Hillel, 'Even [in the case of] produce the processing of which is completed, one can separate produce as heave offering and tithes [may be separated from it] for another batch."** GRA and RiDVaZ, noting this Toseftan continuation is picked up again in the Shammaite lemma at

from fully processed produce, once brought into Jerusalem, may be redeemed and freely eaten in any locale (cf. A above).] For even if you rule [thusly] about produce not yet fully processed—in as much as one may separate second [tithe] on its behalf from [other produce] in another locale—could you rule the same about fully processed produce—[especially since in this case] one may not separate second [tithe] on its behalf from [other produce] in another locale (cf. M. Peah 1:6C–D)?"

[E] [Incidentally], this [argument by the Shammaites] resolves the question spoken by R. Zeira[39] (cf. Y. M.S. 3:3.IV.A): [According to the Shammaites, one may not separate second tithe on behalf of untithed produce in Jerusalem from another batch of produce elsewhere; once the first batch has entered the city, that very food itself is subject to having second tithe set aside.]

[F] R. Ḥanina and R. Jonathan and R. Joshua b. Levi entered [the ruins of] Jerusalem, where [second-tithe] produce happened [to come] into their possession. [Reasoning that, since the city walls were no longer intact, they could remove this food from Jerusalem (contra M. M.S. 3:5B)], they desired to redeem [it after carrying it to] an outlying area. An elderly gentleman said to them, "Your predecessors did not do so! Instead, they discarded [the consecrated produce] over [the ruins of the city] walls; only [having not *carried* it outside Jerusalem] did they redeem it there."

[G] That old one believed that one must view the limits [of Jerusalem] as if [the walls remained] standing, [so that second-tithe produce should not be removed from the city]. These rabbis believed that one need not view the limits [of Jerusalem] as if [the walls remained] standing, [in which case the second-tithe produce could legitimately be carried out of the city]. That old one held the same view as R. Joshua (cf. M. Ed. 8:6C–F); those rabbis held the same view as R. Eliezer (cf. M. Ed. 8:6A–B).[40]

D, simply omit C and the attribution of D, and end this unit with the conclusion of T. M.S. 2:11.

39. So PM, rendering: *hādāʾ peshātāʾ sheʾēlâh ʾāmar rabbî zeʿêrāʾ*.

40. My references here follow PM, who coordinates these opinions with those of Joshua and (by inference) Eliezer at M. Ed. 8:6. The Romm edition reverses the two names. GRA and RiDVaZ take another tack, and here read: "That old one held the same view as R. Simeon b. Judah (cf. M. M.S. 3:6E–H); those rabbis held the same view as the anonymous teacher [to whom Simeon b. Judah responds] (M. M.S. 3:6A–D)." This reading makes the positions taken by those in the narrative match neatly those in the Mishnah, but I see

[H] R. Pinḥas, [in a similar situation, within the ruins of Jerusalem], made second-tithe produce unclean, and then redeemed it [still in Jerusalem], for he wished to scrupulously follow the opinion of both [R. Eliezer and R. Joshua]. [Even if, as Joshua holds, the rules that pertained when the city walls and Temple stood still applied in the ruins, Pinḥas's procedure would be correct.]

[VII.A] R. Jacob bar Idi and R. Joshua b. Levi: "The law follows the opinion of[41] the student, [R. Simeon b. Judah, who rules at M. M.S. 3:6E that, for purposes of the practicable law, unprocessed produce is not subject to tithing; even if brought into Jerusalem, the second tithe eventually separated from it may be redeemed and eaten outside the city]."

[VIII.A] *[But (if) produce has a doubtfully tithed status, (it is appropriate to be lenient, such that the food) may be brought into Jerusalem and then out again, and then redeemed (and eaten in any place)]*[42] (M. M.S. 3:6I). Said R. Zeira, "[This rule is appropriate] so long as the produce in question is in a doubtful status as to whether it had ever been tithed. But if [the produce brought to Jerusalem was separated as second tithe]—even if some doubt has arisen about its status—the [city] limits seize such [produce, and so it must be consumed within Jerusalem forthwith]."

Y. M.S. 3:4 (M. M.S. 3:7–8)[43]

M. M.S. 3:7

[A] *[Consider the cases of] a tree rooted within [the city walls of Jerusalem] but [whose boughs] extend [over the walls and so are located] outside [the city], or a tree rooted outside [the city walls of Jerusalem] but [whose boughs] extend [over the walls and so are located] within [the city].*

[B] *[Produce growing on branches of such trees] that are directly above [the center of] the wall and inwards is [deemed to be] within [Jerusalem, and so, if separated as second tithe, may*

no reason to prefer such an emendation over PM's simple reversal of the two names.

41. Romm edition: 17b.

42. The quote from the Mishnah is added by the translator for clarity.

43. In the Bomberg edition, these materials are numbered Y. M.S. 3:7.

not be removed from the city]. [But produce growing on those branches that are directly over the center of] the wall and outward is [deemed to be] outside [of Jerusalem, and so, if designated as second tithe, may be deconsecrated or taken within the city limits and consumed].

[C] *[As for] olive-press buildings, [which commonly are built into the city walls, so] that their doorways [open] into [the city of Jerusalem, while] their contained spaces are [within the wall and] outside [of the city], or [so] that their doorways [open] outside [of the city of Jerusalem, while] their contained spaces are [within the wall and] within [the city]—*

[D] *The [members of the] House of Shammai say, "[Such a building] is deemed to be entirely within [the city limits]." [As a result, olives and oil within the building must be treated as if already within Jerusalem, and so upon designation as second tithe may neither be removed from the city nor deconsecrated.]*

[E] *The [members of the] House of Hillel say, "[The space within such a building is divided along an imaginary line]: that which is directly along [the center of] the [city] wall and inward is [deemed to be] within [Jerusalem and subject to the appropriate restrictions]. But that which is directly along [the center of] the [city] wall and toward the outside is [deemed to be] outside [of Jerusalem and free from such restrictions]."*[44]

M. M.S. 3:8

[A] *[As regards] Temple chambers built [into the side of the Temple mount, such that their roofs [are continuous with the plane of] the holy [precinct just above them] while [the chamber itself] opens to an unsanctified [area below]—their inner space is [deemed to be] unsanctified, but their roofs, [because they are a continuation of the plane above, are deemed] sanctified.*[45]

[B] *[But if matters are reversed, so that the Temple chambers] are built [with their roofs contiguous with the floor of] an unsanctified [area just above them] while [the chamber itself] opens to the holy [precinct below]—their inner space is [deemed to be part of the] sanctified [precinct] and their roofs are [deemed to be a continuation of the] unsanctified [area].*

44. Cf. Haas, *Maaser Sheni*, p. 85.
45. So Maimonides, *Commentary*, p. 222.

[C] *[As for those Temple chambers] built [straddling the boundary between] the holy [precinct] and the unsanctified [area] and open to [both] the sanctified [precinct] and the unsanctified [area]—[with regard to both] their inner spaces and their roofs, [that part which is] along [the boundary of] the sanctified [precinct] and inward is [deemed to be] sanctified, [and that part which is] along [the boundary of] the unsanctified [area] and outward is [deemed to be] unsanctified.*[46]

[**I**.A] Said R. Yose,[47] "[The rules for olive-press buildings built into the city walls of Jerusalem represent] the teaching of R. Aqiva. But the opinion of the sages differs with regards to all types of chambers: all types of chambers are ruled in accord with their openings; [if one opens to a sanctified area, the restrictions of that area apply to the chamber itself, and if one opens to an unsanctified area, the chamber follows the rules that apply to an unsanctified locale]."

[B] Said R. Eleazar, "[The rules stated in this regard are on the side] of stringency."

[C] R. Yosa inquired, "In what respect are these rulings stringent?"

[D] Said R. Jonah, *"Olive-press buildings [built into the city walls, so] that their doorways [open] into [the city of Jerusalem, while] their contained spaces are [within the wall and] outside [of the city* (M. M.S. 3:7C)*—that which is directly along [the center of] the [city] wall and inward is [deemed to be] within [Jerusalem, and subject to the appropriate restrictions]. But as for the area that is directly along [the center of] the [city] wall and toward the outside* (M. M.S. 3:7E)—in such an area people may not eat items of a lesser consecration, as if the area was outside [the city limits]; nor may they redeem second tithe in such an area, as if it were inside [the city limits].

[E] *"[If] their doorways [open] outside [of the city of Jerusalem, while] their contained spaces are [within the wall and] within [the city]* (M. M.S. 3:7C)*—that which is directly along [the*

46. Cf. Haas, *Maaser Sheni*, pp. 85–86.

47. For this entire unit, I follow the suggested redaction of GRA and RiDVaZ. Tractate Maaser Sheri itself has a different order of stichs and some variants, which together render the argument here incomprehensible to me: the Talmud places A at the end of the unit and splits J so that the attribution precedes F. For a possible explanation and suggested emendations in accord with similar materials at T. M.S. 2:12–15, see PM.

center of] the [city] wall and toward the outside is [deemed to be] outside [of Jerusalem, and free from the city's restrictions]. But as for the area that is directly along [the center of] the [city] wall and toward the outside (M. M.S. 3:7E)—in such an area, people may not eat items of a lesser consecration, as if the area were outside [the city limits]; nor may they redeem second tithe in such an area, as if it were inside [the city limits]." [In such cases, one must follow the restrictions applicable to] *both* regions, [which constitutes the stringency regarding olive-press buildings].

[F] It has been recited on Tannaitic authority: "*[As for those Temple chambers] built [straddling the boundary between] the holy [precinct] and the unsanctified [area]* (M. M.S. 3:8C), and open to the sanctified [precinct]—their inner spaces are [deemed to be sanctified], but their roofs [have a dual status]: *[that part which is] along [the boundary of] the sanctified [precinct] and inward is [deemed to be] sanctified, [and that part which is] along [the boundary of] the unsanctified [area] and outward is [deemed to be] unsanctified* (M. M.S. 3:8C). [If] they open to the unsanctified [area]—their inner spaces are [deemed to be unsanctified], but their roofs [have a dual status]: *[that part which is] along [the boundary of] the sanctified [precinct] and inward is [deemed to be] sanctified, [and that part which is] along [the boundary of] the unsanctified [area] and outward is [deemed to be] unsanctified* (M. M.S. 3:8C).[48] [If] one is built within the sanctified [precinct], but opens to [both] the sanctified [precinct] and the unsanctified [area]—the whole [chamber] is [deemed to be] sanctified. [If] one is built within the unsanctified [area], but opens to [both] the sanctified [precinct] and the unsanctified [area]—the whole [chamber] is [deemed to be] unsanctified."

[G] Said R. Jacob bar Aḥa, "Given that you rule [that] the contained spaces [of such chambers] are [deemed to be] sanctified, then people in them may eat items with an extreme level of consecration, they may slaughter [animals] of a lesser consecration, and any person in a state of uncleanness who enters them is liable, [all as if the chambers were the Temple court itself]."

[H] Rav Judah[49] in the name of Rav: "[An unclean person who enters such a chamber] should not be flogged [unless the chamber

48. Romm edition: 18a.
49. See B. Zev. 55b.

surpasses the size of the Temple court itself, namely], 180 cubits long and 130 cubits wide. For has it not been recited on Tannaitic authority, 'Any [Temple]-chamber built up to the size of the walled courtyard—people in it may eat items with an extreme level of consecration, they may slaughter [animals] of lesser consecration, but any person in a state of uncleanness who enters it is exempt'?"

Y. M.S. 3:5 (M. M.S. 3:9)[50]

M. M.S. 3:9

[A] *[As regards produce in the status of] second tithe that was brought into Jerusalem and then rendered unclean:*

[B] *Whether it was rendered unclean by a primary source of uncleanness or by a secondary source of uncleanness, and whether [it was rendered unclean] inside [Jerusalem] or outside [Jerusalem]—*

[C] *The [members of the] House of Shammai say, "Any such produce must be redeemed [and ritually clean produce bought in its stead, because second tithe must be consumed in a state of ritual cleanness]. [But the unclean produce, even though it no longer has the status of second tithe], itself should be eaten inside [Jerusalem, in accord with the rule that second tithe, once brought into the city, must not be removed]. [This is the appropriate ruling] except for [produce in the status of second tithe] that was rendered unclean by a primary source of uncleanness outside [Jerusalem]. [Given the high degree of ritual uncleanness that affects this food, and given the fact that the food never was brought into Jerusalem while in the status of second tithe, such produce should be deconsecrated and consumed outside the city limits]."*[51]

[D] *The [members of the] House of Hillel say, "Any such produce must be redeemed [and ritually clean produce bought in its stead, because second tithe must be consumed in a state of ritual cleanness]. [Then the unclean produce, since it no longer has the*

50. In the Bomberg edition, these materials are numbered Y. M.S. 3:8.

51. See Maimonides, *Commentary*, p. 222, for the explanations of this dispute.

status of second tithe], should be eaten outside [the city limits of Jerusalem, so as not to defile the city]. [This is the appropriate ruling] except for [produce in the status of second tithe] that was rendered unclean by a secondary source of uncleanness within [Jerusalem itself]. [Given the low degree of ritual uncleanness that affects this food, and given the fact that the food already had been brought into Jerusalem, such produce should be deconsecrated and consumed within the city limits.]"[52]

[**I**.A] It is written [in Scripture], *"should you be unable to transport them, . . . [you may convert them into money]"* (Deut. 14:24–25).

[B] What case do we envision here? If [this particular phrase refers to a farmer who is unable] because of distance, then why does the verse begin, *"Should the distance be too great for you"?* And [if the phrase refers to a farmer who is unable to bring that very produce and consume it] within [Jerusalem],[53] then why does the verse continue, *"[you may convert them into money] . . . . Spend the money [on anything you want]"*?

[C] So then, what case is addressed by the phrase, *"should you be unable to transport them"*? [This means], "You are not permitted to redeem [consecrated produce within Jerusalem itself]." [If, however, such produce is rendered unclean], it is written [in Scripture], *"spend the money [on anything you want]"*—[indicating that only in this case may one redeem and deconsecrate second-tithe produce brought within the city].

[**II**.A] It has been recited on Tannaitic authority: "Bar Qapara said, '[The spread of uncleanness through contact with] a primary source of uncleanness is a matter specified in Torah; [the spread of uncleanness through contact with] a secondary source of uncleanness is a [rabbinic] opinion.' R. Yoḥanan said, '[The spread of uncleanness through contact with] either [a primary or a secondary source of uncleanness] is a matter specified in Torah.'"[54]

[B] There is an apparent contradiction between the opinion of the [members of the] House of Shammai and that of R. Yoḥanan. For *"The [members of the] House of Shammai say, 'Any such produce must be redeemed [and ritually clean produce bought in*

52. Cf. Haas, *Maaser Sheni*, p. 92.
53. So PM, translating: *qêrûv māqôm*.
54. Romm edition: 18b.

its stead, because second tithe must be consumed in a state of ritual cleanness]. [But the unclean produce, even though it no longer has the status of second tithe], itself should be eaten inside [Jerusalem, in accord with the rule that second tithe, once brought into the city, must not be removed]. [This is the appropriate ruling] except for [produce in the status of second tithe] that was rendered unclean by a primary source of uncleanness outside [Jerusalem]. [Given the high degree of ritual uncleanness that affects this food, and given the fact that the food never was brought into Jerusalem while in the status of second tithe, such produce should be deconsecrated and consumed outside the city limits]'" (M. M.S. 3:9C). What difference [would it make if the uncleanness stemmed] from a primary source or a secondary source of uncleanness outside Jerusalem? [On Yoḥanan's view], are not both [types of uncleanness] matters specified in Torah?

[C] And even on the opinion of the [members of the] House of Hillel, is there not an apparent contradiction? For, *"The [members of the] House of Hillel say, 'Any such produce must be redeemed [and ritually clean produce bought in its stead, because second tithe must be consumed in a state of ritual cleanness]. [Then the unclean produce, since it no longer has the status of second tithe], should be eaten outside [the city limits of Jerusalem, so as not to defile the city]. [This is the appropriate ruling] except for [produce in the status of second tithe] that was rendered unclean by a secondary source of uncleanness within [Jerusalem itself]. [Given the low degree of ritual uncleanness that affects this food, and given the fact that the food already had been brought into Jerusalem, such produce should be deconsecrated and consumed within the city limits]'"* (M. M.S. 3:9D). What difference [would it make if the uncleanness stemmed] from a primary source or a secondary source of uncleanness inside [Jerusalem]? [On Yoḥanan's view], are not both [types of uncleanness] matters specified in Torah?

[D] The rabbis, however, only saw a problem with the opinion of Bar Qapara, for there is an apparent contradiction between the opinion of Bar Qapara and that of the [members of the] House of Shammai. For *"The [members of the] House of Shammai say, 'Any such produce must be redeemed [and ritually clean produce bought in its stead, because second tithe must be consumed in a state of ritual cleanness]. [But the unclean produce, even though it no longer has the status of second tithe], itself should be eaten inside [Jerusalem, in accord with the rule that second tithe, once brought into the city, must not be removed]. [This is the appropriate ruling] except for [produce in the status of second tithe] that was rendered unclean by a primary source of uncleanness outside [Jerusalem]. [Given the high degree of ritual uncleanness that affects this food, and given the fact that the food never was brought into Jerusalem while in the status of second tithe, such produce should be deconsecrated and consumed outside the city limits]'* " (M. M.S. 3:9C). What difference [would it make if the uncleanness stemmed] from a primary source of uncleanness,[55] whether outside of [Jerusalem] or inside [Jerusalem]? [On Bar Qapara's view], are not both cases matters specified in Torah, [seeing that both concern a primary source of uncleanness]?

[E] [Yes! Both cases should have the same outcome. But the Shammaites give a special rule for food made unclean by a primary source of uncleanness *inside* Jerusalem], lest people say, "We have seen[56] that [food in the status of] second tithe may be brought into Jerusalem and then taken out." [Hence, the Shammaites hold that, when second-tithe produce is rendered unclean by a primary source of uncleanness, it should be redeemed, but still consumed within the city.]

[F] On this basis, [the Shammaites should rule that such second-tithe produce] should not be redeemed [at all], lest people say, "We have seen that [food in the status of] second tithe may be brought into Jerusalem and redeemed there."

[G] [The Shammaites must allow such produce to be redeemed and other, clean food purchased in its stead, because] having been rendered unclean within [Jerusalem, the city] limits had seized [that very produce, and the owner may not consecrate a separate portion of the same crop]. [Had the second tithe been] rendered unclean outside [Jerusalem, the city] limits would not have seized [that particular food, in which case, even if brought into the city—since it is now unclean and no longer fit for use as second tithe—the food may be taken out and redeemed].

55. So PM, based on Codex Vaticanus. The Leiden Codex, Bomberg edition, and Romm edition read, "What difference [would it make if the uncleanness stemmed] from a primary source or a secondary source of uncleanness, . . . ?"

56. So PM and the Romm edition, reading: *rā'înû*. The Leiden Codex and the Bomberg edition read: *'ênô*, "second tithe does not enter. . . ." The same variation occurs also at F.

[H] Even on the opinion of the [members of the] House of Hillel, is there not an apparent contradiction? For, *"The [members of the] House of Hillel say, 'Any such produce must be redeemed [and ritually clean produce bought in its stead, because second tithe must be consumed in a state of ritual cleanness]. [Then the unclean produce, since it no longer has the status of second tithe], should be eaten outside [the city limits of Jerusalem, so as not to defile the city]. [This is the appropriate ruling] except for [produce in the status of second tithe] that was rendered unclean by a secondary source of uncleanness within [Jerusalem itself]. [Given the low degree of ritual uncleanness that affects this food, and given the fact that the food already had been brought into Jerusalem, such produce should be deconsecrated and consumed within the city limits]'"* (M. M.S. 3:9D). What difference[57] [would it make if the uncleanness stemmed] from a secondary source of uncleanness, whether outside [Jerusalem] or inside [Jerusalem]? [On Bar Qapara's view], are not both cases [mere rabbinic] opinion?

[I] [The Hillelite ruling presumes a case] in which one brings [second-tithe produce] into [Jerusalem] on condition that the [city] limits not seize [that very food, perhaps so as to avoid just the sort of problems under discussion here, should the produce become unclean].

[J] Said R. Zeira, "This [Hillelite ruling] proves that [if] one transports clean second-tithe produce into [Jerusalem] on condition that the [city] limits not seize [that very food], the [city] limits indeed do not seize [the produce; if required, such food may be taken out and redeemed]."

[K] R. Jonah inquired, "[That second-tithe produce in a state of] cleanness [must be kept within Jerusalem and eaten there] is a matter specified in Torah, yet you will rule that [a condition to the contrary is valid]? Rather, the interpretation should be: [if one made such a condition,[58] then] transgressed and redeemed the produce [after removing it from Jerusalem, we nonetheless hold the produce to be validly] redeemed."

[L] R. Jacob the Southerner inquired before R. Yose: "[As explained of the Shammaites above at E, should not the Hillelites

57. The Bomberg edition, through dittography, repeats "What difference."
58. So Haas.

rule that, with regard to second-tithe produce] rendered unclean outside Jerusalem, but then transported inside—such food should not be taken out [no matter what condition one makes], lest people say, 'We have seen that second-tithe [produce] may be brought into Jerusalem and taken out again'?"

[M] [R. Yose replied], "[The condition spelled out at I, that produce is going to be brought into Jerusalem and then taken out, without transgression, is valid only if one] voices [the limitation that] 'taken out' means 'taken out' [physically, but then returned to the city];[such a condition may not] voice [an intention that] 'taken out' means 'to redeem' [the produce outside Jerusalem, for this would clearly be a condition contrary to Scripture]."[59]

[III.A] R. Ḥiyya bar Adda inquired before R. Mana,[60] "[What is the appropriate ruling in this complex case: second-tithe produce inside Jerusalem] is rendered unclean through [contact with] a secondary source of uncleanness; [the food] then is redeemed [in accord with the Hillelite rule at M. M.S. 3:9D, and other produce, now outside Jerusalem, is bought in its stead]. [This other produce] then itself is rendered unclean, now through [contact with] a primary source of uncleanness. [Do we follow the Shammaite ruling—such that this food should be kept outside of Jerusalem altogether (M. M.S. 3:9C)? Or do we follow the Hillelite ruling, which requires the produce's redemption and consumption within Jerusalem?]"

[B] [R. Mana's reply]:[61] It is said: "If the original coins remain available, he may deconsecrate the food with them, [thereby undoing the sale and returning to a simpler state of affairs]. But if [the coins he originally spent] are no longer available, he cannot [deconsecrate the unclean produce at all, for as the Shammaites rule, the produce must be retained as is and kept out of Jerusalem]. [In any case, whether he gets back] the original coins or some new ones, he is not to be flogged [for bringing them out of Jerusalem and spending them there, as instructed by the Shammaites]."

[C] R. Jonah inquired [before R. Mana], "Also: [Do the Shammaites hold the same position] with regard to one [outside Jerusalem]

59. See PM for the meaning of this stich.
60. In the Bomberg edition, Y. M.S. 3:8 continues through F in this unit.
61. Romm edition: 19a.

who buys [unclean food with coins in the status of second tithe; should this food too be kept out of the city]?"

[E] Said R. Mana, "The [city] limits seize [food brought inside Jerusalem]; and a purchaser seizes [any food involved in the transaction]. Just as we rule about [unclean second tithe brought within] the city limits—[according to the Shammaites, such produce must be redeemed, but still eaten inside the city]—so too we rule about the purchaser [of unclean food as second tithe, and the rule applies that this food should be altogether kept out of Jerusalem]."

Y. M.S. 3:6 (M. M.S. 3:10–13)

M. M.S. 3:10

[A] *[If produce] purchased with coins [derived from the sale of second] tithe becomes unclean [and therefore may not be eaten as second tithe]—it should be redeemed.*

[B] *R. Judah says, "It should be buried."*

[C] *[Sages] said to R. Judah, "If [it is the case that produce originally designated as] second tithe, but which then becomes unclean, itself must be redeemed, does it not follow logically that produce purchased with coins [derived from the sale of] second tithe, and which becomes unclean, [also should be redeemed]?" [That is, the original produce itself may be redeemed, despite the unmediated status it had as a sanctified offering. Surely, then, produce later purchased as second tithe, which acquired its sanctified status only secondarily, may likewise be redeemed.]*

[D] *[R. Judah] said to them, "No! [Matters are precisely the opposite of your statement.] Granted that you rule [as above, namely, that produce originally designated as] second tithe, [but which then becomes unclean], itself [must be redeemed]. [That rule applies, however, because if the produce had been] preserved in a state of cleanness, [it could licitly be redeemed while it] remained outside [Jerusalem]. But how could you rule [the same] with regard to produce purchased with coins [derived from the sale of second] tithe, given that such [produce], even when in a state of cleanness, may not be redeemed, even if it still remains outside [Jerusalem]?"*[62]

M. M.S. 3:11

[A] *A deer that one purchased with money [derived from the sale of second] tithe and that [subsequently] died [without proper slaughter, so that its meat is suitable only for consumption by dogs], is to be buried with its hide intact.*

[B] *R. Simeon says, "[Like any other foodstuff in the status of second tithe, such an animal, which has become unfit for human consumption], is to be redeemed."*

[C] *[If] one purchased a live [deer], slaughtered it, and [the meat subsequently] became unclean, it is to be redeemed.*

[D] *R. Yose says, "It is to be buried."*

[E] *[If] one bought [the deer after it already had been] slaughtered, [in effect transferring the sanctified status only to the edible meat], and [that meat subsequently] became unclean, then [the animal] is [to be treated] like produce [in the status of second tithe and should be redeemed].*[63]

M. M.S. 3:12

[A] *[Consider the case of a farmer in the process of selling wine in the status of second tithe, who lends [the purchaser] jugs [in which to transport the wine]. Even if [the seller] corks [the jugs, which might be taken as indicating that he sells the wine and jug as a single whole, nonetheless], he has not transferred [the status of second] tithe [to the jugs]. [This is because he intended merely to loan the jugs, not to sell them.]*

[B] *[What would be the appropriate ruling if] he poured [the wine] into [the jugs] without stating [his intention either to loan or to sell the containers]?*

[C] *[In that case, his actions would serve to indicate whether he considered the wine and jugs to constitute a single whole, as follows]: So long as [the seller] did not cork [the jugs], he has not transferred [the status of second] tithe [to them]. As soon as he*

62. Cf. Haas, *Maaser Sheni*, pp. 95–96.
63. Cf. ibid., p. 98.

corks [the jugs, however], he immediately transfers [the status of second] tithe [to them].

[D] *[In a parallel fashion, consider the case in which a jug full of wine in the status of second tithe is set down together with many other open jugs containing ordinary wine]: So long as [the seller] did not cork [the jug] containing the second tithe, all of the wine in all of the jugs is deemed to be a single, very large batch of liquid]. [Thus, if the amount of wine actually in the status of second tithe is less than] one part in one hundred, [the seller may deem the sanctity of the second tithe to be] diluted [to such an extent that it is null and void]. [He therefore may sell all of the wine as ordinary hooch. But if the seller] had corked [the one jug containing wine in the status of second tithe before it was set down among the other jugs containing ordinary wine, the status of second tithe is not dispersed and diluted]. [Rather, if the seller loses track of which jug is full of second tithe], the consecrated status [of that one jug] is spread [immediately throughout all of the containers], no matter how many there are, [so that he must treat all of the vessels as if they contained sanctified wine].*

[E] *[Building upon the previous rule, consider the case in which the seller had not yet separated heave offering from jugs of wine in the status of second tithe, and those jugs were set down together with other jugs containing ordinary wine]: So long as [the seller] did not cork [the jugs containing the second tithe, all of the wine in all of the jugs is deemed to be a single, very large batch of liquid]. [Thus the seller] may separate the requisite heave offering from any one [of the jugs] on behalf of [the wine contained in] all [of them]. [But if the seller] had corked [the jugs containing wine in the status of second tithe before they were set down among the other jugs containing ordinary wine, the wine in the various jugs does not constitute a single batch]. [Accordingly, if the seller loses track of which jugs are full of second tithe], he must separate the requisite amount of heave offering from each and every [jug].*[64]

M. M.S. 3:13

[A] *The [members of the] House of Shammai say, "[If a merchant wishes to sell ordinary wine in a corked jug to someone purchas-*

64. Cf. ibid., pp. 99–100.

ing edibles with money in the status of second tithe, and the seller wishes to avoid having his jug gain the status of second tithe], he must open [the jug] and pour [the wine] into a vat [before the sale]." [Since in this way the jug is never part of the bargain, it remains unconsecrated.]

[B] *The [members of the] House of Hillel say, "[The merchant must only] open [the jug], but need not pour [the wine into a vat]." [By uncorking the jug, he indicates that he wishes to sell only the wine, but not the vessel. In line with M. M.S. 3:12A, then, the jug itself remains unconsecrated.]*

[C] *To what [situation does the Hillelite] rule apply? [It applies] in locales where it is the custom to sell only corked [jugs of wine]. [By breaking with local custom and selling open jugs, therefore, the merchant indicates that he does not wish to sell each jug together with the wine it contains.] On the other hand, in a locale where it is the custom to sell open [jugs of wine, then the jug itself is deemed part of the sale in any event, so that] the jug does not remain unconsecrated, [but actually gains the status of second tithe].*

[D] *But if [the merchant] wished to impose the strictest [interpretation of the law] upon himself, by selling the wine in exact measure, [saying,*[65] *for example, "I hereby sell you exactly three measures of wine for four pieces of silver," then] the jug remains unconsecrated, [because the merchant's statement indicates that he has no intention of selling the jug at all].*

[E] *R. Simeon says, "Also: [if a merchant explicitly] says to his fellow, 'I hereby sell you this cask [of wine] without [selling] its jug,' the vessel remains unconsecrated."*[66]

[**I**.A] What [scriptural verse supplies] the rationale for R. Judah's ruling[67] [that one should bury produce purchased as second tithe if it becomes unclean (M. M.S. 3:10B)]? [Deut. 14:25 specifies that] *"[You may convert them into] silver"*—once, but not into silver a second time [after produce bought with the coins becomes unclean].

65. So Maimonides, *Commentary,* p. 224.

66. Bomberg edition: 54c. Cf. Haas, *Maaser Sheni,* p. 100.

67. In the Bomberg edition, this unit and all of unit II are numbered Y. M.S. 3:9.

[B] [R. Judah's rationale itself is not expressed clearly in his dispute with sages.] Rather, since they responded to him with an argument *a minori ad majus*, so does he reply to them, [thus proving his view correct even on their assumptions].

[II.A] R. Yose said in the name of R. Yoḥanan, "[The rule at M. M.S. 3:11A] treats a deer [purchased with money derived from the sale of second tithe] like an item sanctified for the upkeep of the Temple, [which may be deconsecrated only] after it has been stood up [before a priest] and appraised. [If such an animal dies, however, it cannot be properly assessed and so is to be buried (M. Tem. 7:3). The sages have made the same rule apply to a second-tithe animal.]"

[B] R. Jeremiah inquired before R. Zeira,[68] "What is the law as to an *unclean* animal [consecrated for the upkeep of the Temple, or by extension, purchased as second tithe]? Must it too be stood up [before a priest] and appraised [before deconsecration]?"

[C] [R. Zeira] said to him, "Had only R. Yose in the name of R. Yoḥanan ruled that a clean animal need not be stood up [before a priest] and appraised, then an unclean animal [also] would not need to be stood up [before a priest] and appraised."

[D] Said R. Hila, "It has been so recited on Tannaitic authority: *'[A firstling of animals, however, which—as a firstling—is the LORD's, cannot be consecrated by anybody; whether ox or sheep, it is the LORD's.] But if it is of unclean animals, it may be ransomed as its assessment, [with one-fifth added]'* (Lev. 27:26–27)—**Just as an unclean beast is a special case because its condition at redemption is the same as at consecration [i.e., it has been and remains unclean from birth], so I would include by analogy a dead animal [declared as a donation for the Temple upkeep or purchased as second tithe *after* its slaughter], since its condition at redemption is the same as at consecration (see M. M.S. 3:11E). I would exclude, by contrast, the animal one declares, 'Consecrated!' which then dies; for its condition at redemption is not the same as at consecration. [Accordingly, just as M. M.S. 3:11A rules, one may not redeem an animal that dies while in the status of second tithe or a donation for the upkeep of the Temple]**" (Sifra Beḥukotai Parshata 4:2).

68. Romm edition: 19b.

[E] Said R. Yose, "[Another] Tannaitic teaching so rules [that an animal consecrated after its slaughter may be redeemed]: *'[As regards] a donkey [dedicated to the Temple]—it is possible to commit sacrilege regarding both it and its milk'* (M. Meil. 3:5). Now isn't milk the same as [the meat of] a dead animal, [such that one might commit sacrilege regarding the meat too]? [And since] any thing that is subject to sacrilege may be redeemed—[we see that an animal consecrated after its slaughter may be redeemed]."

[F] Should you wish to interpret [this ruling] as specifying the laws for dead animals [consecrated after their slaughter, just as the milk was dedicated after milking the donkey]—you may not do so, for we have recited on Tannaitic authority, *"[As regards] a donkey [dedicated to the Temple]."* [The point of M. Meil. 3:5, therefore, is that once dedicated, an animal's milk is subject to the same restrictions as the animal itself.[69] But the ruling says nothing about a dedication of the milk alone, nor does it address a case in which slaughtered meat is dedicated to the Temple.]

[G] Said R. Ḥanina before R. Mana, "You should [rather] explain [the ruling of M. Meil. 3:5] in accord with R. Simeon. For R. Simeon said, 'Items consecrated for the upkeep of the Temple need not be stood up [before a priest] and appraised [before redemption]' (cf. M. Tem. 7:3). [The milk may be redeemed, despite the fact that it cannot be appraised in the approved fashion; Simeon takes this as an indication that such an appraisal is simply not required at all.]"

[H] [R. Mana] responded to him, "If the law follows R. Simeon's opinion, why does [M. Meil. 3:5] specify a donkey [and its milk]? Wouldn't the same rule apply to all other animals? [Hence, the proper understanding of M. Meil. 3:5 is as specified at F above: once dedicated, an animal's milk is subject to the same restrictions as the animal itself.]"

[III.A] Said R. Zeira,[70] "Scripture implies that one should spend [second-tithe money, if] in the sanctified locale [of Jerusalem],[71]—[*'and spend the money on anything you want'* (Deut. 14:26)]; but one should transport [second tithe to Jerusalem], if in the prov-

69. So RiDVaZ.

70. Romm edition: 20a. In the Bomberg edition, the first three stichs of this unit are numbered Y. M.S. 3:10.

71. So PM.

inces— [*'take it with you to the place that the* L*ORD your God has chosen'* (Deut. 14:25). [This distinction underlies the rules at M. M.S. 3:12, which specify in what cases a jug containing wine purchased as second tithe itself becomes sanctified.] Just as, in the sanctified locale [of Jerusalem, where the jug is not needed for carrying the wine from place to place because the liquor may be imbibed immediately,] the jug does not take on a sanctified status, so too in the provinces, [where the jug will be required for transporting its contents to Jerusalem], the jug does enter the status of consecration as second tithe."

[IV.A] R. Ḥiyya in the name of R. Yoḥanan: "Thus must this Tannaitic teaching [be glossed]: *[(What would be the appropriate ruling if) he poured (the wine) into (the jugs) without stating (his intention either to loan or to sell the containers)? (In that case, his actions would serve to indicate whether he considered the wine and jugs to constitute a single whole, as follows)]:*[72] *So long as [the seller] did not cork [the jugs]*—**when he declared them tithe**—*he has not transferred [the status of second] tithe [to them]. As soon as he corks [the jugs, however]*—**if he then declares them tithe**—*he immediately transfers [the status of second] tithe [to them]. [In a parallel fashion, consider the case in which a jug full of wine in the status of second tithe is set down together with many other open jugs containing ordinary wine]: So long as [the seller] did not cork [the jug containing the second tithe, all of the wine in all of the jugs is deemed to be a single, very large batch of liquid]*—***if he then declares them tithe***—*[and if the amount of wine actually in the status of second tithe is less than] one part in one hundred, [the seller may deem the sanctity of the second tithe to be] diluted [to such an extent that it is null and void. He therefore may sell all of the wine as ordinary booze. But if the seller] had corked [the one jug containing wine in the status of second tithe before it was set down among the other jugs containing ordinary wine]*—***and* then declares them tithe**—*[the status of second tithe is not dispersed and diluted]. [Rather, if the seller loses track of which jug is full of second tithe], the consecrated status [of that one jug] is spread [immediately throughout all of the containers], no matter how many there are, [so that he must treat all of the vessels as if they contained sanctified wine]. [Building upon the pre-*

72. The opening portion of this lengthy quote from the Mishnah is added by the translator for clarity.

*vious rule, consider the case in which the seller had not yet separated heave offering from jugs of wine in the status of second tithe, and those jugs were set down together with other jugs containing ordinary wine]: So long as [the seller] did not cork [the jugs containing the second tithe]—**if he then declares them tithe**—[all of the wine in all of the jugs is deemed to be a single, very large batch of liquid]. [Thus the seller] may separate the requisite heave offering from any one [of the jugs] on behalf of [the wine contained in] all [of them]. [But if the seller] had corked [the jugs containing wine in the status of second tithe before they were set down among the other jugs containing ordinary wine, the wine in the various jugs does not constitute a single batch]—**and then declares them tithe**—[if the seller loses track of which jugs are full of second tithe], he must separate the requisite amount of heave offering from each and every [jug]"* (M. M.S. 3:12 with glosses).

[C] **To what case does [M. M.S. 3:12] apply? [It applies] to [jugs containing] wine. But as regards [jugs] of [brine, vinegar, fish brine], oil, [or honey]—whether [he designates the foodstuffs as second tithe] before he corked [the jug] or after he corked [the jug], the jug does not take on [the status of second] tithe; [if this one jug is confused with many others containing unconsecrated liquid], whether [he designated the foodstuffs as second tithe] before he corked [the jug] or after he corked [the jug], [consecration as second tithe] is neutralized in one hundred and one parts [of unconsecrated liquid]; [if the one jug contains heave offering that has yet to be separated and is confused with many others, containing ordinary wine], whether [he designated the foodstuffs as second tithe] before he corked [the jug] or after he corked [the jug], he may remove heave offering from one jug for all [of them together]** (T. M.S. 2:18).

[V.A] Said R. Ḥanina,[73] "[The ruling found at M. M.S. 3:13A—*The (members of the) House of Shammai say, 'He must open (the jug) and pour (the wine) into a vat'*]—raises a question for the [members of the] House of Shammai, [assuming that it refers to a situation in which the householder wishes to separate heave offering from one jug of wine on behalf of all the others (cf. M.

73. In the Bomberg edition, the remainder of this unit is numbered Y. M.S. 3:11.

M.S. 3:12E)]: What difference should there be between this case and one in which five sacks of untithed grain are placed at one threshing floor? If[74] one had five sacks of grain at a threshing floor, would we not set aside heave offering and separate tithes from one sack on behalf of the others? [Why do the Shammaites require the seller to pour all the wine into a single vat, then, in order to sell it without consecrating the individual jugs?]"

[B] R. Joshua b. Levi said, "[The Houses' dispute in M. M.S. 3:13A–B] does indeed refer back to the preceding case [of separating heave offering from one jug on behalf of many others, M. M.S. 3:12E, and the Shammaite ruling seems problematic]."[75]

[C] R. Ba said, "[The Houses' dispute refers to] a second [passage of Mishnah, M. M.S. 3:13C–E; here the question is how the seller should avoid transferring consecrated status to the jugs when he sells large quantities of wine]. [According to this interpretation, there is no apparent contradiction between the Shammaite view and the rules for separating heave offering from large quantities of grain.]"

[VI.A] If [a householder buys a jug of wine with money derived from the sale of second tithe] and specifies,[76] "I wish to have one quarter [*log* of the liquid in this jug as unconsecrated wine]," the jug remains unconsecrated.

[B] R. Ḥiyya in the name of R. Yoḥanan: "[The present] Tannaitic teaching states the same, [that one can avoid the jug's becoming sanctified through an explicit stipulation]: *R. Simeon says, 'Similarly, [if a merchant explicitly] says to his fellow, "I hereby sell you this cask [of wine] without [selling] its jug," the vessel remains unconsecrated.'*"

74. See Y. Ter. 2:1.

75. Romm edition: 20b.

76. So GRA and PM, following Codex Vaticanus (*ʾim ʾāmar*). The Romm edition has an apparent error: (*ʾim rôv*).

4 Yerushalmi Maaser Sheni Chapter Four

Y. M.S. 4:1 (M. M.S. 4:1–2)

M. M.S. 4:1

[A] *One who transports produce [in the status of] second tithe from a place [where it is] expensive to a place [where it is] cheap, or from a place [where it is] cheap to a place [where it is] expensive, redeems it according to the market price of his [current] location.*

[B] *[As regards] one who transports produce [in the status of second tithe] from the threshing floor to the city, or jugs of wine from the winepress to the city, [so as to sell the produce at a higher market value]—the increase [in value accrues to the] second [tithe], but the expenses [involved in transporting the produce are paid out of the farmer's] pocket.*[1]

M. M.S. 4:2

[A] *People may redeem [produce in the status of] second tithe according to its lowest [price in the local market]. [For example, it may be sold at the wholesale rate] at which a shopkeeper buys, but not [at the retail rate] at which he sells; or [at the discount rate] at which a moneychanger breaks [large denominations, so as to rid himself of lots of small coins], but not at [the standard rate] at which he buys [small change].*

[B] *And people may not redeem [produce in the status of] second tithe by estimating [its worth].*

[C] *[Rather, if] its market price is well known, [the produce] may be redeemed for [an offer made in accord with that going rate] by*

1. Cf. Haas, *Maaser Sheni*, p. 109.

one [buyer]. But [if] its market price is undetermined, [the produce] should be redeemed according to the [average of the offers made by] three [buyers]. Examples [of produce in this latter category]: wine that has formed a film, produce that has begun to rot, and coins that are rusty.[2]

[**I**.A] *One who transports produce [(in the status of) second tithe] . . .* (M. M.S. 4:1A): Said R. Jonah, "They specified only *'One who transports'*—[that is, de facto]. But in the first place, it is forbidden [to transport second-tithe produce from one market to another; it should either be redeemed locally or taken directly to Jerusalem]. Furthermore, [the passage of Mishnah refers explicitly to] *'produce [in the status of] second tithe'*—[that is, produce already separated from an untithed batch and consecrated as second tithe]. But if [the batch of] produce has not yet had second tithe separated, [so that some tithe eventually will be designated from within it, but as yet no act of consecration has taken place], even in the first place it is permitted [to transport such a batch from market to market]."

[B] [M. M.S. 4:1A, which allows one to redeem second tithe from one locale in a distant market and at that market's price] accords with the following [narrative]: Rabbi possessed [some untithed] fruit in this locale and also in Kutnayin. He used to designate the tithes for this locale from [the fruit] over there, and then used to redeem the [consecrated produce] according to the [lower market] price found over there.

[C] It has been recited on Tannaitic authority: *"[People may redeem (produce in the status of) second tithe according to its lowest (price in the local market)]*[3] (M. M.S. 4:2A)—[This applies] both [if the price had been] high and then went down, or [if] the price had been low, and then went up.

[D] Granted that if the price had been high and then went down, [one should be able to redeem the second tithe at the current, low market price]. [But why should one be able to use the low valuation in a case where the price] had been low and then went up?

[E] This case is exceptional, [because it attempts to avoid a situation in which, since he feels compelled to redeem his own produce at a premium price, he may try to lower his expenses by] cir-

2. Bomberg edition: 54d. Cf. Haas, *Maaser Sheni*, p. 112.
3. This quote of the Mishnah is added by the translator for clarity.

cumventing the laws requiring him to pay an added fifth (see M. M.S. 4:4–5). [In order to forestall this temptation, sages here rule leniently and allow the householder to redeem his own produce at the lowest recent price.][4]

[F] It has been recited on Tannaitic authority: Abba bar Ḥilfai bar Qiruyah said, "In what case [does the more stringent ruling apply, that one must redeem second tithe at current market rates, no matter how high]? [It applies] in the case of [produce with] an assured status [as second tithe]. But if the produce had a doubtful status [as second tithe, the more lenient rule applies]: 'Whether [the price had been] high and then went down, or the price had been low, and then went up'—he sells it at the lower price (cf. C above)."

[G] Why [is a leniency allowed in the case of doubtfully tithed produce]? Is it because [the food] seems to be worth only a low price, [its status being somewhat in doubt]? Or is it because, [owing to the perishable nature of the produce], he cannot transport the food back to the [more expensive] locale [without its losing some value anyway]?

[H] What would be the difference between [these two explanations]? [Let us assume that the produce had lost some of its value as estimated] in its own local [market], but then [the price] returned to the higher level. If you say [that we allow the sale at the lower price] "because he cannot transport the food back to the [more expensive] locale [without its losing some value anyway]"[5]—the price has already gone up [in the local market, and he need not transport it anywhere to get the higher price]! But if you say [we allow the lower price] "because the food seems to be worth only a low price, [its status being somewhat in doubt]"—even if [the price locally had gone back up], the produce still would appear to be worth only the lower value.

[I] [This lenient ruling is illustrated] by the following [narrative] about R. Ḥiyya bar Vah: When in Rome, he observed some local [merchants] redeeming [the second-tithe portions of] Nicolaos dates from the [Land of Israel] at the [lower] market price [the produce would have had] in Israel [as a homegrown crop]. He

4. So the emendation of PM.
5. Romm edition: 21a.

said, "Who instructed them [to use the lower price in this manner]?"[6] Ḥilfai bar Qiruyah had instructed them.

[J] It has been recited on Tannaitic authority: "[By transporting a golden *dinar* from one locale to another before breaking it for smaller coins, for example, bringing it from a province to Jerusalem for use as second tithe],[7] one may profit up to a *sheqel* (8 percent) or even up to a quarter [of a *dinar*] (25 percent). How could one make [such a profit]? A [golden] *dinar* in our locale is worth 2 *minas* [= 200 *zuz*], but in Arbel [near Sepphoris] it is worth 2 *minas* and 50 *zuz* [= 250 *zuz* in all]. He wishes to change [25 golden *dinars*, here worth] 50 *minas* [= 5,000 *zuz*], and over here [in Arbel] asks them to pay him at the rate of 2 *minas* and 50 *zuz* each. [His profit on such an exchange is 1,250 *zuz* or 25 percent.]"[8]

[II.A] It has been recited on Tannaitic authority: "[When offering to sell] second-tithe [produce], people may not [ask for a] redemption [price] based on [its status as] second [tithe], but only on [its value as] unconsecrated [food]. [As specified at T. M.S. 4:11, this ensures that the buyer will not purposely undervalue the consecrated fruit, knowing that the seller is anxious to redeem it and set off for Jerusalem.]"

[B] R. Saul inquired, "Imagine the case if everyone knew that he was selling second-[tithe produce]. [Would there be a point in asking for offers based on the value of a similar amount of unconsecrated produce?]"

[C] Even in this case [the seller must negotiate the price while upholding the fiction that he sells unconsecrated produce, for the reasons specified above].

6. See PM for an alternative explanation that assumes the Nicolaos dates had an uncertain status as second tithe; apparently the mention of Ḥilfai bar Qiruyah was sufficient for PM to import the distinction in status from F above.

7. See T. M.S. 3:4 and PM.

8. So GRA and RiDvaZ. The Romm edition reads: "A [golden] *dinar* in our locale is worth 2,000 [*peruṭot*]; but in Arbel [near Sepphoris] it is worth 2,000 [*peruṭot*] and one *leqen* [= 2,032 *peruṭot* in all]. He wishes to change 500,000 [*peruṭot* = 250 golden *dinars*] and over here [in Arbel] asks them to pay him 502,000 [*peruṭot*]. [His profit on such an exchange is 2,000 *peruṭot*.]" This reading may be rejected because it indicates a return of only 0.4 percent. As Haas notes, "Rome reads: 'He intends to sell 500,000 [*peruṭot*] and demands in return that he be given here 2,000 *peruṭot* [for each *dinar*], but in Arbel that he be given

[**III**.A] It has been recited on Tannaitic authority: People may not redeem second-tithe [produce through barter], unless [the exchange is for produce] of the same species.

[B] In the absence of this ruling, what might we have said? "People may redeem barley [in the status of second tithe through barter] for wheat, or wheat [in the status of second tithe] for barley, [seeing that both wheat and barley are grains and so the same genre of foodstuff]." Hence, the ruling is required; even [such barter among different types within a single species should be discouraged, for example, one should not redeem] white wheat for dark wheat or dark wheat for white wheat.

[**IV**.A] Said R. Ḥanania,[9] "[In connection with the notion that second-tithe produce may be appraised at a lower price than the going market rate (see Y. M.S. 4:1.I), consider the following story]: When Rabbi would pick the season's first cucumbers [as an exotic gift] for the imperial representatives, [rather than waiting until ten had become ripe, he would pick however few were suitable, but then] designate [one-tenth of each as] second tithe while he cut each and every cucumber. [Then, when redeeming the portion of each he had designated as second tithe], he estimated their [value on the low side], as if they had already been cut [into pieces]."

[B] R. Yoḥanan inquired, "[Even though the plants remain] whole, you maintain they [may be appraised as if] sliced up?!"

[C] Said R. Jonah, "[R. Yoḥanan's question] is well stated. [For imagine the case] if two people were joint owners of a single cucumber—one owning one-tenth and the other owning nine-tenths. Rather than one saying to the other, '[Let's cut it up]; you take your part and I'll take mine,' [which would result in nearly valueless vegetable slices, they would act together to obtain a higher price]; the cucumber would be sold jointly by this one and that one at the highest possible price. So too in this present case [of Rabbi's cucumbers that are partially unconsecrated and partially consecrated], the whole batch should be sold jointly by this one and by that one at the highest possible price."[10]

2,000 [*peruṭot*] plus a *leqen* [or 2,032 *peruṭot* per *dinar*, 508,000 in all].'" This too is an inadequate reading, for the profit here turns out to be only 1.6 percent.

9. In this unit, I follow GRA and RiDVaZ. See also PM.

10. Romm edition: 21b.

[D] [Rabbi's practice of selling his second-tithe cucumbers cheaply] accords with the following [story]: R. Simeon b. Rabbi used to instruct the [Jews] of Rome to underestimate [the redemption price of their second-tithe vegetables]. [But] Bar Qapara took the [vegetables] and cut them up right in front of him. [Bar Qapara] said to him, "Are these worth anything?"

[E] [Bar Qapara's insistence that one not estimate an item as if it had been cut up] thus far applies to anything that, upon being cut up, is worthless; but what about something that, upon being cut up, is worth even more? [In that case, Bar Qapara obviously would allow the cutting, for his general principle seems to be that one must appraise second tithe at its highest possible value.]

[F] R. Joshua b. Levi said, "People should redeem [produce in the status of] second tithe only for its true value,[11] [not higher or lower]."

[G] Said R. Ḥezekiah, "Nothing should be deconsecrated for half a *peruṭah* [even if that is its true worth], so that there not be a case of, *'[They may not] deconsecrate [produce designated as second tithe] with a poorly minted [and therefore nearly valueless] coin'* (M. M.S. 1:2), [but only with money] worth at least a *peruṭah*.

[V.A] Said R. Imi,[12] "How many[13] people have come before R. Yoḥanan and R. Simeon b. Levi [for a ruling on how to value second tithe]? They always say, 'Go forth and uphold the following Tannaitic teaching: *People may redeem [produce in the status of] second tithe according to its lowest [price in the local market]. [For example, it may be sold at the wholesale rate] at which a shopkeeper buys, but not [at the retail rate] at which he sells; or [at the discount rate] at which a moneychanger breaks [large denominations, so as to rid himself of lots of small coins], but not at [the standard rate] at which he buys [small change]* (M. M.S. 4:2A)."

11. So GRA and RiDVaZ; the Talmud itself reads: "only up to thirty-six [*peruṭot*." I follow GRA and RiDVaZ because their reading allows F to make sense in context of varying valuation schemes for redemption of second tithe. PM and *Mareh Ha-Panim* explain that the printed version seems to address a new concern and stands as an independent unit: if one desires to purposely *over*value second-tithe produce when redeeming it, one should not overpay by too high a value. But for further support of the emendation followed here, see also *Mareh Ha-Panim*, p. 22b, s.v. *maʿaser shenî*.

12. In the Bomberg edition, this unit is numbered Y. M.S. 4:2.

13. The Romm edition erroneously reads *bamāh* instead of *kamāh*.

[B] Thus far [the rule at M. M.S. 4:2 seems to apply clearly to] a large quantity of produce [which in any case might be sold at wholesale prices]. [But] if it were a smaller amount? So too: *[it may be sold at the wholesale rate] at which a shopkeeper buys, but not [at the retail rate] at which he sells; or [at the discount rate] at which a moneychanger breaks [large denominations, so as to rid himself of lots of small coins], but not at [the standard rate] at which he buys [small change]* (M. M.S. 4:2A).

[C] [In illustration of this wholesale valuation, consider the following stories]: (1) Rav Naḥman bar Jacob once showed a reed matting[14] [used to wrap a bundle of dates] to a carpenter, and then redeemed it at the price he named.

[D] (2) R. Yannai once showed a quarter [*kav*] of wheat to a miller,[15] and then redeemed it at the price he named.

[E] (3) R. Simon once showed fruit to R. Ḥilqiah [for an appraisal]. [Ḥilqiah] said to him, "[You're asking me? Sell it] for whatever it is worth!" [Angrily, R. Simon] said to him,[16] "People should not redeem produce [in the status of] second tithe at the valuation [given it] by fools!"

[F] (4) R. Pinḥas once showed fruit[17] to a grist dealer [for an appraisal]. [The grist dealer] said to him, "[You're asking me? Sell it] for whatever it is worth!" [R. Pinḥas] said to him, "Thus has R. Ḥilqiah said in the name of R. Simon, 'People should not redeem produce [in the status of] second tithe at the valuation [given it] by fools!"

[G] (5) Said R. Shimmi, "[The wholesale price is] the same as would be charged [for perishable goods] in the summer months, during the hottest heat of the day after bathing time, when [a vendor] gathers up the remnants [of his stock],[18] at which time one can take out a few *peruṭot* and redeem all of it."

[H] (6) Said R. Jeremiah, "[The wholesale price is] the same as one could charge [Friday] afternoon as [the Sabbath] evening is

14. So Jastrow, vol. 1, p. 441, s.v. *ḥôtāl*.

15. So PM, transposing two letters so that *ḥaṭônayā*ʾ (meaningless in context) would read *ṭeḥônayā*ʾ (miller). Codex Vaticanus, for its part, reads *sîṭônayā*ʾ, which may be translated "provisioner" (see Jastrow, vol. 2, p. 978, s.v. *sîṭonā*ʾ).

16. Here I follow the emendation suggested by PM. The Talmud itself, apparently through dittography based on F, inserts: "Thus did R. Ḥilqiah say in the name of R. Simon, 'People should not . . .'" See also B. Sanh. 14b.

17. Romm edition: 22a.

18. So Jastrow, vol. 1, p. 389, s.v. *zûrayā*ʾ; see also vol. 1, p. 174, s.v. *balînêi*.

spreading, from women who are braiding their [hair and already preparing for the Sabbath]; one must pass [the hat] to each of them, gathering a few *peruṭot* and thereby redeeming the produce."

[I] (7) Said R. Yudan bar Gadia, "[The wholesale price is the same as received by] R. Jacob bar Bun, [who came into possession of some second-tithe produce just before Sabbath, when there was insufficient time to find a buyer]; he set [the produce] aside even though it withered, but then redeemed it immediately [after the Sabbath]."

[J] (8) R. Mana had [some second-tithe] oil [that he sent for] storage in Acco. [Upon hearing of this], said to him R. Ḥiyya b. Adda, "Oil [such as yours] from Beit Maᶜaqa does not keep; this is your last opportunity to redeem it, for it is only worth six *minas*!"

[K] Said R. Yoḥanan, **"People should redeem [produce in the status of] second tithe according to [the valuation of] three bidders . . ., even if one of them is a gentile, even if one of them is the owner [of the produce]"** (T. M.S. 3:5).

[L] R. Jonah inquired: "[If] two [of the bidders] are gentiles, [what is the law]?" [Yoḥanan responded], "[Such a valuation may] not [serve as an appraisal]."

[M] [Jonah then asked], "[If] two [of the bidders are joint] owners [of the produce, what is the law]? [Yoḥanan responded], "[Such a valuation may] not [serve as an appraisal]."

[N] [Jonah then asked], "[If] one [of the bidders was a gentile] and one was the owner [of the produce, what is the law]?" [Yoḥanan responded], "[Such a valuation may] not [serve as an appraisal]."

[O] Rather, [the Tannaitic teaching cited by Yoḥanan must be taken] disjunctively; [at least two of the three bidders must therefore be Israelites with no proprietary interest in the food being appraised].

Y. M.S. 4:2 (M. M.S. 4:3)[19]

M. M.S. 4:3

[A] *[If while attempting to deconsecrate second-tithe produce] the householder [who owns it] announces, "[This produce is worth]*

19. In the Bomberg edition, this passage is numbered Y. M.S. 4:3.

a sela^c *[and I wish to deconsecrate it at that price]," and someone else says, "[I too wish to deconsecrate the produce you own for]* a sela^c*," the householder has priority, since [by statute] he must add an extra fifth [of the redemption price to what he must pay (cf. Lev. 27:31), thereby increasing the total amount of food that will eventually be eaten in Jerusalem as second tithe].*

[B] *[But if] the householder announces, "[This produce is worth] a* sela^c *[and I wish to deconsecrate it at that price]," and someone else says, "[I too wish to deconsecrate the produce you own, but I am willing to pay]* a sela^c *and an* issar*," the other person has priority, since it actually increases the principal [representing the produce's market value].*

[C] *One who redeems his own [produce in the status of] second tithe must add a fifth [to its selling price], whether [the produce grew as] his own or whether it was given to him as a gift.*[20]

[**I**.A] But is not [the seller's own bid of one *sela*^c, after figuring in] the added fifth he [must pay] (= 96 *issars* + 19 *issars*), greater than [the independent bid of one *sela*^c] plus [an *issar*] (= 96 *issars* + 1 *issar*)?

[B] Said R. Avin, "[Even though the greater amount, the seller's own bid is evaluated] differently, for he is able to circumvent [the laws stated with regard to second tithe], and [thereby render his own redemption of that produce] exempt from the added fifth (cf. M. M.S. 4:4), [in which case, of course, the independent bid is higher.]"

[C] [Hence]: *"[The bid of a* sela^c *plus an* issar*] has priority, since it actually increases the principal [representing the produce's market value]"* (M. M.S. 4:3B).

[**II**.A] R. Jacob bar Ida in the name of R. Simai: "[As regards] any [batch of] second-tithe [produce][21] that is intrinsically worth less than a *peruṭah*—one need not pay the added fifth [when redeeming it for oneself]."

[B] R. Yose b. R. Simon in the name of R. Yoḥanan:[22] "[As regards] any [batch of] second-tithe [produce] for which the added fifth would be less than a *peruṭah*—one need not pay the added fifth [when redeeming it for oneself]."

20. Cf. Haas, *Maaser Sheni*, p. 126.
21. See Y. B.M. 4:5 and B. B.M. 53b.
22. So the Bomberg edition; other editions have the abbreviation "R. Y."

[C] R. Ba bar Memel responded,[23] "Have[24] we not recited on Tannaitic authority: *'There are five [cases that turn on something being worth at least] a* peruṭah,*'* (M. B.M. 4:7)? If we include the opinion of R. Simai (A above), let it be recited that there are six [such cases]! [M. B.M. 4:7 would be supplemented as follows]: *'The intrinsic worth of [a batch] of second-tithe [produce] must be at least a* peruṭah *[for the laws of the added fifth to come into play].'* And, including the opinion of R. Yoḥanan, there would be seven [such cases]: *'The added fifth pertaining to a batch of second-tithe [produce] must be at least a* peruṭah, *[or the seller may simply ignore that additional payment].'*"

[D] And furthermore, on the basis of that which R. Yose said in the name of R. Mana bar Tanḥum; R. Abbahu in the name of R. Yoḥanan, [we can add an eighth case that turns on something being worth at least a *peruṭah*]: **"Real[25] estate may not be acquired for sums of money less than a *peruṭah*"** (Y. Qid. 1:3).

[E] And furthermore, on the basis of the following, [we can add a ninth case that turns on something being worth at least a *peruṭah*]: "[As regards a batch of] second-tithe [produce, the value of which is unknown, and so potentially less than a *peruṭah*]—[any valuation is sufficient, if the seller says, '[The second-tithe produce] itself and its added fifth are hereby deconsecrated with this *selaᶜ*."

[J] R. Yose in the name of R. Qrispa; R. Jonah in the name of R. Zeira: "This does not constitute a ninth case involving a *peruṭah*], for the Tannaitic teaching just cited refers to [using] a *selaᶜ* that [itself is partially consecrated as] second tithe, it being implausible that some part of its value is not unconsecrated. [We allow the redemption of the unknown—and potentially trivial—amount of second tithe merely to 'fill up' the partially consecrated *selaᶜ*; that fact sets no precedent in general for batches of produce worth less than a *peruṭah*.]"

[III.A] Said R. Yoḥanan,[26] "[As regards] an item consecrated [for Temple use] that was redeemed for more than its actual worth, [thus, in a roundabout fashion, giving an extra donation to the Temple]—[the status of consecration] seizes all [of the money]. [As for] second-tithe produce that was redeemed for more than its

23. Romm edition: 22b.
24. See B. B.M. 55b.
25. See B. Qid. 13b.
26. See Y. Sanh. 1:2 for this entire unit.

actual worth—[the status of consecration] does not seize all [of the money, but only the portion corresponding to the value of the second tithe itself]."

[B] [In such cases of overpayment], what is the difference between an item consecrated [for Temple use] and second-tithe [produce]?

[C] Said R. Imi, "A person commonly will increase [the amount paid when redeeming] a consecrated item, [often explicitly giving this additional money as an extra donation]. [In the case of second tithe, however, people usually try to reduce the amount of money they spend in deconsecration (see above, Y.M.S. 4:1), and so we may assume that any sum over and above the actual worth of the food was simply spent in error.]"

[D] R. Zeira inquired before R. Imi: "[Shall we not] interrogate such a person, who might then say, 'That [extra Temple-donation] was not my intention'?"

[E] [R. Imi] said to him, "Once he has been asked, [we may take into account his explicit intentions; in the absence of such questioning, we presume that, like most people, he intended the additional amount to constitute an extra donation to the Temple]."

[F] R. Jonah inquired: "[The ruling above at A, which presumes that people usually prefer to underpay when redeeming second tithe], accords with the opinion[27] that [second-tithe produce] is not personal property. But on the opinion that [second-tithe produce remains] one's personal property, [so that overpayment merely means that the purchaser will have more second-tithe money to spend in Jerusalem], what[28] is the difference between an item consecrated [for Temple use] and second-tithe [produce]?"

[G] Said R. Yose, "Has not the [following] rationale already been stated, 'A person commonly will increase [the amount paid when redeeming] a consecrated item, [often explicitly giving this additional money as an extra donation]' (C, above)? [By silence, is it not clear that people do not commonly do the same when deconsecrating second tithe?]"

[H] Said[29] R. Yoḥanan, "[As regards] an item consecrated [for Temple use] that was redeemed [by its original donor], who neglected to

27. See B. Qid. 54a.
28. Bomberg edition: 55a.
29. See B. B.M. 54a.

pay the added fifth, [thereby shortchanging the Temple]—this [consecrated item] nonetheless is redeemed. [As for] second-tithe [produce] that was redeemed [by its owner], who neglected to pay the added fifth—this [produce] is not redeemed, [but remains in the status of second tithe]."

[I] [In such cases of underpayment], what is the difference between an item consecrated [for Temple use] and second-tithe [produce]?

[J] Said R. Hila, "An item consecrated [for Temple use is guarded by] claimants, [namely, the Temple treasurers, who see to it that the added fifth is paid when appropriate; if they slip up, the purchaser should not be held accountable]. Second-tithe [produce, by contrast, is not guarded by] claimants, [but only by the good faith of the Israelite who dedicated it; should he neglect the added fifth, he nonetheless remains responsible for carrying out a proper act of deconsecration]."

[K] R. Jonah inquired: "[The ruling above at H, which presumes that people usually prefer to underpay when redeeming second tithe, and so might purposely neglect the added fifth], accords with the opinion that [second-tithe produce] is not personal property. But on the opinion that [second-tithe produce remains] one's personal property, [so that payment of the added fifth merely means that the purchaser will have more second-tithe money to spend in Jerusalem], what is the difference between an item consecrated [for Temple use] and second-tithe [produce]?"

[L] Said R. Yose, "Has not the [following] rationale already been stated, 'An item consecrated [for Temple use is guarded by] claimants, [namely, the Temple treasurers, who see to it that the added fifth is paid when appropriate; if they slip up, the purchaser should not be held accountable]. Second-tithe [produce, by contrast, is not guarded by] claimants, [but only by the good faith of the Israelite who dedicated it; should he neglect the added fifth, he nonetheless remains responsible for carrying out a proper act of deconsecration]' (J, above)?"

[**IV**.A] *One who redeems his own [produce in the status of] second tithe must add a fifth [to its selling price], whether [the produce grew as] his own or whether it was given to him as a gift* (M. M.S. 4:3C).

[B] **This Tannaitic teaching represents the opinion of R. Meir, for R. Meir ruled that a gift is not [legally equivalent to] a sale** (see Y. Maas. 2:1). [Since a gift is legally distinct from a sale, the recipient will be the first to sell/redeem the second-tithe food, and so must pay the added fifth, even though the produce was not originally his own.]

[C] Said R. Jonah, "This [Tannaitic teaching] reflects the view of the entire [rabbinic consistory]. You may interpret [the two cases mentioned in this rule differently; in the first case, the farmer grows the food from seed and designates the second tithe; in the second case, however, he is given] untithed produce. [Both cases are mentioned not because the gift-produce is 'his own,' but because the two types of produce have a different status of consecration.]"[30]

[D] Yet have we not recited on Tannaitic authority: *"One who redeems[31] his own [produce in the status of] a four-year-old planting must add a fifth [to its selling price, whether (the produce grew as) his own or whether it was given to him as a gift]"*[32] Could you actually say [that the separate mention of a gift, as against homegrown produce, here too refers to a gift of produce in the status of a fourth-year planting,[33] [but not yet so designated] (cf. C, above)? [No, for such a category—consecrated but not yet designated—simply does not exist in this case. The question remains, therefore: why mention gifts separately from produce that grew while in the redeemer's possession? Just as here you would have to say that this special mention is] not due to [the nature of] fourth-year produce itself, so too [in the current case of second] tithe, you likewise must finally agree [that the separate mention of gifts is due to their distinct legal standing, not the consecrated status of a particular batch of second-tithe produce].

Y.M.S. 4:3 (M.M.S. 4:4–5)

M. M.S. 4:4

[A] *People may circumvent [the laws stated with regard to the added fifth, even while redeeming produce they own in the status of] second tithe.*

30. Romm edition: 23a.
31. See B. Qid. 54a and B. B.M. 55a.
32. The last phrase of the quote from the Mishnah is added by the translator for clarity.
33. So Codex Vaticanus, followed by GRA and RiDVaZ. Other manuscripts and the Romm edition insert: "here too refers to a gift of untithed produce. Have we not recited on Tannaitic authority."

[B] *How [might a householder do this]?*

[C] *A person may direct his companion,*[34] *adult son or daughter, [or] his Hebrew servant or handmaid, "Take these coins as your own, and use them to redeem this [produce in the status of second] tithe." [Although his dependants, these people are deemed separate legal personae; hence, the householder avoids paying the added fifth.]*

[D] *However, one should not direct his minor son or daughter, [or] his Canaanite servant or handmaid, along these same lines, for their doings are considered to be his own [and so he cannot avoid the added-fifth penalty in this way].*[35]

M. M.S. 4:5

[A] *[Another example of the artifice that might be used to avoid payment of the added fifth].*[36] *[If the householder] was working at the threshing floor but had no coins with him [to give to a dependant for purposes of redeeming the produce], he may say to his companion, "This produce is hereby given to you as a gift," and then immediately say, "It also is hereby deconsecrated with coins that I have at home." [Again, since the householder does not own the second-tithe produce when he redeems it, no added fifth penalty is due, even though he fully expects his friend to return the gift.]*[37]

[**I**.A] Rabbi Avun said,[38] "R. Eleazar and R. Yose bar Ḥaninah disputed [over the meaning of Deut. 14:24's claim that second-tithe produce constitutes a 'blessing,' as follows]:

[B] "One says, 'Why is it that *"People may circumvent [the laws stated with regard to the added fifth]"* (M. M.S. 4:4A)? [We may infer that Scripture intends this money-saving leniency], because [second-tithe produce] is described [at Deut. 14:24] as a blessing."

[**II**.A] [When one follows the procedure for avoiding payment of the added fifth (M. M.S. 4:4–5)], what case do we envision? If the case is one in which he said to [his adult child or slave], "Go and redeem [the second tithe] for me," [then the child or slave] is his agent! [In light of M. Ber. 5:5, *"A person's agent (legally) acts*

34. The Mishnah itself lacks: "companion."
35. Cf. Haas, *Maaser Sheni*, p. 129
36. So Maimonides, *Commentary*, p. 226.
37. Cf. Haas, *Maaser Sheni*, p. 129.
38. The Bomberg edition numbers the next two units Y. M.S. 4:4.

as the person himself," how could this avoid liability for paying the added fifth? So too, if he had said], "Go and redeem [The second tithe] for yourself," it still would belong to him, [so even here he does not avoid paying the added fifth].

[B] Rather, we must envision a case in which he said to [the adult child or slave], "Redeem some of your [second tithe] for me," "Redeem some of my [second tithe] for yourself." [In either of these cases, the owner is not redeeming the consecrated produce himself, so no added fifth is due; at the same time, the farmer gets full benefit from the deconsecrated produce, which now can be used by his dependents.]

[C] And it has been so recited on Tannaitic authority: [If the owner of second tithe says to one of his dependents], "Redeem some of your [second tithe] for me," "Redeem some of my [second tithe] for yourself," he need not pay an added fifth.

[D] Said R. Yoḥanan, "In[39] any case regarding [second] tithe: one need not pay an added fifth unless both it [the second tithe] and its redemption [money] belong to the [same person]."

[E] R. Yose b. R. Bun in the name of R. Ḥanina: "The [scriptural] rationale for R. Yoḥanan's [ruling has to do with the wording of Lev. 27:31]: *'If anyone wishes to redeem any of his tithes, he must add his own*[40] *one-fifth to them.'* [This careful wording] assures that [the added fifth only applies if] both it [the second tithe] and its redemption [money] belong to the [same person]."

[**III.**A] [When one follows the procedure for avoiding payment of the added fifth (M. M.S. 4:4–5), what[41] case do we envision? If the case involves an adult [Hebrew handmaid], has she [not] already gained [the capacity to act independently of her master upon] puberty? [No added fifth therefore should be due if she redeems the produce.] If the case involves a minor [Hebrew handmaid], can a minor acquire [anything, so as to be able to independently redeem the second tithe]?

[B] Said R. Yudan bar Shalom in front of R. Yose, "You may interpret this case in accord with the opinion that a minor may validly separate [and consecrate] heave offering; [similarly, the

39. See B. Qid. 24a.

40. NJPST lacks: "his own"; I add this to render the pronominal suffix on the Hebrew *ḥamîshātô,* which is the Talmud's clear interest here.

41. See Y. Eruv. 7:6 for this entire unit. See also B. Giṭ. 65b.

minor should have sufficient legal independence to deconsecrated second tithe]."

[C] [R. Yose] said to [Yudan], "Even on the opinion that a minor may validly separate [and consecrate] heave offering, can a minor acquire [anything, so as to be able to independently redeem the second tithe]?"[42]

[D] According to the opinion of the rabbis over there,[43] [in Babylonia, the status of a minor] is settled, [as follows at D–J]. For over there they say in the name of Rav Naḥman bar Jacob, "In any case in which (1) one offers a minor a nut, which he discards, and a stone, which he takes—[since the child has little concept of value], that which is taken by him [is not to be considered a case of theft], but has the status of something taken from the garbage.

[E] "(2) [If the minor] takes the nut and discards the stone—that which he steals is [at least partially to be] considered theft [despite the fact that he remains a child], for purposes of protecting the peace [and allowing people to recover such items].

[F] "(3) [If the minor] takes both the nut and the stone, stores them, and then retrieves them after some time—that which he steals is considered a true theft, [for the individual has a clear understanding of his actions]. [Such an individual, however, owing to his youth], may acquire items for himself, but not for others."

[G] Rav Huna said, "Just as [a minor with full understanding] may acquire items for himself [notwithstanding his youth], so may he acquire items for others."

[H] The entire [rabbinic consistory] concedes that anything [such a minor distributes as] a gift has not been validly given away, [as follows]: "In as much as it is written [in Scripture], *'When a man gives . . .'* (Exod. 22:6).[44] [Hence]: 'That which an adult [distributes as] a gift has been validly given away, but that which [such a minor distributes as] a gift has not been validly given away,' the opinion of the sages."

42. Romm edition: 23b.

43. See Y. Giṭ. 5:9 for the remainder of this unit.

44. The full verse reads: *"When a man gives money or goods to another for safekeeping, and they are stolen from the man's house—if the thief is caught, he shall pay double."* The rabbis' deductions about the validity of gifts given by minors thus should be seen only as mnemonic prooftexting.

[I] R. Judah bar Pazzi in the name of R. Yoḥanan; R. Jacob bar Aḥa in the name of R. Yoḥanan: "Anything [a minor with full understanding] steals is considered a true theft only if [the child] has at least two pubic hairs, [for this is the standard indication of legal responsibility]."

[J] R. Abbahu in the name of R. Yoḥanan: "The [ruling that thefts by minors with full understanding are true thefts (F, above)] refers to impounding [the item] in a legal process. But [such a minor is not fully an adult; for example], everyone agrees that [if he were to take an oath and then back out], he would be required to bring the sacrifice for breaking an oath only if he had at least two pubic hairs."

[K] But as for the rabbis here [in the Land of Israel, the status of a minor is dealt with differently]. The associates[45] in the name of R. Yose inquired: "On the basis [of the verse you cite], he cannot even acquire ownership of an item for himself! For it is written [in Scripture], *'[When a man gives money or goods] to his associate. . .'*[46] (Exod. 22:6):—[this cannot apply, then] until he is comparable to his associate."

[L] R. Yose b. R. Bun in the name of Rav Samuel bar Rav Isaac: "Resolve [the uncertain status of a minor] by analogy to [children who have just learned] to talk sensibly.[47] For in another context we have recited on Tannaitic authority: *'[As regards[48] children who have just learned to] talk sensibly—purchases and sales they make are valid, in the case of chattels, [but not with regard to real estate]'* (M. Giṭ. 5:5)."

[M] But have we not also recited on Tannaitic authority: "*[(How do people) establish a partnership in an alley, (for purposes of carrying items on the Sabbath)? One (of the residents) sets out a jar (containing food) and states, 'This now belongs to all the residents of the alley.']*[49] . . . *But*[50] *he cannot effect possession on behalf [of the other residents by so transferring ownership] to his minor son or daughter, or to his Canaanite slave or hand-*

45. The Bomberg edition lacks: "The associates."

46. NJPST: "to another." My rendition of the Hebrew *reʿêhû* attempts to emphasize the parity that underscores the Talmud's point.

47. So Jastrow, vol. 1, p. 102, s.v. *ʾifyôtôt*.

48. See B. Giṭ. 59a and 65a.

49. The first portion of the quote from the Mishnah is added by the translator for clarity.

50. See B. B.B. 155a–b.

maid, because their doings are considered to be his own" (M. Eruv. 7.6).

[N] The rabbis of Caesarea say, "[There is no contradiction in fact between these two Tannaitic teachings.] The first case refers to a minor with full understanding, [who therefore may make valid sales and purchases, cf. M. Giṭ. 5:5]. The second case refers to a minor without full understanding, [who therefore cannot effect Sabbath-partnership in an alley, cf. M. Eruv. 7:6]."

[O] In another context,[51] we have recited on Tannaitic authority: *"A person asked [to borrow] a cow, and [the lender] sent it under the supervision of his son, slave, or agent. [(If the cow) died (before it was delivered, the borrower) is exempt (from any liability)]"* (M. B. M. 8:3). Does this not prove [in sharp contrast to most of the foregoing] that a slave may validly transfer ownership of something [upon delivering it] from his master to another?

[P] Said R. Eleazar, "You should interpret this [ruling] as referring [only] to a Hebrew salve; [Canaanite slaves, by contrast, do not have this independent legal power]."

[Q] Said R. Yohanan, "You may even interpret this [ruling] as referring to a Canaanite slave, [who indeed does have the legal power to transfer ownership of the cow upon delivering it, for even the cow itself can transfer its own ownership]! Interpret [this last reference to the following situation]: [The borrower said to the lender], 'Open [the barn door] for [the cow], and it will come over [to my pasture] of its own accord.' [In this case, from the moment it walks out of its own farmyard, and into the neighbor's pasture, it has validly transferred its own ownership.] And so has it been recited on Tannaitic authority: '[When transferring a cow from lender to borrower, if the borrower] himself drives it along [from behind], leads it, or calls to it so that it follows along after him—[if the animal dies before reaching the borrower's farmyard, the borrower nonetheless] is responsible [for the animal], and must pay [any damages according to the usual procedures] for a borrower.' [The upshot, at any rate, is that any slave, Hebrew or Canaanite, may transfer ownership from his master to another in this case, and by extension, in other cases too.]"

51. See Y. Qid. 1:3 for the remainder of this unit. See also B. B.M. 98b.

[R] R. Zeira deduces [his version of the ruling regarding a slave's validly transferring an item] as follows: " '*[(How do people) establish a partnership in an alley, (for purposes of carrying items on the Sabbath)? One (of the residents) sets out a jar (containing food) and states, "This now belongs to all the residents of the alley."]*[52] . . . *But he cannot effect possession on behalf [of the other residents by so transferring ownership] to his minor son or daughter, or to his Canaanite slave or handmaid, because their doings are*[53] *considered to be his own'* (M. Eruv. 7:6). Does this not[54] prove that a slave may not validly transfer ownership of something from his master to another?"

[S] You must interpret [this ruling] as corresponding to the opinion of R. Meir, [but not to that of the other sages]. For R. Meir[55] [is the one who] considers the doings of a slave equivalent to the deeds of his master, [so that transferring to them part ownership in the food or drink is legally a meaningless act].

[T] [Is this really R. Meir's view?] Has it not been recited on Tannaitic authority: *"[(How do people) establish a partnership in an alley, (for purposes of carrying items on the Sabbath)? One (of the residents) sets out a jar (containing food) and states, 'This now belongs to all the residents of the alley.'] [And thus he may effect possession on behalf (of the other residents by transferring ownership)]*[56] *. . . to his own wife"* (M. Eruv. 7:6)?! Now wouldn't R. Meir consider the doings of a wife equivalent to those of her husband, [so that transferring to her part ownership in the food or drink should also be legally a meaningless act]?

[U] R. Ḥananiah in the name of R. Pinḥas: "You must interpret [R. Meir's opinion about the independent legal standing of a wife and husband] in accord with this Tannaitic teaching, which has been recited: **'A person's wife**[57] **may not redeem second-tithe [produce belonging to her husband, without incurring liability to pay the added fifth].' R. Simeon b. Eleazar says in**

52. The first portion of the quote from the Mishnah is added by the translator for clarity.
53. So the emendation of PM. The Talmud itself erroneously reads: "are not."
54. See B. B.M. 99a–b.
55. See B. Qid. 32b.
56. The first portion of the quote from the Mishnah is added by the translator for clarity.
57. See B. Qid. 24a.

the name of R. Meir, 'A person's wife may redeem [second-tithe produce belonging to her husband, without incurring liability to pay the added fifth]'" (T. M.S. 4:7).[58]

[V] This teaching [thus shows that] R. Meir considers the doings of a slave equivalent to those of his master; [but he] does not consider the doings of a wife equivalent to those of her husband.

[IV.A] Originally,[59] people would [circumvent the laws of the added fifth through an actual transfer] of coins [from the owner of the second tithe to a stranger, who would first use the cash to deconsecrate the produce and then return the produce as a gift] (as at M. M.S. 4:5A). [But] when [these strangers realized they could] take the money and run, [the rabbis] ordained that [avoiding the added fifth] should be accomplished [through the transfer of unconsecrated] produce [to a stranger, who would first trade it for the second tithe, and then return the second-tithe produce as a gift]. [But] despite this, [these strangers realized they could] take the produce and eat it [capriciously, without trading for the consecrated produce; the rabbis] ordained that [avoiding the added fifth] should be accomplished by transferring [to a stranger] ownership of one-tenth of [the owner's] land; [such land is of no immediate use to the stranger, who would therefore undoubtedly trade it forthwith for the second-tithe produce and return the whole lot as a gift] (cf. T. M.S. 4:3).

[B] R. Inaya bar Sisai went before R. Jonah and offered "I will buy your [second-tithe produce] with that *sela*^c [you have, so as to help you avoid payment of the added fifth]." [R. Jonah] said, "If you wish to pick it up, so do!" [thereby giving it to R. Inaya as a gift], and [R. Inaya] went ahead and took it from him.[60] Said R. Jonah, "[Despite the rabbis' ordaining that one not transfer money in this manner when avoiding payment of the added fifth], I had assessed his intentions: if I reclaimed [both] the [coin and the deconsecrated produce] he would not object; for that reason, I gave it to him."

58. Tosefta reverses the order of these two stichs and lacks the attribution to R. Meir.

59. In the Bomberg edition, this unit is numbered Y. M.S. 4:5.

60. Romm edition: 24a

Y. M.S. 4:4 (M. M.S. 4:6–7)

M. M.S. 4:6

[A] *[Consider a case in which a purchaser bargained to redeem some second]-tithe produce for one* selaᶜ *and took over possession [of the produce] from [the farmer]. [If the buyer] had not yet paid [the redemption price of one* selaᶜ, *and the produce's market value went up and] now stands at two* [selaᶜs, *what should the buyer do]?*

[B] *He should pay [the farmer] one* selaᶜ *and earn a profit of one* selaᶜ, *[for he now owns produce worth double the purchase price fixed when he took possession of it]. But [one-half of the produce he acquires, that is, the one* selaᶜ's *worth for which he never paid any cash whatsoever, and which therefore never actually was deconsecrated, retains the status of] second tithe, and he now owns [it and must dispose of it properly].*[61]

[C] *[Now consider a case in which a purchaser bargained to redeem some second]-tithe produce for two* selaᶜs *and took over possession [of the produce] from [the farmer]. [If the buyer] had not yet paid [the redemption price of two* selaᶜs, *and the produce's market value went down and] now stands at one* selaᶜ, *[what should the buyer do]?*

[D] *[So as to avoid confusion regarding the status of the coins paid], he should pay [the farmer] one* selaᶜ *in unconsecrated coin, [which then becomes consecrated in place of the second tithe]; [he should also pay] one* selaᶜ *from his own coins [that already have the status of] second tithe. [In this way, the farmer knows that all of the coins he receives have the special status and restrictions of second tithe.] Now if [the farmer] was an* ᶜam hāʾāreṣ, *[who could not be trusted to properly dispose of second-tithe coins, the purchaser should] give him money [in the status of doubtful second tithe].*[62]

M. M.S. 4:7

[A] *[As regards] one who redeems [produce in the status of] second tithe, but does not declare [that the money now has] the status [of a consecrated item]—*

61. See Haas, *Maaser Sheni*, p. 213, n. 26.

62. Cf. Haas, *Maaser Sheni*, p. 139. For the interpolation, "[in the status of doubtful second tithe]," see Maimonides, *Commentary*, p. 226, and PM.

[B] *R. Yose says, "His [actions] suffice [to effect the transfer of holiness from produce to coin]."*

[C] *R. Judah says, "He must make [the exchange] explicit, [by verbally declaring his intentions]."*

[D] *[As for a person who] was speaking to a woman [either] about her divorce document, [assuming they were married], or about her bridal price, [assuming they were contemplating marriage], and then gave her the divorce contract*[63] *[itself, or money for] the bridal price, without explicitly [stating what the writ or cash was for]—*

[E] *R. Yose says, "His [actions in this context] suffice [to effect the divorce or betrothal]."*

[F] *But R. Judah says, "He must make [his intentions] explicit, [by verbally declaring that the woman is divorced or betrothed]."*[64]

[**I.**A] The current Tannaitic teaching,[65] [which holds that when purchasing second-tithe produce whose value is rapidly rising, some of the food will remain consecrated even while being transferred in ownership], does not represent the opinion of R. Simeon b. Gamaliel. For we have recited on Tannaitic authority: **"Rabban**[66] **Simeon b.Gamaliel [and R. Ishmael b. R. Yoḥanan b. Beroqa] say, 'Acquisition of second-tithe produce constitutes its redemption'"** (T. Arakh. 4:4). [Hence, if the second-tithe produce changes ownership, on this view it would necessarily have been deconsecrated in the process.]

[**II.**A] R. Yose in the name of Eleazar: "[In the situation envisioned at M. M.S. 4:6B, where people come into possession of an extra selaᶜ's worth of second-tithe produce as profit due to rapidly rising prices], they need not pay the added fifth [if they themselves deconsecrate that] second selaᶜ's [worth of produce]."

[B] R. Eleazar just glared at him.

[C] [R. Yose] asked him, "Why are you staring at me? Even my master[67] must concede to that which **R. Yoḥanan said, 'In any**

63. The Romm edition Talmud lacks: "the divorce contract."
64. Romm edition: 24b. Cf. Haas, *Maaser Sheni*, p. 142.
65. The Bomberg edition numbers the next two units Y. M.S. 4:6.
66. Cf. Y. M.S. 5:1.
67. The Talmud itself reads: "Even R. Hila would concede . . ." I follow GRA and RiDVaZ which claim that the current reading is incomprehensible and emend here simply by dropping the single word "Hila." A possible explanation

case regarding [second] tithe: one need not pay an added fifth unless both it [the second tithe] and its redemption [money] belong to the [same person]' (Y. M.S. 4:3.II.D). [Since this second sela^c's worth of second tithe does not really belong to him, but is mere profit, he does not meet the double requirement laid forth by Yoḥanan.]"

[III.A] Precisely what[68] does [R. Judah mean when he says that] *"He must make [the exchange] explicit, [by verbally declaring his intentions]"* (M. M.S. 4:7C, F)? [He should say], "This [writ] constitutes your divorce document"; "This [money] constitutes your bridal price." In the current context: "This [money] constitutes the redemption price for that second tithe."

[IV.A] R. Zeira,[69] Ḥiyya bar Bun; Abba bar Taḥlifah in the name of R. Hoshaiah: "In what case did [R. Yose and R. Judah] dispute [as to whether a verbal declaration is required when handing over divorce documents or the bridal price] (M. M.S. 4:7)? [They disagreed only about this requirement if those discussing marriage or divorce] strayed on to other topics [before the actual transfer].

[B] But [Yose and Judah agree that] if they kept to the business at hand [during the transfer, then no statement of intention is required]: the divorce document [or the bridal price] is legitimate."

[V.A] R. Ḥaggai inquired of R. Yose: "[Is it not the case that] Rabbi agrees with R. Yose, while R. Nathan agrees with R. Judah?

[B] "For in another context we have recited on Tannaitic authority: *"[If[70] the husband said to (his wife's agent)], 'You are not to accept [this divorce document on her behalf]; take it and give it to her instead'—if he wishes to recant [before the agent has actually delivered the writ], he may do so [and there is no valid divorce]"* (M. Giṭ. 6:1).

---

of the Talmud's reading would be that even though R. Hila takes an exceptionally stringent line toward the proper deconsecration of second tithe (cf. Y. M.S. 4:2.III.J), he too agrees with R. Yoḥanan's double requirement for paying the added fifth. Nonetheless, this would not account for the larger sense of the narrative, which has Yose apparently misquoting Eleazar, then defending his citation.

68. The Bomberg edition numbers the next two units Y. M.S. 4:7.

69. See Y. Giṭ. 6:1 for the next two units.

70. See B. Giṭ. 62b.

[C] "And this Tannaitic teaching represents the opinion of Rabbi, for it is recited on Tannaitic authority: **'[A wife] said [to her agent], "Bring my divorce document [from my husband]," and [the agent] went and told [the husband], "Your wife said [to me], 'Bring[71] my divorce document [from my husband],'" [and the husband responded], "Take it to her"; "Give it to her"; "Acquire it for her"—"[Even] if he wishes to recant [before the agent has actually delivered the writ], he may not do so [and the divorce document remains valid in any case]," the opinion of Rabbi'** (T. Giṭ. 4:1a). [As R. Yose in M. M.S. 4:7, so too Rabbi does not require any explicit statement by the husband, 'This writ constitutes your divorce document.']

[D] "[The quotation of Tosefta continues]: **'Rabbi Nathan[72] says, "[If the husband responded], 'Take it to her'; 'Give it to her'—if he wishes to recant [before the agent has actually delivered the writ], he may do so [because such a statement does not constitute a formal declaration that he thereby has transferred the divorce document; the divorce therefore is not valid until she actually takes possession of the writ]. [But if the husband responded], 'Receive it for her'; 'Acquire possession of it for her'—[even] if he wishes to recant [before the agent has actually delivered the writ], he may not do so; [the divorce document remains valid because he explicitly specified that the divorce was valid as of that moment]." Rabbi says,[73] "In all these cases, [the husband] may not recant [once he has given the writ to the agent], unless he explicitly stipulates, 'You are not to accept [this divorce document on her behalf]; take it and give it to her instead'** (T. Giṭ. 4:1b). [Again, Rabbi, like R. Yose at M. M.S. 4:7, holds that the action of giving over the divorce document alone suffices, no statement of the husband's intention is required, and once handed over to the agent the divorce document is fully in effect; R. Nathan, like R. Judah at M. M.S. 4:7, holds the opposite, namely, the divorce document cannot be in force before its delivery unless the husband makes an explicit statement of his intention to the contrary.]"

71. So Tosefta itself, endorsed by PM. The Talmud here reads: "receive," an apparent confusion from the previous case in Tosefta. It also inserts: "Receive it for her," at the end of the list of the husband's responses, again through probable mistake.

72. Tosefta itself reads: "R. Simeon b. Gamaliel."

73. Bomberg edition: 55b.

[E] But there is a problem with Rabbi's view: [If the husband employs his wife's messenger as his own agent, by saying], "Take this [to my wife][74] under my commission," and if he then wished to recant [before the writ was delivered], may he not recant? [Given that his own agent remains in possession of the divorce document, this should be permitted, yet Rabbi's clear opinion is that the husband would not be able to back out of the divorce.]

[F] And there is a problem with R. Nathan's view: [If the husband makes his intentions known to the agent, but indirectly, for instance by saying], "Take this [to my wife] under her commission," and if he then wants to recant, he should not be allowed! [Since the agent accepts the writ under the wife's commission—and the husband seems to be fully aware of this—the wife should be fully divorced immediately; nonetheless, R. Nathan's clear view would be that, in the absence of an explicit statement by the husband, the divorce will not take effect until the wife actually receives the writ.]

[G] R. Ḥuna said, "[If the husband commissions his wife's messenger, as at E above,[75] the outcome is that] he becomes both his agent and her agent! [How then should we determine the outcome?]"

[H] Issa[76] said, "All of this accords with that which we have recited on Tannaitic authority: '[If the writ is in the possession of someone serving as both] his agent and her agent, [then the status of the wife is a matter of incertitude]; she is both divorced and not divorced.'"

[I] [Said R. Ḥaggai before R. Yose, "Is the current dispute (regarding the status of a divorce document in transport from husband to wife via an agent] really parallel to that other dispute we have recited on Tannaitic authority elsewhere? (Consider these two disagreements): '(If the husband) was speaking to the wife on matters pertaining to her pending divorce or marriage and then gave her the divorce document or bridal price without specifying (what he was giving to her)—R. Yose says, "(The context) suffices (to make clear his intention to divorce or to marry her)."

74. Romm edition: 25a.

75. So GRA, whom I follow for consistency with the Talmud's statement that the messenger becomes the agent of both parties. PM, however, relates Ḥuna's statement to the situation at F, where the husband simply endorses his wife's commission of the agent. See also B. Giṭ. 62b.

76. GRA attributes this stich to "R. Assi." PM renders: "R. Yissa."

R. Judah says, "(Despite their ongoing discussion), he must specify (his intended consequence in giving her the writ or money)." It turns out that Rabbi agrees with R. Yose, while R. Nathan agrees with R. Judah.'"][77]

[J] [R. Ḥaggai further] said to him, "And what [dispute] do you have in your hand [that is supposed to be wholly parallel to the foregoing]? [Is it not the following]: 'R. Zeira; Ḥiyya bar Bun; Abba bar Taḥlifah in the name of R. Hoshaiah: "In what case did [R. Yose and R. Judah] dispute [as to whether a verbal declaration is required when handing over divorce documents or the bridal price] (M. M.S. 4:7)? [They disagreed only about this requirement if those discussing marriage or divorce] strayed on to other topics [before the actual transfer]. But [Yose and Judah agree that] if they kept to the business at hand [during the transfer, then no statement of intention is required]: the divorce document [or the bridal price] is legitimate"' (Y. M.S. 4:4.IV.A–B).

[K] "[But now we can see that the two disputes are not really parallel at all.] For in the one context, [T. Giṭ. 4:1, Rabbi and R. Nathan's] dispute [over the necessity of a formal declaration of intention applies] even if [husband and wife] continue to discuss the [pending divorce or marriage; in the other case, M. M.S. 4:7, R. Yose and R. Judah's disagreement applies only if the husband and wife have begun to discuss other matters in the meantime]."

[VI.A] R. Ezra inquired of R. Mana, "[Consider the practice of gift giving, specifically, the case where one person appointed an agent to accept the gift on his behalf, but the giver told the agent merely to bring the item to the person, but did not instruct him to accept it. Does Rabbi's opinion that one cannot recant (above, Y. M.S. V. EC–D)] apply also to the transfer of a gift [from one person to another]? [For in both cases, the] person [who commissions the agent, whether wife or gift-recipient], would have appointed an agent to accept something that did not, as yet, belong to the person."[78]

[B] [R. Mana] said to him, "[The two cases are not fully parallel, for] in the one context, the Torah itself has already accorded her

77. The Talmud itself lacks this bracketed material, which I supply based on the parallel in Y. Giṭ. 6:1.

78. Cf. RiDVaZ for the meaning of this unit.

ownership of the divorce document, so she really only appoints the agent to accept something that already belongs to her; [that is why, on Rabbi's view, the husband cannot retract, no matter what he stated]. But in the case of the gift, you would have to say that [the recipient] commissions the agent to accept something that does not, as yet, belong to him; [accordingly, given the giver's stipulation, the gift could be retracted before its delivery, contrary to Rabbi's ruling for divorce documents]."

[C] Furthermore, [we can see the appropriate ruling for gift giving] on the basis of something said by R. Yose, R. Jacob bar Zevadi, [and] R. Abbahu in the name of R. Yoḥanan: "[A person][79] stated he was giving [something] to his friend as a gift, but then wished to recant [before the gift was delivered]—he may recant, [for until the delivery, the gift remains his property]."

[D] R. Yose arose before R. Jacob bar Zevadi: "Would such a person's *hin*-measure [accord with this verse of Scripture], '*[You shall have] . . . an honest* hin' (Lev. 19:36)? [Once he promised the gift, how could he recant?]"[80]

[E] They responded, "[That verse applies to] a case in which someone explicitly stated that [a given volume] is honestly a *hin*."

Y. M.S. 4:5 (M. M.S. 4:8)[81]

M. M.S. 4:8

[A] *[Consider a case in which a person] deposited a [second-tithe coin worth one]* issar *[with a food merchant in Jerusalem], and [over time] consumed [produce purchased] against half its value, [thus discharging the holiness within half the coin]. [The person] then went to another [food] establishment [in Jerusalem], where [his coin] was valued at one* dupondium, *[twice its previous value, so that the remaining consecrated money is worth a full* issar*]. [Such a person] should consume, [as second tithe], another full* issar *[and only then deem the coin to be fully deconsecrated].*

79. See Y. Shevi. 10:5, Y. B.M. 4:2, and B. B.M. 49a.
80. So RiDVaZ.
81. In the Bomberg edition, this unit is numbered Y. M.S. 4:8.

[B] *[Consider a case in which a person] deposited a [second-tithe coin worth one]* dupondium *[with a food merchant in Jerusalem], and [over time] consumed [produced purchased] against half its value, [thus discharging the holiness within half the coin]. [The person] then went to another [food] establishment [in Jerusalem], where [his coin] was valued at one* issar, *[only half its previous value, so that the remaining consecrated money is worth only one-half an* issar*]. [Such a person] should consume, [as second tithe], another one-half [*issar, *and only then deem the coin to be fully deconsecrated].*

[C] *[A person] who deposited a second-tithe coin worth one* issar *[must consume food worth the overwhelming majority of the coin's value before deeming it deconsecrated]. [That is, he] must eat [food worth all but] one-eleventh of*[82] issar's *value, [if the coin had doubtful second-tithe status], or [all but] one-hundredth of the* issar's *value [if it surely had the status of second tithe].*

[D] *The [members of the] House of Shammai say, "[In] any [case, no matter what the certainty of the status of the second-tithe coin, the householder must consume all but] one-tenth [of the* issar's *value before deeming it deconsecrated]."*

[E] *But the [members of the] House of Hillel say, "[If the coin] certainly [had the status of second tithe, he must consume all but] one-eleventh [of its value before deeming it deconsecrated]; and [if its status as second tithe were] doubtful, [he must consume all but] one-tenth [of its value]."*[83]

[**I.**A] R. Ḥiyya recited on Tannaitic authority: "Two *issars* equal one *dupondium*."

[B] Said R. Mateniah,[84] "The present Tannaitic teaching makes the same point: *[Consider a case in which a person] deposited a [second-tithe coin worth one]* issar *[with a food merchant in Jerusalem], and [over time] consumed [produce purchased] against half its value, [thus discharging the holiness within half the coin]. [The person] then went to another [food] establishment [in Jerusalem], where [his coin] was valued at one* dupondium,

82. Romm edition: 25b.
83. Romm edition: 25a. Cf. Haas, *Maaser Sheni*, pp. 144–45.
84. So the Leiden Codex and Romm edition, perhaps through the similarity of the next word *matnîta*ʾ. The Bomberg edition attributes this stich to "R. Yose."

[twice its previous value, so that the remaining consecrated money is worth a full issar*]. [Such a person] should consume, [as second tithe], another full* issar *[and only then deem the coin to be fully deconsecrated]* (M. M.S. 4:8A).

[**II**.A] Samuel said,[85] "This teaching (cf. M. M.S. 4:8C) cannot be [calculated, for one-eleventh of an *issar* is a repeating fraction, $.\overline{09}$]. [Hence], if one [consumes] all but one-tenth [of the *issar* (= .10), he has left too much and the *issar* is not yet deconsecrated], so he needs to consume an additional one-hundredth [of an *issar*]. [But this would leave him with .09 *issar,* and he would have eaten more than necessary to deconsecrate the coin], so he would have to leave an additional one one-thousandth. [But this would leave him with .091 *issars,* more than one-eleventh, and the coin would not yet be deconsecrated], so he would have to eat an additional one ten-thousandth. [But this would leave him with .0909 *issars,* and again he would have eaten more than required to deconsecrate the coin. Owing to the repeating fraction, this problem continues *ad nauseam.*]"

[**III**.A] *The [members of the] House of Hillel*[86] *say, "[If the coin] certainly [had the status of second tithe, he must consume all but] one-eleventh [of its value before deeming it deconsecrated]; and [if its status as second tithe were] doubtful, [he must consume all but] one-tenth [of its value]"* (M. M.S. 4:8E).

[B] Bar Qapara recited on Tannaitic authority: "Whether the money has a doubtful or an assured status [as second tithe], *'[He must consume all but] one-eleventh [of its value before deeming it deconsecrated]'* (M. M.S. 4:8E)." R. Yudan b. R. Shalom instructed [people] in accord with this teaching of Bar Qapara.

[**IV**.A] **[The (members of the) House of Hillel say, "A person may separate first tithe from doubtfully tithed produce, remove the heave offering (of the tithe), and then eat (the remainder of the first tithe), but need not separate second tithe (from that first-tithe produce)." But the (members of the) House of Shammai say, "He must separate second tithe (from the batch of first-tithe produce before he eats it)." And the practicable**

85. See Y. Dem. 7:5, which appears to be the original context for Samuel's statement. See also PM.

86. So the emendation of PM. The Talmud itself reads: "The House of Shammai."

law follows the opinion of the House of Shammai] (T. M.S. 3:15).[87]

[B] The [opinion of] the House of Shammai accords with that of R. Eliezer, for **R. Eliezer said,**[88] **"[If a person] is trusted [to have properly separated] second [tithe], he may be trusted [to have properly separated] first [tithe]"** (T. M.S. 3:16, with minor variations).

[C] Said R. Yose, "[This ruling, that one who has separated second tithe should be trusted to have properly designated first tithe], represents the opinion of the entire [rabbinic consistory, not just R. Eliezer]. For they compared it to first fruits offered together with a supplement, [above and beyond the required minimum]. Just as: *'The supplement to the first-fruits offering is [fully in the status of first fruits, so that it] must be eaten in a state of cleanness and is exempt from a doubtfully tithed status'* (M. Bik. 3:10), so this [produce properly consecrated as second tithe] may be eaten as second [tithe] and is [assumed to be] exempt from [any further separation of] first [tithe]."

[D] R. Ḥanania came forward in the name of R. Yose: "This [is the opinion] of R. Eliezer [alone]. [For **sages say, 'If a person is trusted (to have properly separated) first (tithe), he may be trusted with regard to second (tithe); (but if he) is trusted (to have properly separated) second (tithe), he is not (automatically) trusted (to have separated) first (tithe)'** (T. M.S. 3:16).]"[89]

Y. M.S. 4:6 (M. M.S. 4:9–12)[90]

M. M.S. 4:9

[A] *Any coins discovered [in Jerusalem] are deemed unconsecrated. [This is the case] even if [one finds a cache containing] gold* dinars, *as well as silver and copper coins, [and, because of the mixture of denominations, believes that the collection may have been designated as tithe].*

87. For the insertion of this bracketed Toseftan passage, see PM.
88. See Y. Dem. 4:3.
89. The entire quote of the Tosefta is added by the translator for clarity.
90. In the Bomberg edition, this unit is numbered Y. M.S. 4:9.

[B] *[But if the person] found a potsherd marked*[91] *"tithe" [among the coins], the [entire cache] is [accorded the status of] tithe.*[92]

M. M.S. 4:10

[A] *[As regards a person] who finds a jug marked "offering"—*

[B] *R. Judah says, "If [the jug is made] of clay, it is unconsecrated, but its contents are accorded [the status of] an offering. If [the jug is made] of metal, it is accorded the status of an offering, while its contents remain unconsecrated."*

[C] *They said to him, "It is not the usual practice for people to put unconsecrated material into [a container that has the status of] an offering."*[93]

M. M.S. 4:11

[A] *[As for a person] who finds (1) a jug marked with [the letter]* qof*—[the produce it contains is accorded the status of] an offering* (qōrbān)*; (2) [a jug marked with the letter]* mem*—[the produce contained is accorded the status of] tithe* (maᶜasēr)*; (3) [a jug marked with the letter]* dalet*—[the produce is] doubtfully tithed* (demai)*; (4) [a jug marked with the letter]* ṭet*—[the produce is] certainly untithed* (ṭevel)*; (5) [a jug marked with the letter]* tav*—[the produce is accorded the status of] heave offering* (terûmâh)*;*

[B] *For in times of persecution, [people abbreviated such labels, for example], writing* tav *instead of the full word* terûmâh.

[C] *R. Yose says, "All [such abbreviations stand for] people's names, [not the status of the jar's contents]."*

[D] *Said R. Yose, "Even if one found a barrel full of produce, [clearly] marked 'heave offering,' the contents are unconsecrated, because I say that although it may have been filled with heave offering last year, [since then, the vessel] could have been emptied [and refilled with unconsecrated produce]."*[94]

M. M.S. 4:12

[A] *[If a person] tells his son, "[I have placed some] second-tithe [coins] in a particular corner," but [the son] finds [some coins] in a different corner, the [coins he finds] are unconsecrated.*

91. Romm edition: 26b.
92. Cf. Haas, *Maaser Sheni*, p. 148.
93. Cf. ibid., p. 148.
94. Cf. ibid., pp. 148–49.

[B] *[If the householder told his son], "[I have placed] one* maneh *[of second-tithe coins] in a particular [corner], but [the son] found two hundred [*zuz, *that is, two* manehs, *in that same corner], the extra [one* maneh*] is [deemed to be] unconsecrated.*

[C] *"[I have placed] two hundred [*zuz *of second-tithe coins in the corner]," [but the son] found [only one]* maneh *[i.e., only one hundred* zuz*], all [the money is deemed to have the status of second] tithe.*[95]

[I.A] [By their rule, *"Any coins discovered [in Jerusalem] are deemed unconsecrated"* (M. M.S. 4:9A), the rabbis intended] that one not reason as follows: since people do not ordinarily act [so as to leave unconsecrated money lying around in Jerusalem, hoards of coins that are indeed found in the holy city] ought to be considered [second] tithe, [stored in the city for later purchases of food and drink]. For this reason one must rule [to the contrary, that such coins, owing to the very uncertain status, are to be considered] unconsecrated.

[II.A] It has been recited on Tannaitic authority: **[If a jug found in Jerusalem was marked]** ***alef, dalet, ḥet, ṭet, resh,*** or ***tav***[96]**—[the produce it contains is deemed to be] heave offering** (T. M.S. 5:1).

[B] *ʾAlef,* [the number one, indicates heave offering], the first [offering designated from a batch of produce].

[C] *Dalet,* [representing *demai,* indicates that, like food with a] doubtfully tithed status, [the contents of the jug are prohibited, except as the very first offering to be separated].

[D] *Ḥet* [representing *ḥelbô,* refers to Lev. 4:19], "*[He shall heave*[97]*] all its fat.*"

[E] *Ṭet* [would represent *ṭûvô*], its best part.

[F] *Resh* [represents *rêshît*], the first [offering].

[G] And *tav* [represents the word *terûmâh*], literally, "heave offering."

95. Cf. ibid., p. 153.

96. So the Talmud's version. Tosefta itself reads only: ***ʾalef, dalet, resh,* or *tav*.** Note also that the Talmud, apparently through scribal confusion, adds *mem,* appropriate not to items in the status of heave offering but of tithe (*maʿasēr*) and at any rate included below at I in the continuation of the Tosefta's list.

97. NJPST, taking the verse in context, renders: "He shall remove all its fat."

[H] **[If the jug was marked] *pe-shin,*[98] [representing the words *pidyôn,* "redemption," and *shēnî,* "second"]—[the produce is deemed to be] second [tithe].**

[I] **[If marked] *yod,* [indicating the number ten, hence a tenth of the crop], or *mem,* [representing the word *maᶜasēr*]—[the produce is deemed to be first] tithe** (T. M.S. 5:1).[99]

[J] **[If a jug is found outside of Jerusalem, marked] "tithe for the city"—[the jug's contents] should be redeemed [as second tithe and the proceeds brought to Jerusalem in the usual manner].**

[K] **[If a jug full of produce is marked] "for Joseph"[100] or "for Simeon"**—I say [such personal names simply indicate the owner of each] picnic basket.[101]

[L] **[If the jug is marked] "to be brought up and eaten"—[the produce remains] unconsecrated** (T. M.S. 5:3, with minor variations).

[M] [The Toseftan rules cited] thus far [apply to] new [jugs of produce, since the inscriptions cannot be last year's, but must refer to the food now found in the jug]. [But if we speak of] well-worn jugs—*"I say that although it may have been filled with heave offering last year, [since then, the vessel] could have been emptied [and refilled with unconsecrated produce]"* (M. M.S. 4:11D).

[N] Such[102] [principles are illustrated by] the following [story involving] R. Jonah[103] and R. Yose, who jointly owned some bottles [of wine]. R. Jonah died, and [his student and heir] R. Mana said to R. Yose, "Every bottle inscribed 'R. Jonah' now belongs to me." [R. Yose] responded, "[Perhaps] last year [those bottles were so marked, and they] would have been your inheritance; but this year they are mine, [notwithstanding the old labeling]."

[O] If one found [a bottle full of wine] with its stopper, and upon the

98. So Tosefta itself. Codex Vaticanus reads only *shin*. Printed editions of the Talmud add ***"bet-shin,* [representing the number two and the word *shenî,* second]."**

99. Tosefta reverses the order of stichs at H and I.

100. So Tosefta itself. The Talmud reads: "for Yose."

101. So Jastrow, vol 2, p. 974, s.v. *sîbôlet*. Tosefta itself ends this stich: "**—[nothing special need be done with the produce].**" The Talmud misplaces its ending here by one line, following L.

102. See B. Yev. 115b.

103. The Bomberg edition here reads: "R. Judah."

stopper was inscribed "tithe"—[what is the law]? Is [the wine] in fact consecrated, [in as much as it remains sealed]? [Or should we allow for the possibility that the stopper was simply reused and is an outdated label?][104]

[P] [In accord with R. Yose's general outlook, one may assume] that the [stopper] was transferred [from another bottle that did in fact contain consecrated wine; the current contents of this bottle, however, may be deemed unconsecrated].[105]

[III.A] In another context, we recite on Tannaitic authority: *[On the eve of a festival]*[106] *a person set aside some black figs [for one of the holiday meals] but then [at meal time] found white figs; or he set aside some white figs but then found black figs; or he set aside two figs but then found three figs—[this food is] forbidden [for use on the festival, since it surely is not the same produce he designated and prepared beforehand for his meal]. [Had he set aside] three figs but then found two—[these figs are] permitted [for festival use, since in all likelihood, they are a portion of the food he prepared for the holiday meal]. [(Had he set aside a few chicks) inside the nest, but then found them in front of the nest—(the chicks are) prohibited (for use on the festival). But if there are no other (chicks) present—(the chicks found outside the nest) are permitted]*[107] (M. Beṣ. 1:4).

[B] R. Jacob bar Aḥa in the name of R. Yose: [This Tannaitic teaching represents the opinion of] Rabbi. For it has been recited on Tannaitic authority. ***[If the householder told his son] . . ., "[I have placed] two hundred [zuz of second-tithe coin in the corner]," [but the son] found [only one]* maneh *[i.e., only one hundred* zuz*]*—"[(We assume) that one *maneh* was left behind and] one *maneh* was carried off," the opinion of Rabbi. But sages say, "[All (of the coins)] are unconsecrated"**[108] (T. M.S. 5:7).

[C] [Jacob bar Aḥa] retracted and ruled that [M. Beṣ. 1:4] represents the opinion of the entire [rabbinic consistory], for chicks [set aside for use in a festival meal] differ [from second-tithe coins] in that the former are capable of flying away. [Not only

104. So PM and RiDVaZ.
105. Romm edition: 27a.
106. See Y. Beṣ 1:5 and B. Beṣ. 10b.
107. The concluding portion of the quote of the Mishnah is added by the translator for clarity.
108. Portions of the Toseftan passage are added by the translator to fill out this elliptical quote.

Rabbi, but all sages would therefore agree that if only two of three birds were found, the two that do remain would be permitted for festival use.]

[D] But has not R. Ḥalafta b. Saul recited on Tannaitic authority: "The same law applies to both chicks and eggs [set aside in a particular number for use on the festival, if later fewer are found]—both cases follow the opinion of Rabbi, [and the eggs or chicks that remain may be used on the festival]." [This ruling cannot stem from the ability of the eggs to fly away, and so M. Beṣ. 1:4 again seems to represent the opinion of Rabbi alone, not that of the entire rabbinic consistory.]

[E] [Again, the ruling at M. Beṣ. 1:4 may be viewed as representing the general opinion, not just that of Rabbi at T. M.S. 5:7.] In the former case, the person who set aside [the eggs within the nest also returned on the festival and] found [the eggs outside the nest]. [Since he would be able to discern if they were in fact the same eggs, all of the rabbis would agree that he could use them on the festival.] But in the other case, the father placed [the coins in storage], but his son[109] found [the coins]. [Since the son would have no way to determine if those that remained were some of the same coins, sages rule that none of the coins should be deemed consecrated; Rabbi, by contrast, simply presumes that a portion of the coins were taken improperly in the interim.][110]

[F] R. Bun bar Cohen said before R. Yasa in the name of R. Aḥa, "In regard to second tithe, R. Abba b. Zeveda instructs [that the law] follows the opinion of Rabbi."

[IV.A] [Upon his father's death a young man] was wondering [where] his father had [hidden] his money, and [the father] appeared to him in a dream [and said], "[My money is in the status of] such-and-so [an offering] and [is stored] in thus-and-such a place."[111] When the case came before the rabbis, they ruled,

109. So Y. Beṣ. 1:5, as required by context. the Talmud itself reads: "but the father"

110. The parallel in Y. Beṣ. 1:5 attributes this stich to R. Yosa.

111. The phrase, "*When the case came before the rabbis,*" seems to be an Aramaic paraphrase of Tosefta itself, which reads: **"This is what happened: they went and found the coins just there. So they came before the sages and inquired. [The sages] ruled, 'These coins are unconsecrated, for matters learned in a dream cannot serve to elevate or diminish [the status of the coins].'"**

"Matters learned in a dream cannot serve to elevate or diminish [the status of the coins]" (T. M.S. 5:9).

[B] R. Jonah inquired, "[The son] was wondering, had this vision, yet you rule [such dream-evidence inconsequential]?"

[C] Said R. Yose, "[Allowing such evidence] would be unreasonable: it is not as if he had a vision regarding something he was not wondering about. Instead, the dream here was precisely [on the topic of] what the person [had been thinking about; it thus was only a reflection of his own thoughts and not a true revelation]."[112]

[D] Said R. Avin, "One who wishes to act properly will follow the advice of R. Yose."

[V.A] A person once came before R. Yose b. Ḥalafta and told him, "In a dream-vision, I was told, 'Go to Cappodocia and you will find your father's property [awaiting your claim as heir].'" [R. Yose] said to him, "Had the gentleman's father in all his days ever gone to Cappodocia?" to which he responded, "No." [R. Yose] told him, "Count off ten roof-rafters in your house and you will find your father's property [hidden there]"—[for "Cappodocia" means] *kappa dekoria* ["ten rafters" in Greek].

[B] A person once came before R. Yose bar Ḥalafta and told him, "In a dream-vision, I was wearing a crown of olive branches." [R. Yose] said to him, "You will soon be exalted." Another person came and told him, "In my dream-vision, I was wearing a crown of olive branches." [R. Yose] said to him, "You're going to be flogged." He said [to R. Yose], "You told him he would soon be exalted, but you told me I'm going to be flogged!?" [R. Yose] explained, "[I discerned that] his [olives] were budding; yours, by contrast, were ready to be pressed [for their oil]."

[C] (1) A person once came before R. Ishmael b. R. Yose and told him, "In a dream-vision, someone was watering an olive tree with oil." [R. Ishmael] said to him, "The gentleman's soul will soon expire, for he has been intimate with his own mother."

[D] (2) A person[113] once came before R. Ishmael b. R. Yose and told him, "In a dream-vision, one of my eyes was watering the other [with its tears]." [R. Ishmael] said to him, "The gentleman's

112. So Haas.
113. See B. Ber. 56b.

soul will soon expire, for he has been intimate with his own sister."

[E] (3) A person once came before R. Ishmael b. R. Yose and said to him, "In a dream-vision, I had three eyes." [R. Ishmael] said to him,[114] "You are destined to make ovens: two of the eyes [you saw] are your own, and one eye is the oven's [vent hole]."

[F] (4) A person once came before R. Ishmael b. R. Yose and said to him, "In a dream-vision, I had four ears." [R. Ishmael] said to him, "You are destined to fill [wine casks]: two of the ears [you saw] are your own, and two ears are the cask's [handles]."

[G] (5) A person once came before R. Ishmael b. R. Yose and said to him, "In a dream-vision, living creatures ran away from me." [R. Ishmael] said to him, "You will [have great power;[115] even when] you carry a mere prickly twig everyone will flee before you."

[H] (6) A person once came before R. Ishmael b. R. Yose and said to him, "In a dream-vision, I was wearing a book with twelve pages!" [R. Ishmael] said to him, "The gentleman's blanket [must be threadbare], with twelve patches."

[I] (7) A person[116] once came before R. Ishmael b. R. Yose and said to him, "In a dream-vision, I swallowed a star." [R. Ishmael] said to him, "The gentleman's soul will soon expire, for he has killed Jews, as it is written [in Scripture], *'A star rises from Jacob'* (Num. 24:17)."

[J] (8) A person once came before R. Ishmael b. R. Yose and said[117] to him, "In a dream-vision, this gentleman's vineyard grew only lettuce." [R. Ishmael] said to him, "The gentleman's wine will turn out so sweet you will have to dip bitter lettuce in it."[118]

[K] (9) A person once came before R. Ishmael b. R. Yose and said to him, "In a dream-vision, I was told this: 'Let your finger sprinkle down.'" [R. Ishmael] said to him, "Pay me first, and I will interpret it to you." [The next morning], the person told [R.

114. Romm edition: 27b.
115. So Jastrow, vol. 1, p. 46, s.v. *ʾîzāʾ*.
116. See B. Ber. 56a.
117. Bomberg edition: 55c.
118. So PM. Jastrow, vol. 1, p. 178, s.v. *bāsîm* and *basîn*, renders an opposite meaning: "this man's wine shall turn sour (ferment); thou wilt take lettuce and dip in vinegar" (as a condiment).

Ishmael], "In a dream-vision, I was told this: 'It shall swell in your mouth.'" [R. Ishmael] said to him, "Pay me first, and I will interpret it to you." [On the third morning], the person told [R. Ishmael], "In a dream-vision, I was told this: 'Your finger shall straighten,'" [R. Ishmael] said to him, "Didn't I tell you to pay me first, and then I would interpret it for you? [Now you have lost everything!] When you were first told, ['Let your finger sprinkle down'], water was dripping onto your stored wheat. When you were next told, ['It shall swell in your mouth'], your wheat had already swelled [prematurely germinating]. And when you were finally told, ['Your finger shall straighten'], your wheat had sprouted [in the storage vat]."

[L] A Samaritan once decided, "I shall mystify the Jewish elder, [R. Ishmael, by falsely reporting a dream that no one can interpret]." He came before him and said, "In a dream-vision, I saw four cedars, four sycamores, a bundle of reeds, a cow hide, and this gentleman was sitting and thrashing." [R. Ishmael] said to him, "The gentleman's soul will soon expire; even though this was no dream, you will not leave without [an interpretation]! Four cedars represent the four posts of your death bed. Four sycamore trees represent its four legs. A bundle of reeds represents its bolster. The hide supports the straw. The cow represents the lattice [that holds the mattress]. And the gentleman sitting and thrashing—that gentleman languishes upon it, neither dead nor alive." And it came to pass just [as R. Ishmael predicted, and the Samaritan trickster died a slow, disease-ridden death].

[M] A woman once came before R. Eliezer and said to him, "In a dream-vision, the upper lintel in my house was shattered." [R. Eliezer] told her, "This means that you will bear a son [who will watch over you in place of the broken lintel]."[119] She went away, and after a time gave birth to a son. After a few days' [recovery], she came looking for [R. Eliezer to inform him of her son's birth], but his students said to her, "He is not here; what do you want of him?" She told them, "[A year ago], in a dream-vision, this woman saw that the upper lintel in her house was shattered." [Before she could tell them that R. Eliezer's partial interpretation had come true], they blurted out [the full meaning of the dream]: "You will bear a son [as a new protector], but the

119. So PM.

woman's husband, [the old lintel], will die." When R. Eliezer returned, they gave him a full report, and he said, "You have killed someone! Why? Because[120] a dream is fulfilled only in accord with the interpretation [given by a sage], as it is said: *'And as he interpreted for us, so it came to pass'* (Gen. 41:13). [You should never have told her the part about her husband dying!]"

[N] Said R. Yoḥanan, "Dreams are fulfilled in accord with the interpretation [given by a sage], except for wine-[induced pink elephants]."

[O] One sort of person drinks wine with good results; another sort drinks wine with disastrous results. A student of the sages drinks [their advice] with good results; an ignoramus drinks [the advice of sages and ignores it], with disastrous results.

[P] A person once came before R. Aqiva and said to him, "In a dream-vision, my leg (*raglî*) was shortened!" [R. Aqiva] told him, "During the upcoming festival (Aramaic: *môʿadā'*; but in Hebrew, *regel*), you will not have meat to eat." Another person came before him and said, "In a dream-vision, my leg was huge!" [R. Aqiva] told him, "During the upcoming festival, you will eat a lot of meat."

[Q] One of R. Aqiva's students was sitting with a long face. [R. Aqiva] asked him, "What's all this?" [The student] said to him, "In a dream-vision, I got three pieces of bad news: 'In [the month] of *Adar* you will die'; 'In [the month] of *Nisan* you will be blind'; and 'You will not gather that which you plant.'" [R. Aqiva] said to him, "[Interpreted properly], these are actually three pieces of good news: ['In (the month) of *Adar* you will die'] means 'In the splendor (*hadārā'*) of Torah, you will be taken up'; ['In (the month) of *Nisan* you will be blind'] means 'You will not see a need for miracles (*nîsîn*)'; and 'You will not gather that which you plant' means 'You will not bury the children you raise.'"[121]

120. See B. Ber. 55b.
121. Romm edition: 28a.

5 Yerushalmi Maaser Sheni Chapter Five

Y. M.S. 5:1

M. M.S. 5:1

[A] *(1) [As regards] a vineyard in its fourth year [of growth]—[people] should mark its [boundaries] with clumps of earth.*

[B] *(2) But [to mark the boundaries of a vineyard] in its first three years of growth, [people should use lumps of] clay.*

[C] *(3) [To mark] a grave[yard, people should use] lime dissolved in water, then poured [along the boundary].*

[D] *Said Rabban Simeon b. Gamaliel, "To what [case] do these [rules about marking off vineyard with a special status, M. M.S. 5:1A], apply? [They apply] during the Sabbatical year. [Since the produce of the seventh year is available for any Israelite to take, people must mark these special vineyards to alert others against taking consecrated fruit.]—During the other years of the Sabbatical cycle, let the wicked robber glut on it and die.*[1]*—But [to avoid this Sabbatical year problem altogether], conscientious people set aside coins and declare, 'Any [grapes] plucked [from this vineyard by passersby during this Sabbatical year] hereby are deconsecrated with these coins.'"*[2]

[**I.**A] *[As regards] a vineyard in its fourth year [of growth]* (M. M.S. 5:1A)—

1. So the Talmud's interpolation, but this sentence is lacking in the Mishnah itself. See Jastrow, vol. 2, p. 714, s.v. *lāʿat*.
2. Bomberg edition: 55d. Cf. Haas, *Maaser Sheni*, p. 165.

[B] Zona asked Rabbi,[3] "What precisely shall we recite [on this topic]: 'A *vineyard* in its fourth year of growth' or more generally, 'A *field* in its fourth year of growth'?" He told them, "Go ask R. Isaac the Elder, for he has scrutinized the entire collection of Tannaitic teachings." They went and asked [R. Isaac], who told them, "The opening [passages, M. M.S. 5:1–3][4] concern a vineyard in its fourth year [of growth]; the subsequent [passages] concern a field in its fourth year [of growth]."

[C] R. Zeira had received a tradition from an old one, a contemporary of R. Isaac the Elder, that he had not in fact scrutinized *every* Tannaitic teaching.

[**II**.A] It has been recited on Tannaitic authority: *[As regards] a vineyard in its fourth year [of growth]—[people] should mark its [boundaries] with clumps of earth* (M. M.S. 5:1A), for these are temporary [and will have completely degraded as the year goes by].

[B] *But [to mark the boundaries of a vineyard] in its first three years of growth, [people should use lumps of] clay* (M. M.S. 5:1B); [they should use] white, [bisque-fired clay], for this last longer [than mere earth, up to the three years necessary].

[C] *[To mark] a grave[yard, people should use] lime . . .* (M. M.S. 5:1C), for this lasts the longest of all.

[**III**.A] R. Taḥlifa b. Saul recited on Tannaitic authority: "If [one needed to mark] individual vines, [but not the whole vineyard], he should tie jug handles [along the vine]."

[**IV**.A] R. Zeira inquired, "Why don't we rule that [one should mark] each [vine] according to its particular status, [rather than lumping them all together in a possible confusion]? [Such an individual system would] accord with the following, which has been recited on Tannaitic authority: **A tree [the fruit of which has been declared] holy, [dedicated to the Temple]—people should dye it red. A house of idolatrous worship—people should blacken it with charcoal. A leprous house—people should place hardwood ash on it. Where a corpse [has been found—people should mark the spot of the unsolved murder] with blood, [so they easily can locate the nearest town, whose citi-**

3. See B. Ber. 35a–b.
4. So PM.

zens will have to break a cow's neck and proclaim their innocence]. The place where they break the calf's neck—[people should mark it] with a circle of stones (T. M.S. 5:13)."

[B] He then thought better of so ruling, lest [someone mistake a consecrated tree that had been dyed red] for a tree that fails to mature its fruit, [which also is dyed red].

[C] Is it not, however, recited on Tannaitic authority: **"[As regards][5] a tree that does not mature its fruit—people should dye it red and weight it down with stones [tied to its boughs], thereby reordering [its boughs so that sunlight will reach them and so the tree will] produce properly"** (T. Shab 7:15)? [The two cases, then, do not correspond perfectly.] In the one context, [of a tree whose fruit is dedicated to the Temple, we dye the tree red] so that no [ordinary Israelite] will take its produce; but in this other context, [of a tree bearing only immature fruit, which no one would want to pick, we dye and weight the tree] so that it will produce [fruit] in the first place.[6]

[D] R. Jonah inquired, "[In order to differentiate the two types of trees dyed red], why don't we rule [that we should use] a red *ring* [to mark a tree dedicated to the Temple, which would be] reminiscent of [the red line marking] the altar [in the Temple], as in the following passage, which we recited in another context, on Tannaitic authority: *A red*[7] *line goes around it at the middle, to isolate the blood sprinkled on the top from the blood sprinkled on the bottom* (M. Mid. 3:1)."

[E] R. Ḥiyya recited on Tannaitic authority: "[In order to allow this differentiation], people should paint [the word] 'Dedicated' in red [on consecrated trees; trees that bear immature fruit, by contrast, would be dyed over a large portion of their trunk and weighted as above at C]."

[V.A] R. Yose and R. Simeon b. Gamaliel each have made the same ruling.[8] For: *"[One who gives (his tithed produce) to the mistress of an inn (for preparation as dinner) must tithe both that which he gives to her and that which she returns, because she is suspected of exchanging (untithed produce for that which he*

5. See Y. Shevi. 4:4, B. Shab. 67a, and B. Ḥul. 77a.
6. Romm edition: 28b.
7. See B. Zev. 53a.
8. See Y. Dem. 3:5 for this entire unit.

gives her)].[9] *R. Yose said, 'We are not responsible for the actions of deceivers. [He tithes only that which she returns to him]'* " (M. Demai 3:5).

[B] And similarly, R. Simeon b. Gamaliel says, "We are not responsible for the actions of deceivers."

[C] It seems reasonable to assert that R. Yose would agree with R. Simeon b. Gamaliel, but R. Simeon b. Gamaliel would not agree with R. Yose.

[D] R. Yose would agree with R. Simeon b. Gamaliel, because he holds that we are not responsible for the actions of deceivers, [and we certainly do not need to mark fields so that, when they steal, they can avoid fields full of prohibited foods].

[E] R. Simeon b. Gamaliel would not agree with R. Yose [that one need not tithe produce given to an innkeeper]. [For even though the innkeeper will undoubtedly attempt to switch the produce and thereby deceive the guest, still] it should not be the practice of a trustworthy person (*ḥāvēr*) to dispense untithed produce from his possession.[10]

[**VI.**A] What [verse of Scripture serves as the basis for the requirement] to mark [graveyards]?[11]

[B] R. Berekhiah b. R. Jacob bar Bat Jacob in the name of R. Ḥunia from Bet Ḥoron;[12] R. Yose cites it [with this attribution]: R. Jacob bar Aḥa in the name of R. Ḥanania from Bet Ḥoron; R. Ezekiel,[13] R. Uziel the son of R. Ḥunia from Bet Ḥoron in the name of R. Ḥunia of Bet Ḥoron: "[The scriptural basis is found at Lev. 13:45]: *'[As for the person with a leprous affection], . . . he shall call out, "Unclean! Unclean!"'* [In like fashion, you should mark off a graveyard] so that the uncleanness calls out to you with its own mouth, 'Keep your distance!' "

[C] R. Hila in the name of R. Samuel b. R. Naḥman: "[A far more specific scriptural basis for marking a graveyard is found at Ezek. 39:15]: *'As those who traverse the country make their rounds, any one of them who sees a human bone shall erect a*

9. The first portion of the quote from the Mishnah has been added by the translator for clarity.

10. See PM's comments upon Y. Dem. 3:5.

11. See Y. M.Q. 1:2, Y. Sheq. 1:1, Y. Soṭ. 9:1, B. Pes. 9a, and B. B.Q. 5a.

12. So Codex Vaticanus. See Klein, *Ha-Yishuv*, pp. 14–15.

13. The Bomberg edition here reads: "R. Ḥezekiah."

marker beside it'—this implies that people should mark [any place where] a skeleton [of any type is found]. *'A human* [*bone*]*'*—this implies that people need mark [a place only if a human] spine or skull [is found, i.e., clearly *human* remains]. *'Erect'*—this implies that people must place a fixed headstone, for if you allow people to mark the grave with a loose stone, it could be moved and [improperly proclaim] another spot unclean [as a grave]. *'Beside it'*—that is, in a clean locale, [adjacent to, but not upon the grave itself]. *'A marker'*—this [is the basis of the entire practice of] marking [graves].

[D] It has been recited on Tannaitic authority: **"If one found a loose stone marking [a grave]: even though that is not the approved manner, [for the grave should be marked with a fixed headstone placed on clean ground nearby, nonetheless], anyone who overshadows [the stone] becomes unclean"**[14] (T. Sheq. 1:5)—for I say that a mangled body[15] may have been placed under it; [since such a case of disfigurement is at least possible, it will be impossible to predict precisely where the corpse actually is, and so we must assume that the stone actually rests directly over the grave].

[F] **"If one found two [loose stones marking off a grave]: anyone who overshadows either of them remains clean, [but anyone who overshadows] the area between them becomes unclean"**[16] (T. Sheq. 1:5)—if, [however, the area] between them has been cultivated, [we treat each stone] as if it were separate [from the other, so that they mark two graves]. [In accord with the foregoing rule, then, one who overshadows the area] between them remains clean, [but one who overshadows the ground] immediately surrounding [each stone] becomes unclean.

[G] It has been recited on Tannaitic authority: "People need not mark [a burial site containing only a small amount of] flesh, [but no bone], for the flesh may decompose."

[H] R. Justi bar Shunam inquired of R. Mana, "Won't it turn out that, [if it is discovered that the flesh has not in fact decom-

14. So the Romm edition. The Leiden Codex and the Bomberg edition, however, read "is clean."

15. So PM, Jastrow (vol. 2, pp. 1386–87, s.v. *qamṣûṣ*), and Haas. The Leiden Codex amd the Bomberg edition have the similar *qamṣûn*. The Romm edition, however, reads: "a marked body" (*meṣûyîn*).

16. T. Sheq. 1:5 reverses the order of the two cases.

posed], you will retroactively declare objects in a state of cleanness to have been unclean [if they have overshadowed the unmarked burial site]?"

[I] [R. Mana] said to him, "Better to render objects unclean temporarily—[while we reasonably await the decomposition of the flesh]—than to [allow the grave site to] render objects unclean for all time."

[VII.A] The associates say, "R. Simeon b. Gamaliel has spoken well, [when he rules that people need mark off a fourth-year vineyard only during the Sabbatical year, for that is the only time a passerby who does not know the special status of the crop might legitimately pick the fruit] (cf. M. M.S. 5:1D).

[B] "But there is an apparent contradiction [in the opinion] of the rabbis. [They hold that such a vineyard should be marked off as having a special status at all times, apparently to warn potential thieves of the added prohibitions attendant upon this particular produce (cf. M. M.S. 5:1A).] For doesn't one mark [the vineyard so that the marker is visible] by day, and doesn't [the thief] steal [its produce] by night, [when he cannot see the markers]? [What purpose, then, can such markers serve?]"

[C] Said to them R. Mana, "[Thieves case houses and fields] by day, [returning at night to accomplish the actual theft], just as in the following, which R. Ḥanina[17] said, *'In the dark they break into houses; by day they made a sign for themselves;*[18] *they do not know the light'* (Job 24:16). *'By day they made a sign for themselves'*—the same was done by the generation destroyed by the Flood: [by day] they would identify [expensive items by swathing them] with balsam oil;[19] at night they would come by and steal them."

[D] When R. Ḥanina gave this explanation [of how thieves operated just before the Flood] in Sepphoris, three hundred break-ins were committed.[20]

[VIII.A] *[(Said Rabban Simeon b. Gamaliel), "But conscientious people set aside coins and declare, 'Any (grapes) plucked (from this vineyard by passersby during this Sabbatical year) hereby are*

17. See B. Sanh. 109a.
18. Hebrew: *ḥitmû lāmô*; NJPST renders: "by day they shut themselves in."
19. So the Bomberg edition, which reads *ʾapôbalsemôn*; other versions read *ʾapkhôlsemîn*. See Jastrow, vol. 2, p. 100, s.v. *ʾapôbalsemôn*.
20. Romm edition: 29a. So Jastrow, vol. 1, p. 513, s.v. *ḥatîrtāʾ*, who suggests striking out the following word, *bātîm*, as a scribal error.

deconsecrated with these coins'"][21] (M. M.S. 5:1D). Let [someone who would like to be conscientious simply] mark [the vineyard at all times, not just during the Sabbatical year]! And if it had been so marked, how could one [who set aside money only in connection with the Sabbatical year] be called conscientious?

[B] Said R. Yoḥanan, "It turns out that R. Simeon b. Gamaliel's ruling—[limited as it is to the Sabbatical year alone]—represents [the opinion of] one who says [that produce mistakenly gathered by the poor should be declared ownerless] only at evening time, as it has been recited on Tannaitic authority: **R. Judah**[22] **says, "[In the morning, the householder must] declare, 'Whatever the poor will gather during today's binding process**[23]**—[even though they have no right to this grain, which therefore should remain subject to the designation of all tithes]—is hereby rendered ownerless [and the poor or anyone else who gathers the food may consume it without incurring liability for eating untithed produce].'" R. Dosa says, "[He must make this declaration] at evening time, [so that the statement refers only to the specific produce taken by the poor]." But sages say, "[Produce declared] ownerless under pressure [that people otherwise might steal it and consume it without separating the tithes due from it] has not [validly been declared] ownerless property, since people are not responsible for [the actions of] deceivers"** (T. Peah 2:5). [Like Dosa, Simeon b. Gamaliel suggests not taking blanket precautions, which might protect even thieves who steal from a fourth-year vineyard, but only more limited measures that refer to those who have some legitimate rationale for taking the produce, for example, during the Sabbatical year.]

[C] But[24] [Simeon b. Gamaliel's suggestion for conscientious people] does not cohere with one who rules [that the householder should make his declaration] in the morning, [before the produce has in fact been taken by the poor]. For, [in the case at hand, of fourth-year vines], can a person deconsecrate[25] [such produce while it remains] attached to the ground?!

21. This quote of the Mishnah is added by the translator for clarity.

22. So the Tosefta itself. The Talmud reverses the opinions of Judah and Dosa. See also B. B.Q. 69a.

23. The Talmud inserts here: "as ownerless property."

24. Bomberg edition: 56a.

25. So the emendation of PM. He attributes the reading found in the Talmud, "declare ownerless" to dittography based on B, above.

[D] Said R. Jeremiah, "[Rabban Simeon b. Gamaliel's opinion does in fact cohere], even with one who rules [that the householder should make his declaration] in the morning, only R. Simeon b. Gamaliel does not agree [with the following Toseftan ruling]: **[The (members of the) House of Shammai say, 'People may not redeem (produce from a vineyard's fourth year of growth when it is still in the form of) grapes, but only (after it has been processed into) wine.' But the (members of the) House of Hillel say, '(People may redeem such produce either as) wine or as grapes.' However, both (houses) agree that people may not redeem (produce from a vineyard's fourth year of growth while it remains) attached to the ground]**[26] (T. M.S. 5:19). Furthermore, he is of the opinion that **'Acquisition of second-tithe produce constitutes its redemption'** (T. Arakh. 4:4; see also Y. M.S. 4:4.I.A); [by analogy, if a person erroneously takes some fourth-year grapes, through his acquisition he would have deconsecrated them in any case]."

[E] Said R. Yose, "Would [Simeon b. Gamaliel] really allow [the householder to make such a statement, that *'Any (grapes) plucked (from this vineyard by passersby during this Sabbatical year) hereby are deconsecrated with these coins']* (M. M.S. 5:1D)? [If the grapes are going to have left his possession, how can his deconsecration be effective?] [Or]: What if a person realized that a loaf of his bread was rolling down the bank of a river—if he [attempted to limit his damages by paying off a Temple debt], and said, 'That loaf of bread is hereby dedicated [to the Temple],' would his declaration have effect? [Obviously not, since the bread is in the very process of leaving his possession. So too, the owner of a fourth-year vineyard should not be able to make the declaration that Simeon b. Gamaliel specified!]"

[F] Said R. Jeremiah, "Before you question [whether R. Simeon b. Gamaliel's[27] suggestion for conscientious folk is coherent] with the opinion that [the householder's declaration should be made] in the morning, [in as much as the produce is about to leave his possession (cf. E)], you must raise the same question about the opinion [that the householder should make his declaration] at evening time (cf. B)! [If the problem with a morning declaration

26. The quote of the Tosefta is added by the translator for clarity in light of the question posed at C.

27. So PM; the Talmud itself reads: "Before you question me."

is that the produce is about to leave the householder's possession, how much more should this be deemed a problem at evening time, when the produce has already been taken away! How can the householder's declaration in such a case have any effect whatsoever?]"

[G] [R. Yose] said [to R. Jeremiah], "One who holds that [the declaration should be made] at evening time is not subject to any of these questions; [for the form of his declaration, which refers to the specific produce improperly taken by the poor, makes clear that he retains the legal right of ownership, which he then gives away]."[28]

Y. M.S. 5:2 (M. M.S. 5:2–3)

M. M.S. 5:2

[A] *[Produce of] a vineyard in its fourth [year of growth] was to be brought to Jerusalem [if it was grown in an area] within one day's [journey from the city] in any direction. [Such a trip constituted no significant hardship; accordingly, the farmer was not to deconsecrate the produce and merely transport the coins.]*

[B] *And what is the extent [of this area]? Eilat to the south, Aqravah to the north, Lod to the west, and the Jordan River to the east.*

[C] *Now when produce became [very] abundant, the [sages] ordained that [all fourth-year produce] should be redeemed [and only the money brought to the Temple, even if the fruit grew] a short distance from the walls [of Jerusalem]. But there was a stipulation on this [ordinance]: Whenever the [sages] wanted [to reverse their decision, for example, due to low yields],*[29] *the law would revert to its original form.*

[D] *R. Yose says, "This stipulation was made when the Temple was destroyed. And the stipulation [had this form]: Whenever the Sanctuary would be rebuilt—May it occur speedily and in our own day!*[30]*—the law would revert to its original form."*[31]

28. Romm edition: 29b.
29. So Maimonides, *Commentary*, p. 229.
30. So the Talmud's scribal interjection. The Mishnah itself lacks this phrase.
31. Cf. Haas, *Maaser Sheni*, pp. 167–68.

M. M.S. 5:3

[A] *[As regards] a vine in its fourth year [of growth, the fruit or proceeds of which must be eaten only in Jerusalem, just as is the case with produce in the status of second tithe (cf. Lev. 19:24)]—*

[B] *The [members of the] House of Shammai say, "[If the owner converts this produce to its value in coins, which he will bring to Jerusalem, the cash] is not [subject to the law of] the added fifth,*

[C] *"And [if the fruit of the four-year-old vine remains in one's home after Passover of the fourth and seventh years of the Sabbatical cycle], it is not [subject to] removal." [The Shammaites thus treat the fruit of a four-year-old vine as analogous to second tithe in one respect only: such fruit must be consumed in Jerusalem. Unlike second tithe, however, such fruit is exempt from the rules of the added fifth and of removal.]*

[D] *The [members of the] House of Hillel say, "[The produce of a vine in its fourth year of growth] is subject to the laws [of the added fifth and removal, for the fruit is deemed fully analogous to food in the status of second tithe]."*

[E] *The [members of the] House of Shammai say, "[Unlike produce in the status of second tithe, the fruit of a four-year-old vine is subject to both the law of] the separated grape and [the law of] the defective cluster. [Second tithe is deemed holy, and so poor offerings need not be designated from it. As at B–C, the Shammaites claim that the grapes of a four-year-old vine are not governed by the rules that apply to second tithe.]*

[F] *"And [since poor offerings must be separated from the produce of a four-year-old vine, it is] the poor [who] redeem [the produce they receive as separated grapes and as defective clusters] for themselves, [and they bring the cash to Jerusalem and use it to buy other food]." [All food in the status of second tithe, by contrast, is redeemed by the householder, for the poor have no claim on it (see D).]*

[G] *But the [members of the] House of Hillel say, "[In contrast to E–F], all [of the produce of a vine in its fourth year of growth is to be taken by the householder] to the winepress." [Just as with second tithe, the householder is the one who must prepare the wine and then take it to Jerusalem.]*[32]

32. Cf. ibid., p. 171.

[**I**.A] Said R. Hila, "Originally, [people outside Jerusalem] would process [their fourth-year grapes into] wine, maintaining a state of cleanness, for use in libations [when they traveled to the holy city]. [But since this meant that] no grapes were available [in the city, for everyone transported libation wine instead], they ordained that *'[(Produce of) a vineyard in its fourth (year of growth)] was brought to Jerusalem [if it was grown in an area] within one day's [journey from the city] in any direction'* (M. M.S. 5:2A)."

[B] **[And when such fruit was transported to Jerusalem], people would distribute it among relatives, neighbors, and acquaintances.**[33] [If] there was a small amount remaining after distribution, **people decorated**[34] **the marketplace, [rather than selling such produce in violation of the law]** (T. M.S. 5:14 with gloss).

[**II**.A] This [Tannaitic teaching, which defines the boundaries of a one-day journey from Jerusalem (M. M.S. 5:2B)], disputes [the regular practice of] Nikkai, who was a servant in Migdal Ṣavaʿaya, [farther east of Jerusalem than the Jordan River].[35] On the eve of Sabbath, after preparing his candles, he would travel [to Jerusalem], greet the Sabbath in the Temple, return [home], and kindle [the candles, all in far less than a day's trip]. Others say: [Nikkai] was a scribe. On the eve of Sabbath, he would travel [to Jerusalem], lay forth his lesson in the Temple, return [home], and greet the Sabbath there, [again, after far less than a day's trip].

[B] Ṭarṭiroy of Mahalol,[36] [a village in lower Galilee, north of Lod], would travel [to Jerusalem] and spend the Sabbath in the Temple, yet no one preceded him to the fig trees [in Mahalol Sunday morning, even though he had to arrive from Jerusalem]. [Others say]: The women of Sepphoris, [north of Lod], would travel [to Jerusalem] and spend the Sabbath in the Temple, yet no one preceded them to the fig trees [in Sepphoris on Sunday morning, even though they had to arrive from Jerusalem].

33. The Tosefta itself reverses "relatives" and "neighbors."

34. So Tosefta itself. The Leiden Codex, apparently through scribal error, reads *meʿasēr* instead of *maʿatēr*.

35. So Klein, *Ha-Yishuv*, p. 104, s.v. *migdal ṣavāʿayāʾ*, who identifies the city with Migdal Geder, in Transjordan. PM claims that Migdal Ṣavaʿaya is north of Lod, apparently linking it to the city Migdal Nunia, perhaps because the other stories at B and C all speak of villages north of Lod, but apparently less than one day's journey.

36. See Klein, *Ha-Yishuv*, p. 104, s.v. *mahalôl*.

[C] The women of Lod, [according to M. M.S. 5:2B, exactly a day's trip from Jerusalem], would knead dough, travel to Jerusalem for prayer, and return [to Lod] even before the dough had risen.

[D] A person once was ploughing when his ox got loose and ran. He ran after it, it ran farther, and he ran after it,[37] and soon he wound up in Babylonia! [When he told people of this quick trip], they asked, "When did you leave [Israel]?" "[Earlier] today," he replied. They asked, "What [route] did you travel?" He said to them, "This one." They said to him, "Show us!" He attempted to indicate [the roadway], but didn't know which one.

[E] Conclude [that these stories] dispute [the definition of a day's journey found in the Mishnah-passage at hand].[38]

[F] Even so, there is no contradiction, for there used to be tunnels [that allowed unbelievably fast passage from one place to another], but [the entrances] have become hidden, [and only occasionally are rediscovered, quite by accident]. This accords with what is written [in Scripture]: *"He has walled in my ways with hewn blocks, He has made my paths a maze"* (Lam. 3:9).

[III.A] R. Jonah in the name of R. Zeira, "[In accord with the sages' ruling (M. M.S. 5:2C)], even [the fourth-year fruit from] a vineyard planted next to the very walls of Jerusalem may be redeemed."

[IV.A] Said R. Aḥa, "[The following verse of Scripture] implies that the Temple itself will be rebuilt before the [reestablishment of the] Davidic monarchy [that rules from it]:[39] as it is written [in Scripture]: *'[He set (your father) atop the highlands, to feast on the yield of the earth]. . . . And grape-blood you shall drink as wine'*[40] (Deut. 32:14). [Grape juice that eventually turns into wine is taken as a hint that the Temple building will turn into the seat of the Davidic monarchy.][41] Yet you, [R. Yose], can rule that [not until the rebuilding of Jerusalem will people be required to bring the grapes themselves to the city, rather than just the proceeds of the redemption sale] (M. M.S. 5:2D)?!"

37. The Leiden Codex does not duplicate this phrase.
38. The Leiden Codex lacks this stich.
39. Romm edition: 30a.
40. So the literal translation required by the Talmud's context. NJPST renders: "And foaming grape-blood was your drink."
41. So PM.

[V.A] It has been repeated on Tannaitic authority,[42] "Rabbi says, '**To what case does [the Shammaite exemption of fourth-year produce from the laws of the added fifth and removal] apply? It applies to [produce growing in] the Sabbatical year. [Since during the Sabbatical year the farmer has no claim of ownership on the crop, he likewise has no responsibility for utilizing the produce properly.] But during the other years of the Sabbatical cycle, [the Shammaites] rule that [the produce of a planting in its fourth year of growth] is subject to the laws of the added fifth and of removal. [As in the Hillelite view, the farmer here is deemed the owner of the crop and so responsible for the proper dispensation of the fruit'**] (T. M.S. 5:17)."

[B] In the opinion of this Tannaitic authority, [namely, Rabbi], one derives [the Sabbatical laws applicable to] a planting in its fourth year of growth only from [the Sabbatical laws governing produce in the status of] second tithe. Since [by definition the laws of the added fifth and of removal] do not apply to second-tithe produce [grown during] the Sabbatical year, so too [these laws] do not apply to [the fruit of] a four-year-old planting in the Sabbatical year. [That is to say, in Rabbi's opinion, following the Hillelites, the two types of produce are precisely analogous. Whatever laws govern the dispensation of second tithe therefore govern the use of the fruit of a four-year-old planting.]

[C] [But treating these two types of produce as entirely analogous itself creates a problem!] On the basis of the foregoing analogy, [one would have to claim that the produce of a four-year-old planting during the Sabbatical year] has no sanctified status whatsoever. [Since during the Sabbatical year, no one owns the produce of the Land of Israel, no one possesses a portion of the grain or is required to set aside second tithe. If the two types of produce are fully analogous, therefore, just as second tithe never is consecrated during the Sabbatical year, so too the produce of a four-year-old planting never should become consecrated! But this reasoning cannot hold], for we may derive the consecrated status [of the produce of a four-year-old planting] from the following verse: *"[When you enter the land and plant any tree for food, you shall regard its fruit as forbidden. Three years it shall*

42. See Y. Peah 7:6 for the remainder of this unit with slight variations. See also Brooks, *Talmud of the Land of Israel: Tractate Peah,* pp. 290–302.

be forbidden for you, not to be eaten. In the fourth year, all its fruit shall be] set aside for jubilation [before the LORD]" (Lev. 19:23–24). [This verse suggests that such produce] has the consecrated status of all items that [Scripture] describes as worthy of "*jubilation.*" [The point is that unlike second tithe, Scripture specifically calls produce of a four-year-old planting "*set aside for jubilation,*" i.e., holy. All the laws governing the use of such produce therefore should apply to it.]

[D] [The Talmud explores another possible analogy between second tithe and the produce of a four-year-old planting.] [Once again assuming that the two types of produce are analogous, and that during the Sabbatical year the produce of a four-year-old planting is completely free of holy status], then it should be deemed permitted for [consumption by] a person in mourning [who has not yet buried his relative]. [Under ordinary circumstances, such individuals are not allowed to come in contact with sanctified food, lest they render it unclean. If the produce of a four-year-old planting truly is unconsecrated, then this should not be a consideration.]

[E] [As above, the analogy breaks down.] It has been recited on Tannaitic authority: [Scripture itself terms the produce of a four-year-old planting "*set aside,*"] thereby indicating that [such fruit] is in fact forbidden to a person in mourning [who has not yet buried his dead].

[F] [The analogy now is tested a third time. Given the analogy imputed to these two types of produce], then [the produce of a four-year-old planting in the Sabbatical year] should be subject to removal! [Second tithe, like first fruits and other items specifically set aside as holy, is subject to removal even during the Sabbatical, as stated at M. M.S. 5:6F: *(During the seventh year of the Sabbatical cycle) . . . produce in the status of second tithe or first fruits is destroyed under all circumstances (i.e., even outside of Jerusalem, since the farmer has no time to take it to the city).*]

[G] But what of R. Simeon's [ruling regarding first fruits]? For [at M. M.S. 5:6G] R. Simeon exempts [first fruits, and by analogy produce of a four-year-old planting], from [the requirements of] removal, [claiming instead that the owner may simply give the fruit to a priest for his consumption during the Sabbatical year].

[H] [Finally, if the two types of produce indeed are analogous, and if the produce of a four-year-old planting therefore need not actually be removed], then one should allow [the produce] to be redeemed with [grain] that remains unharvested. [Yet at T. M.S. 5:19, this is explicitly forbidden: **"The (members of the) House of Shammai say, "They do not redeem (i.e., deconsecrate by selling produce from a vineyard's fourth year of growth when it remains in the form of) grapes, but only (after it has been processed into) wine." But the (members of the) House of Hillel say, "(They redeem such produce either as) wine or as grapes." However, both (Houses) agree that they do not redeem, (i.e., deconsecrate, produce from a vineyard's fourth year of growth while it is still) unharvested."** This last attempted analogy never is answered. The upshot seems to be that the opinion attributed to Rabbi at A is untenable. The Shammaites cannot maintain that second tithe and the produce of a four-year-old planting are analogous in all respects except during the Sabbatical year.]

[I] [Continuing the foregoing train of thought, the Talmud now cites the remainder of the Toseftan passage that included Rabbi's opinion. As we shall see, the opposing interpretation of Simeon then leads to proof that in the Shammaite view, second tithe and the produce of a four-year-old planting in fact are subject to precisely *opposite* rules.] It has been taught on Tannaitic authority: **"Rabban Simeon b. Gamaliel says, 'As regards both the Sabbatical year and the other years of the Sabbatical cycle—the [members of the] House of Shammai say, "The law of the added fifth does not apply and the law of removal does not apply" ' "** (T. M.S. 5:17H–I).

[J] According to the opinion of this Tannaitic authority,[43] [namely, Rabban Simeon], one does not derive [the laws applicable to] produce of a four-year-old planting from [the laws applicable to] second tithe at all. [Rather, the two are deemed subject to entirely opposite sets of laws.]

[K] [On this basis, the Talmud now repeats the entire discussion regarding the analogous character of the two types of produce. Here, however, the point is that the analogy breaks down not only during the Sabbatical year, but in fact during all years of the Sabbatical cycle.] On the basis of the foregoing analogy, [one would have to claim that the produce of a four-year-old planting] has no sanctified status at any time. [Just as second tithe itself is

43. See B. Qid. 54b.

not actually consecrated, so too the produce of a four-year-old planting never should become consecrated. But this reasoning cannot hold], for we may derive the consecrated status [of the produce of a four-year-old planting] from the following verse: *"[When you enter the land and plant any tree for food, you shall regard its fruit as forbidden. Three years it shall be forbidden for you, not to be eaten. In the fourth year, all its fruit shall be] set aside for jubilation [before the LORD]"* (Lev. 19:23–24). [This verse suggests that such produce] has the consecrated status of all items that [Scripture] describes as worthy of *"jubilation."* [The point is that unlike second tithe, Scripture specifically calls produce of a four-year-old planting *"set aside for jubilation,"* i.e., holy. All the laws governing the use of such produce therefore should apply to it].

[L] [Another version of the analogy between second tithe and the produce of a four-year-old planting follows. Once again assuming that the two types of produce are entirely analogous, so that the produce of a four-year-old planting is completely free of holy status], then it should be deemed permitted [for consumption by] a person in mourning [who has not yet buried his relative]. [Under ordinary circumstances, such individuals are not allowed to come in contact with sanctified food, lest they render it unclean. If the produce of a four-year-old planting truly is unconsecrated, then this should not be a consideration.]

[M] [As above, the analogy breaks down.] For [Scripture itself terms the produce of a four-year-old planting "*set aside*," i.e., holy, thereby] indicating that such fruit is forbidden to a person in mourning [who has not yet buried his dead].

[N] [The analogy now is tested a third time. Given the analogy imputed to these two types of produce], then [the produce of a four-year-old planting] should be subject to removal [at the beginning of the fourth and seventh years]! [Second tithe, like first fruits and other holy items, is subject to removal at these times as stated at M. M.S. 5:6F: *"(During the seventh year of the Sabbatical cycle) . . . produce in the status of second tithe and first fruits are removed (i.e., destroyed) under all circumstances (i.e., even outside of Jerusalem, since the farmer has no time to take them to the city)."]*

[O] But what of R. Simeon's [ruling regarding first fruits]? For [at M. M.S. 5:6G], R. Simeon exempts [first fruits, and by analogy produce of a four-year-old planting], from the requirements of removal, [claiming instead that the owner may simply give the fruit to a priest for his consumption].

[P] [Finally, if the two types of produce indeed are analogous, and if the produce of a four-year-old planting therefore need not actually be removed], then one should allow [the produce] to be redeemed with grain that remains unharvested. [Yet at T. M.S. 5:19, this is explicitly forbidden: **"The (members of the) House of Shammai say, 'They do not redeem (i.e., deconsecrate by selling produce from a vineyard's fourth year of growth when it remains in the form of) grapes, but only (after it has been processed into) wine.' But the (members of the) House of Hillel say, '(They redeem such produce either as) wine or as grapes.' However, both (Houses) agree that they do not redeem (i.e., deconsecrate produce from a vineyard's fourth year of growth while it is still) unharvested."** At the end of two cycles of attempted analogies, the conclusion must be drawn that produce in the status of second tithe and the produce of a four-year-old planting are analogous in all respects, except during the Sabbatical year, when they are subject to precisely opposite rules.]

[**VI**.A] R. Zeira inquired before R. Abbahu, "On the basis of what [verse of Scripture may we determine that produce of a planting in its fourth year of growth] requires deconsecration [before it may be utilized]?"

[B] [Scripture states], *"[In the fourth year, all its fruit shall be] set aside for jubilation [before the LORD]" (qōdesh hilûlîm)* (Lev. 19:23–24). [This phrase must be understood as] "*deconsecratable before the LORD*," (*qōdesh ḥilûlîm*) for the sages did not distinguish for exegetical purposes between the letter *hey* and the letter *ḥet*.

[**VII**.A] R. Ayyvu bar Nagri taught in the presence of R. La, according to R. Ishmael, "[Scripture states], *'If anyone wishes to redeem any of his tithes, he may redeem it,*[44] *but he must add one-fifth to them'* (Lev. 27:31). [This verse] excludes [the case of the produce of] a four-year-old planting, for [such produce] is not subject to [the law of] the added fifth."

44. NJPST omits this redundant phrase. I retain it in my translation because the Talmud relies upon it for its interpretation at B.

[B] [Later, R. Ayyvu] recanted and ruled in [R. La's] presence. "There are two separate redemptions [referred to in the verse]; [*'If anyone wishes to **redeem** any of his tithes, he may **redeem** it, but he must add one-fifth to them'* (Lev. 27:31)]. The first refers [to the redemption of produce in the status of] second tithe, the second [to produce of] a planting in its fourth year of growth."

[**VIII.**A] In another context, we have repeated on Tannaitic authority, "*R. Judah says, '[The laws governing the use of] a four-year-old planting's [produce] do not apply to [plantings owned by] gentiles. [Israelites may consume such food even though the plantings are in their fourth year of growth.]' But sages say, 'These laws do apply; [since the grapes grow in the Land of Israel, during the fourth year of the plantings' growth, the fruit may not be consumed by an Israelite]'*" (M. Ter. 3:9).

[B] Said R. Eleazar, "This Tannaitic teaching must be interpreted as follows: [In Rabbi Judah's opinion, the law governing the use of] four-year-old plantings does not apply to [plantings owned by] gentiles at all." [This position stands in contrast to an unstated assumption that Judah's exemption of the law applies only to plantings owned by gentiles within Syria. According to this interpretation of Judah's statement, Syria, under a strict definition of the Land of Israel, is not subject to tithing laws at all; since the extension of such rules to its produce is but a rabbinic enactment, we may waive these laws for land owned by gentiles within Syria. Thus Judah, for his part, seems to render a superfluous ruling, that gentiles are not subject to the rules of four-year-old plantings; Eleazar claims that Judah's opinion therefore must exempt any gentiles who own plantings, even those within the Land of Israel itself.][45]

[C] Rav Bebai said in the presence of R. Zeira in the name of R. Eleazar, "It turns out that R. Judah follows the opinion of the [members of the] House of Shammai, as reported before by Rabbi (see above, Y. M.S. 5:2.V.A). For the [members of the] House of Shammai have ruled, 'One derives [the rules governing the produce of] a planting in its fourth year of growth only from [the rules governing] second tithe; and just as [the laws regarding produce in the status of] second tithe are not operative dur-

45. For this interpretation, see PM to Y. Peah 7:5.

ing the Sabbatical year, so too [the laws governing the produce of] a four-year-old planting are not operative in the Sabbatical year.' And similarly R. Judah rules, 'They derived [the rules governing the produce of] a planting in its fourth year of growth only from [the rules governing produce in the status of] second tithe; just as [the laws regarding produce in the status of] second tithe are not operative in Syria, so too [the laws regarding the produce of] a four-year-old planting are not operative in Syria.' [Again, the point of this lemma is that Judah has followed Rabbi's version of the Shammaite view, namely, that second tithe and the produce of a four-year-old planting are in fact analogous, and so subject to precisely the same rules.]"

[D] [R. Zeira] said to them, "Take a careful look at [the Shammaite position]. They said only that '[Produce of a four-year-old planting] is not subject to the laws of the added fifth and of removal.' With regard to other matters—such produce is governed [by the usual laws]." [Zeira's point is that the analogy between second tithe and the fruit of a four-year-old planting extends only to these two areas of law. The Shammaites therefore would hold that the laws of the four-year-old planting *do* apply in Syria. Judah's rule does not follow the Shammaite lead; rather, Judah himself, following his own opinions, has made this ruling]:

[E] *"R. Judah says, 'The law of produce of a four-year-old planting does not apply to plantings belonging to a gentile within Syria' "* (cf. M. Ter. 3:9).

[F] Samuel bar Abba inquired, "But the [members of the] House of Shammai have ruled, 'One only derives [the rules governing the produce of] a four-year-old planting from [the laws governing] second tithe'; just as one says that [the laws governing] second tithe do not apply during the Sabbatical year, so too [the laws governing produce of] a four-year-old planting are not operative during the Sabbatical year, and since [the laws of] second tithe do not apply during the third and sixth years [of the Sabbatical cycle], so too [the laws governing the produce of] a four-year-old planting should not apply [during the third and sixth years of the Sabbatical cycle]."

[G] Said R. Yose,[46] "Even though [the laws of] second tithe do not apply to [crops grown during] the third and sixth years [of the

46. See Y. Shevi. 7:2.

Sabbatical cycle], still, [in those same years, in place of second tithe, farmers must obey the restrictions of] other tithes.[47] [Hence, it should be clear that the laws governing the produce of a four-year-old planting, by analogy to those other tithes, in fact *do* apply during the third and sixth years of the Sabbatical cycle, contra Samuel bar Abba, F.]

[H] "[But in] the Sabbatical year [itself], none of the rules of tithes applies whatsoever! [How then might we in any way rule that the laws of four-year-old plantings apply during the Sabbatical year?]"

[I] Ḥefah asked: "R. Judah ruled, 'One only derives [the rules that govern] produce of a four-year-old planting from [the rules that govern] second tithe; and just as [the rules governing] second tithe are not operative in Syria, so too [the laws governing] produce of four-year-old plantings are not operative in Syria.' [May we also make the following] analogy? 'One may derive [the rules governing] heave offerings of thanks only from [the rules governing] heave offering of the tithe; and just as [the rules of] heave offering of the tithe did not apply [while Israel wandered] in the desert, [but only after the fourteen-year process of conquering and settling the Land], so too heave offerings of thanks did not apply in the desert.' "

[J] Said R. Yose, "[The analogy indeed is valid], but it extends only to deriving the proper measure [of produce to be set aside as heave offering of thanks]. [Just as heave offering of the tithe is set at one-tenth part of the first tithe, so too heave offerings of thanks should be one part in ten.]"

[K] It has been recited on Tannaitic authority, **"R. Yose b. R. Judah said; R. Eleazar b. R. Simeon says, '"The Israelites became subject to [the laws governing] produce in its fourth year of growth only after fourteen years"** (T. Men. 6:20)—the seven in which they conquered [the Land of Israel], and the seven in which they divided [the Land into tribal parcels].' "

[L] Said Rav Ḥisda, "It turns out that R. Yose b. R. Judah in fact follows the opinion of his father R. Judah. For just as R. Judah said, 'One may derive [the laws governing produce of a four-year-old planting only from [the laws governing] second tithe,' and just as he says, 'The laws of second tithe are not applicable in Syria,' likewise the laws of produce of a four-year-old planting

47. The parallel in Y. Peah 7:6 reads: "poor person's tithe."

do not apply in Syria! Similarly, R. Yose b. R. Judah says, 'They derive the rules applicable to the produce of a four-year-old planting only from those applicable to second tithe. Just as the rules governing second tithe are operative only after the fourteen years, so too the rules governing the produce of a four-year-old planting are operative only after the fourteen years.' "

[M] Said R. Yose, "He follows the opinion of his father?! For you may indeed infer [which rules govern the province of] Syria by [noting which rules govern the Land of Israel] before the fourteen years; but you may not derive [the rules governing the Land of Israel] before the fourteen years from observing which rules govern the province of Syria."

[N] It is written [in Scripture], *"and only in the fifth year may you use its fruit, that its yield to you may be increased"* (Lev. 19:25). R. Yose the Galilean says,[48] "[Why has Scripture stated this obvious point? For if we are forbidden to eat the fruit of a tree for the first four years of its growth, isn't the clear implication that we may eat during the fifth year? Instead, the purpose of this phrase is] to add the produce of the fifth year to that of the fourth year; just as the produce of the fifth year clearly belongs to the householder, so too the produce of the fourth year should belong to the householder."[49]

[O] R. Zeira, R. Yasa in the name of R. Yoḥanan, "It turns out that R. Yose the Galilean follows the opinion of R. Judah. Just as R. Judah says, 'He may treat [the produce of the fourth year] as his own,' so too R. Yose the Galilean [rules], 'He may treat [the produce of the fourth year] as his own property.' "

[P] R. Jeremiah inquired before R. Zeira, "In the opinion of one who considers [the produce of the fourth year as the householder's] own property, what is the law as to that produce itself being subject to [the separation of] tithes?"

[Q] [R. Zeira] replied, "[Your question] accords with [an answer] of R. Joshua b. Levi. For R. Avin said in the name of R. Joshua b. Levi,[50] 'Your question has far greater implications. In fact,[51] in

48. See Sifra Vayiqra 3:9.

49. So PM to Y. Peah 7:5. In that context Sirillo adds: "R. Aqiva says, 'The Torah speaks here in opposition to human inclination, so that a person would not think that for four years he might mistakenly eat from the vine with no penalty. For that reason, the verse continues, "that its yield to you might be increased." ' "

50. See Y. Yev. 7:3.

51. See also B. Ber. 45a, B. Eruv. 14b, and B. Men. 35b.

any issue on which a court vacillates, and [in which] you cannot determine what the proper rule [should be], go and see what the people are doing, and follow [their example]. [If] we look at what the general public does [in this case, we see that] they do not separate [tithes from this fourth-year produce].' "

[R] Said R. Mana, "If we are to consider [the notion that the produce of a four-year-old planting belongs to the householder] as a Shammaite opinion, [then we must ask the following]: is there a [single] general public [whose practice follows the opinion] of the [members of the] House of Shammai? [No! Therefore Zeira's point that, in general practice, people do not separate tithes from the produce of a four-year-old planting has no bearing on the case at hand, which must be settled by appeal to Shammaite opinion.]"

[S] Said R. Avin, "[Even in the Shammaite opinion], we may derive [the rules governing the produce of] a four-year-old planting only from [the rules governing] second tithe; and just as second tithe is not subject to [further separation of] tithes, so too [the produce of] a four-year-old planting is not subject to [further separation of] tithes." [Zeira's claim thus may be asserted even on the basis of Shammaite principles.]

[T] R. Ba, R. Ḥiyya in the name of R. Yoḥanan, "**[As regards] a loaf of bread made from flour [in the status] of second tithe in Jerusalem—according to R. Meir, [the loaf] is exempt from [the separation of the] Ḥallah offering. But according to R. Judah, [the loaf] is subject to [the separation of the] Ḥallah offering**" (T. Ḥal. 1:5, with slight formal variations).

[U] Said R. Judah,[52] "This dispute applies only [to loaves of bread baked within] Jerusalem [itself]. But it does not apply [to loaves baked] in the outlying areas [of the Land of Israel]. [Such loaves of bread are subject to separation of the Ḥallah offering]."

[V] R. Ba bar Cohen inquired before R. Yose, "In the opinion of a person who claims that [the produce of a planting in its fourth year of growth] is subject to [the restrictions of] separated grapes, is [a loaf flavored with those grapes] subject to [the separation of the] Ḥallah offering?"

[W] [R. Yose] replied, "Is this not the opinion of R. Judah? And have we not argued throughout this entire discussion that

52. Codex Vaticanus and Y. Peah 7:5 read: "R. Jonah."

R. Judah rules in accord with the [members of the] House of Shammai?" [The questions never are answered, but the clear implication is that in line with the Shammaite view and with his own earlier opinion, Judah would regard such a loaf of bread as subject to the separation of the Ḥallah offering.][53]

Y. M.S. 5:3 (M. M.S. 5:4–7)

M. M.S. 5:4

[A] *What [is the procedure for] redeeming fourth-year produce?*

[B] *(1) [The farmer] sets a basket*[54] *[containing some of the fruit] before three [potential buyers], and asks, "How many [baskets of such produce, as yet unharvested in the field], are you gentlemen willing to redeem at the price of one* selaʿ*, plus paying the [harvesting] expenses out of your own pocket?"*

[C] *Then [any one of the three] may set down his money and declare, "All [produce] of this type, to be picked [at my expense], is hereby deconsecrated with these coins at the rate of so many baskets to a* selaʿ*.*[55]

M. M.S. 5:5

[A] *(2) But during the Sabbatical year [the buyer] redeems [such produce] at its full value [i.e., he may not deduct what it will cost to harvest it, for during that year one may not contract to work the land].*

[B] *(3) If, [during the six ordinary years of the Sabbatical cycle], an entire [fourth-year crop had been declared] ownerless, [and someone wants to claim it, reap it, sell the produce, and finally bring the consecrated money to Jerusalem, he receives] compensation only for [what it cost him to] harvest [the crop].*

[C] *[A person] who wishes to redeem his own fourth-year produce must add a fifth [to the redemption price he charges himself], whether [the produce grew in] his own [field] or was given to him as a gift.*[56]

53. Romm edition: 30b.
54. So the Mishnah itself and the emendation of PM, who notes that printed editions of the Talmud, through scribal error, read not *sal* but *selaʿ*.
55. Cf. Haas, *Maaser Sheni*, pp. 173–74.
56. Cf. ibid., p. 174.

M. M.S. 5:6

[A] *[The rite of] removal [of consecrated items not yet transferred in accordance with the law was performed on] the day preceding the last*[57] *festival day of Passover in the fourth and seventh [years of the Sabbatical cycle].*

[B] *What [was the procedure for] removal [of tithes]?*

[C] *(1) People give [produce in the status of] heave offering and [in the status of] heave offering of the tithe to those entitled [i.e., to the priests]. (2) [They give produce in the status of] first tithe to those entitled [i.e., to the Levites]. (3) [They give produce in the status of] poor person's tithe to those entitled [i.e., to the poor]. (4) [As for produce in the status of] second tithe and first fruits, [these are] to be destroyed under all circumstances.*

[D] *R. Simeon says, "First fruits are given to the priests, just as is the case with heave offering."*

[E] *[As regards] a cooked dish [containing produce in a consecrated status]—*

[F] *The [members of the] House of Shammai say, "[The householder] must remove it [and give it to the appropriate persons]."*

[J] *The [members of the] House of Hillel say, "[Since it has been transformed by cooking], it already has been adequately 'removed.' "*[58]

M. M.S. 5:7

[A] *In contemporary times, [i.e., since the destruction of the Temple, what is the rule if] one possesses produce [in the status of second tithe] and the time for removal arrives?*

[B] *The [members of the] House of Shammai say, "[The householder] must deconsecrate [the produce by transferring its status] to silver coins."*

[C] *The [members of the] House of Hillel say, "It makes no difference whether [the farmer removes his consecrated food in the form of] silver coins or [in the form of] produce."*[59]

57. So PM and Haas, *Maaser Sheni*, p. 218, n. 22. The Talmud and many manuscripts of Mishnah read, "first festival day."

58. Cf. Haas, *Maaser Sheni*, pp. 177–78.

59. Cf. ibid., p. 181.

[I.A] *[How*[60] *many (baskets of such produce, as yet unharvested in the field) are you gentlemen willing] to redeem, at the price of one* sela^c . . . (M. M.S. 5:4B)—[in fact, he should ask if the bidders are willing] to buy [the fourth-year produce] at the price of one *sela*ᶜ; [this proposed price then would not include additional expenses, such as the added fifth, which the buyers themselves would incur].

[B] *[If, (during the six ordinary years of the Sabbatical cycle), an entire (fourth-year crop had been declared) ownerless, (and someone wants to claim it, reap it, sell the produce, and finally bring the consecrated money to Jerusalem, he receives)]*[61] *compensation only for [what it cost him to] harvest [the crop]* (M. M.S. 5:5B)—[to be precise, he receives] compensation only for [what it cost him to] pluck [the crop; for one is not permitted to harvest fourth-year produce in the normal manner, but only in a more piecemeal fashion].

[C] R. Hoshaiah used to convene three grain-dealers[62] [for the bidding] and redeem [fourth-year produce] based on their assessment.

[II.A] It is written [in Scripture]:[63] *"After each three-year period*[64] *you shall bring out the full tithe of your yield of that year, but leave it within your settlements; [then the Levite, who has no hereditary portion as you have, and the stranger, the fatherless, and the widow in your settlements shall come and eat their fill]"* (Deut. 14:28). One might have thought that you are responsible for bringing out tithes and the poor person's tithe once during the Sabbatical cycle, [at the end of any three-year period therein]. [To indicate that] one must do so twice in the Sabbatical cycle, in the third year and in the seventh year—once in every three years, not once in the Sabbatical cycle [at the end of some three-year period]—Scripture explicitly states, *"After each three-year period."*

60. In the Bomberg edition, this unit is numbered Y. M.S. 5:4.

61. The first portion of the quote from the Mishnah is added by the translator for clarity.

62. So Jastrow, vol. 1, p. 57, s.v. *ʾîstônensîn.*

63. In the Bomberg edition, this unit is numbered Y. M.S. 5:5. For parallels, see Sif. Deut. Re'eh 109 (pp. 169–70) and Sif. Deut. Ki Tavo 302 (pp. 320–21).

64. While NJPST renders, "every third year," its footnote proposes a more literal rendering, "after a period of three years." My translation combines the intent of these two in order to better fit the Talmud's point.

[B] Similarly, I may have recited [this verse to mean that the removal of tithes and poor person's tithe from my home should occur during the] New Year's [festival following the three-year period at hand, i.e., at the beginning of the fourth and eight years of a Sabbatical cycle], since by the New Year it is required to destroy undistributed [first and second] tithe, and to bring poor person's tithe out [of the house]. So Scripture explicitly states, *"After each three-year period"*—"After each" implies that you must remove [the poor person's tithe] at the end of the appropriate year, but not at the beginning [of the next year].

[C] Given [that one must do so] at the end of the appropriate year, I might have thought that you are responsible for removing the tithes and for taking the poor person's tithe out [of your home precisely on the last day of the year], right at the beginning [of the next] year. So Scripture explicitly states, *"When you have completely set aside*[65] *the tenth part of your yield"* (Deut. 26:12)—[which implies that you must bring out the tithe] immediately upon completing the tithing process.

[D] Given [that one must do so] at the completion of tithing the produce, I might have thought [that one should do so] even [as early in the year] as Hanukkah. But [Scripture] states here, *"After each . . . "* and it states in another context, *"After each seven-year period, during the year set for remission, at the Feast of Booths, [. . . you shall read this teaching aloud in the presence of all Israel]"* (Deut. 31:10–11); just as *"After each"* in the context [of public proclamation of Moses' teaching] refers to a festival, so too *"After each"* in the current context, [of removal of tithes], refers to a festival.

[E] Given that *"After each"* in the context [of the proclamation of Moses' teaching] refers [in particular] to the Festival of Booths, [I might have thought that *"After each"*] in the current context [of removing tithes] also refers to [accomplishing the removal during] the Festival of Booths. So Scripture explicitly states, *"When you have completely set aside the tenth part of your yield"* (Deut. 26:12). When has one set aside the tithes from all his yield? During Passover of the fourth year. [Only at Passover of the fourth] year is one required to remove [the tithes]; but one is not responsible during any other year.

65. NJPST renders: "When you have set aside in full."

[F] **"[Only at Passover of the fourth] year is one required to remove [the tithes]"** (cf. E above)—[in particular, those designated from produce grown during years one through three of the Sabbatical cycle]. But you need not [at this point] remove [the consecrated portion separated from] greens that grew between New Years and Passover [of the fourth year, even if this produce is ready to hand; rather, you may await the next period of removal, during the seventh year].

[G] The associates say that one declares [*"I have cleared out the consecrated portion from the house; and I have given it to the Levite, the stranger, the fatherless, and the widow, just as You commanded me"* (Deut. 26:13)], not during the fourth year, but during the fifth year, [even though Scripture commands this Confession be made *"When you have set aside in full the tenth part of your yield"* (Deut. 26:12).

[H] Said R. Hila that the declaration is not necessary in the fourth but only in the fifth year.

[I] What case illustrates the practical difference between these two views? A case in which a person transgressed and declared [during the fourth year that he had removed the tithes]—according to the associates, such a declaration is invalid; according to R. Hila, it is proper [even if earlier than necessary].[66]

[III.A] [When separating tithes] during the year [of removal], you may bring forth [some produce] in a state of uncleanness and [designate it] on behalf of [produce] in a state of cleanness, [so that at least some food will be properly designated, rather than simply destroyed in the process of removal]; in other years, however, you may not bring out unclean [produce] on behalf of clean [produce, for the threat of the removal does not press at this point].

[B] Said R. Eleazar, "This Tannaitic teaching must be interpreted as follows: [When separating tithes] during the year [of removal], you should bring [the produce] from a place of uncleanness to a place of cleanness, [so that the priests can access it directly]; in other years, however, you need not bring [the produce] from a place of uncleanness to a place of cleanness, [for the Levites will gather the tithes and pass on the appropriate portions to the priests]."

66. Romm edition: 31a.

[C] It turns out that R. Eleazar accords with the opinion of one who says that one may not give[67] tithes [directly] to the priests, [but should give them to the Levites for distribution; as explained above, during the year of removal, even Eleazar holds that one should assure easy priestly access to the consecrated food].

[D] During the days of R. Joshua b. Levi, [the sages] arranged to vote that people no longer would be permitted to give [first] tithe directly to the priestly caste, [but would hand it over solely to the Levites, who then would apportion an appropriate amount for the priests]. [In an effort to pack the room for the vote, the sages] asked [the doorkeepers], "Who's coming?" "R. Joshua ben Levi; he supports our Levitical [legislation]!" But when he came in, he [voted] in support of the priests, claiming, "In twenty-four[68] separate places [in Scripture], priests are called 'Levites, [so priests legitimately may receive the tithes directly]. Here is one such example: '*But the priests*[69]*—Levites descended from Zadok* (Ezek. 44:15).' "

[E] R. Benjamin bar Gidol and R. Aḥa were in session discussing [the propriety of giving first tithe directly to the priests]. "Is it not written [in Scripture], *'An Aaronite priest must be with the Levites when they collect the tithe'* (Neh. 10:39a)—[the priest's presence is required so that the Levites] can immediately turn over to him heave offering of the tithe, [but not the entire tithe, which therefore should be given only to the Levites, who will properly distribute it]. Yet is it not also written [in the very same passage], *'and the Levites must bring up . . . the tithe [to the House of God]'* (Neh. 10:39b), [which seems to indicate that all of the first tithe should be given directly to the priests]."

[F] R. Ḥuna and the associates [had the following dispute]: One side said, "[In order to make its point fully, Num. 18:21 need only have specified], *'To the Levites [I hereby give all the tithes in Israel as their share].'* So why would [the verse] in fact specify, '*And* to the Levites,' if not to indicate that first tithe may be given directly to the priests ['*And*' to the Levites]?" The other side said, "Even if [Num. 18:21] specified only *'To the [Levites],'* [still one could] give first tithe directly to the priests. For

67. So Codex Vaticanus. Other versions read: "bring forth."

68. See B. Ḥul 34b.

69. Hebrew: *ve-ha-kōhanîm ha-leviîm;* NJPST reads the apposition as an adjectival phrase: "*the Levitical priests.*"

if a person specified [in his will], 'My son, So-and-so, shall inherit thus-and-such a portion; the remainder of my possessions are inherited by my sons,' would not [the named son] inherit [both the special amount designated for him and his fair] share [of the remainder of the father's estate]? [In like fashion, even if the Levites are singled out for a special share of the tithes, their brothers the priests also should receive their fair share.]"

[G] R. Jonah used to give his first tithes to R. Aḥa b. Ulla, not because [Aḥa] was a priest, but because he was devoted solely to Torah. What [scriptural verse provides his] rationale? *"He ordered the people, the inhabitants of Jerusalem, to deliver the portions of the priests and the Levites, so that they might devote themselves to the Teaching of the LORD"* (2 Chron. 31:4).

[H] [Denying themselves], R. Huna, [a priest], did not accept first tithe, and R. Aḥa, [also a priest], did not accept first tithe, [despite the fact that both were devoted solely to Torah].

[I] R. Ḥiyya bar Ba[70] stringently ruled that he himself should leave the land of Israel—[abroad the rules of tithing are not in effect]—so he would not have to accept the tithes [to which he, as a priest, was entitled at least by some opinions].

[J] Someone asked R. Samuel bar Naḥman, [a priest, if he wished to receive the person's first tithe]. [Uncertain what the correct ruling was, R. Samuel] asked R. Jonathan, "What is the law as to my accepting [these tithes]?" [Jonathan] said to him, "Accept them, for that which rightfully falls to your tribe falls to you."

[K] R. Yannai, [a priest], instructed his relatives: "Should you wish to sharecrop a piece of land, rent it only from ordinary [Israelites, nonpriests and non-Levites; in this way, you will not be tempted to keep the tithes for yourselves as priests, rather than turning them over, as is appropriate, to Levites]."

[L] Now, even though you say, "People should not give [first] tithe directly to the priests," you would surely agree that [a portion of a priest's crop] need not be taken away from him [and turned over to a Levite as first tithe]! What [scriptural verse provides the] rationale? *"When you receive from the Israelites their tithes, which I have assigned to you as your share, you shall set aside from them one-tenth of the tithe as a gift to the LORD"*

70. See Y. Shevi. 3:1.

(Num. 18:26)—you should take [tithes] from ordinary Israelites, but you may not [take tithes] from goods belonging to the priestly or Levitical caste.

[M] It turns out that this accords with something R. Eleazar said: " '*When you receive from the Israelites their tithes*' (Num. 18:26)—you should take [tithe] from ordinary Israelites, but you may not [take produce grown] by gentiles."

[N] R. Abbahu said, "R. Joshua b. Ḥananiah and R. Eleazar b. Azariah disputed [the propriety of giving first tithe directly to the priests]. R. Joshua b. Ḥananiah said, 'People should not give [first] tithe directly to the priestly caste.' R. Eleazar b. Azariah said, 'People may give [first] tithe directly to the priestly caste.'

[O] "R. Joshua b. Ḥananiah objected to R. Eleazar b. Azariah, 'Is it not written [in Scripture], *"You [and your households] may eat it anywhere"* (Num. 18:31)—let a priest go right ahead and eat of it in a graveyard! [Such a gift is absurd, since the priest—owing to his need to preserve a personal state of cleanness—cannot *"eat it anywhere."*] [R. Eleazar] responded to him, 'What is the meaning of *"anywhere"*? [This allows tithes to be consumed even in the Temple] courtyard, [usually the preserve only of Most Holy offerings]! [Since only priests may enter the courtyard, first tithe surely may be given to them.]'

[P] "[R. Joshua] said to him, 'Is it not written [in Scripture], *"You and your households [may eat it anywhere]"* (Num. 18:31)—[I suppose] a woman may enter the [Temple] courtyard?!' [With this rejoinder, the dispute was apparently settled in Joshua b. Ḥananiah's favor; first tithe should be given solely to Levites, who will distribute a portion to the priests.]"

[Q] R. Ba used to tell this story: "R. Eleazar b. Azariah, [a priest], used to accept [the first] tithes separated from a particular garden with two entrances, one [opened onto] an area contaminated with uncleanness, the other opened into a clean area. [Believing that priests in general—and R. Eleazar in particular—have no right to directly accept first tithe], R. Aqiva went and told [the gardener],[71] 'Keep the [unclean entrance] open, but close the [clean entrance]. If [Eleazar] comes [to collect the tithes], tell him to go in this entrance, [which he will not be able to do, be-

71. Romm edition: 31b.

ing a priest]!' He further said, 'And if he appoints his students [as collection agents], tell him that *"You [and your households may eat it]"* is what is written [at Num. 18:31, but the students have no right to gather the food in his behalf].' R. Eleazar b. Azariah heard this and said, 'The penetrating mind[72] of Aqiva b. Joseph has been [at work] here.'[73] At that very moment, R. Eleazar b. Azariah returned [to the Levites] all the tithes he had ever taken."

[R] Said R. Isaac bar Eleazar, "[Eleazar b. Azariah's immediate remedy can be compared] to a wall that needs repair: take an [extra] timber from [another part of] the wall and [fix] it [on the spot, before further damage occurs]. For a coal that does not burn you early never will."

[**IV**.A] All[74] [members of both Houses] agree that the householder must remove [and appropriately distribute] any bread or oil [made out of fourth-year or second-tithe produce]. [Furthermore, both Houses agree that] wine and spiced dishes [made out of consecrated produce] are deemed already to be removed, [owing to the cooking process].

[B] What, [then, was the substance of the Houses'] dispute? [They disputed] about: *A cooked dish [containing produce in a consecrated status]—the [members of the] House of Shammai say, "[The householder] must remove it [and give it to the appropriate persons]." The [members of the] House of Hillel say, "[Since it has been transformed by cooking], he need not remove it"* (M. M.S. 5:6D–F, with slight variations in the Hillelite phrasing).

[**V**.A] *[In contemporary times, (i.e., since the destruction of the Temple, what is the rule if) one possesses produce (in the status of second tithe) and the time for removal arrives? The (members of the) House of Shammai say, "(The householder) must deconsecrate (the produce by transferring its status) to silver coins." The (members of the) House of Hillel say, "It makes no difference whether (the farmer removes his consecrated food in the form of) silver coins or (in the form of) produce"]* (M. M.S. 5:7).[75]

72. Bomberg edition: 56c.
73. So Haas.
74. In the Bomberg edition, this unit begins Y. M.S. 5:6.
75. The quote of Mishnah is added by the translator for clarity.

[B] What [scriptural verse provides] the rationale for the [members of the] House of Shammai? *"Wrap up the money [and take it with you]"* (Deut. 14:25)—[money] alone should one have in one's possession.

[C] What is the rationale behind the [members of the] House of Hillel? Even if one were to deconsecrate the produce, [given the Temple's absence], what benefit could there be?

Y. M.S. 5:4 (M. M.S. 5:8–9)[76]

M. M.S. 5:8

[A] *Said R. Judah, "Originally, they would send [reminders] to householders in the provinces, to this effect: 'Hurry! Properly complete processing your produce [so as to make it ready for tithing]*[77] *before the time of removal arrives.'*

[B] *"[But they ceased this practice] once R. Aqiva instructed that any produce not yet liable to tithes remains exempt, even from [the law of] removal."*[78]

M. M.S. 5:9

[A] *[If a person is away from home at the time of removal, so that] the produce he owns is unavailable to him, he must orally declare [the requisite agricultural gifts to be transferred to their proper recipients].*

[B] *Once Rabban Gamaliel and the elders were traveling on a ship [when the time for removal arrived]. Said Rabban Gamaliel, "The tenth I intend to measure out [and designate as first tithe] is given to Joshua [who is a Levite], and the place [in which it is located] is rented to him. The other tenth which I intend to measure out [and designate as poor person's tithe] is given to Aqiva, who will make it available to the poor, and the place [in which it is located] is rented to him."*

[C] *Said R. Joshua, "[Of the first tithe I will receive from Rabban Gamaliel], the tenth I intend to measure out [and designate as*

76. In the Bomberg edition, Y. M.S. 5:6 continues.
77. So Maimonides, *Commentary*, p. 231.
78. Cf. Haas, *Maaser Sheni*, p. 182.

heave offering of the tithe] is given to Eleazar b. Azariah, [who is a priest], and the place [in which it is located] is rented to him."

[D] *And they exchanged rent payments with one another.*[79]

[I.A] [How could R. Aqiva claim that unprocessed produce is exempt from the law of removal (M. M.S. 5:8B)?] Isn't such produce untithed, [so that it clearly contains foodstuffs subject to removal]?

[B] R. Hila in the name of Samuel: "[Aqiva's view can be proven correct by a *reductio ad absurdum*]. [For if we held as yet untithed produce subject to the law of removal], it would mean we deem untithed produce to be consecrated, [in line with Scripture's declaration after removing tithes from the home: *'I have cleared out the consecrated portion from the house'* (Deut. 26:13)]. [Since such produce certainly is not consecrated, Aqiva must be correct.]"[80]

[C] Said R. Judah,[81] "**Once [when Passover was approaching], Rabban Gamaliel and the elders once were in session on the steps of the portico of the Temple Mount and Yoḥanan the Priest—at that time**[82] **a scribe—was sitting before them. They told him, 'Write: "To our brethren in Upper Galilee and Lower Galilee: May your peace increase! I hereby inform you that the time of removal approaches. Separate tithes from the vats of olive [oil]!" And: "To our brethren in the Upper South and the Lower South: May your peace increase! I hereby inform you that the time for removal approaches. Separate tithes from the sheaves of grain!" And: "To our brethren of the Babylonian Diaspora, of the Medean Diaspora, and of the other Israelite Diasporas: May your peace increase! I hereby inform you that the lambs are still weak and the pigeons are still tender, [so that 'the Month of Spring' has not yet arrived]. It therefore seems proper to me and to my associates that we add thirty days to this year"** '[83] (T. Sanh. 2:6)."

79. Cf. ibid., p. 183.
80. For this interpretation, see RiDVaZ. But cf. also PM, who links this stich to the end of the preceding unit.
81. See Y. Sanh. 1:2 and B. Sanh. 11a.
82. See Jastrow, vol. 1, p. 352, s.v. *halāz*.
83. Throughout I follow the version found in the Tosefta itself. See also PM.

[**II**.A] *[Once Rabban Gamaliel and the elders were traveling on a ship (when the time for removal arrived). Said Rabban Gamaliel to the elders, "The tenth I intend to measure out (and designate as first tithe) is given to Joshua (who is a Levite)"]*[84] (M. M.S. 5:9B)—this [selection of Joshua instead of Eleazar b. Azariah, a priest], proves that people should not give [first] tithe directly to the priestly caste.

[B] [In fact], this was a special case, because R. Joshua b. Hanania happened to be present, [and as a Levite, his claim took precedence; had he been absent, however, R. Eleazar could just as well have received the tithes].

[C] Said R. Ḥananiah, "[The manner in which they transferred the tithes to one another] indicates[85] that Rabban Gamaliel was required to award [part ownership of the place where tithes were stored; only in this way could the designation be completed without physically transferring the produce to the recipients' domain]."

[D] Said R. Joshua, "[Awarding the recipient part-ownership in the place where the tithes are located would suffice only if] the produce were still attached to the ground. [But what would be the result if] a basket [full of produce] belonging to R. Gamaliel were placed in R. Joshua's house and [if Gamaliel] said, 'The tenth [I intend to designate] from within it [as first tithe] is hereby given [to Joshua],' would he have done anything meaningful at all unless he completes [the transaction, either by physically removing the produce from the basket, or by awarding Joshua part ownership of the basket itself]?!"

[E] R. Rediphah said:[86] "R. Jeremiah[87] and R. Yose disputed. One said, 'Anyone who is eligible *to gather* [the poor offerings may] acquire [them on behalf of another poor person],' and the other said, 'Anyone who is in a position *to set aside* [poor offerings may] acquire [them on behalf of a poor person].'

[F] "The one who said, 'Anyone who is eligible to gather' certainly would agree [that a person who was in a position] to set aside [the offerings could acquire them on behalf of a poor person].

84. This quote of the Mishnah is added by the translator for clarity.
85. Romm edition: 32a.
86. See Y. Peah 4:6 for the remainder of this unit. See also Brooks, *Talmud of the Land of Israel: Tractate Peah*, pp. 197–99.
87. The parallel at Y. Peah 4:6 reads: "R. Jonah."

[But] the one who said, 'Anyone who is in a position to set aside' would not agree [that a person who was] eligible to gather [the poor offerings could acquire them on behalf of another poor]."

[G] A Tannaitic teaching contradicts the one who said, "Anyone who is eligible to gather [the poor offerings] may acquire them [for another poor person]." For in another context, we recite on Tannaitic authority, *"A person may say, 'Give this writ of divorce to my wife!' because [the agent to whom he passes the writ] may even accept his own daughter's writ of divorce. [Hence he acquires the writ on the wife's behalf. Similarly, a person may say], 'Give this writ of emancipation to my slave!' for [the person to whom he passes the writ] may even accept his own writ of emancipation [in this manner]. [Hence he acquires the writ on behalf of the slave]"* (M. Giṭ. 1:5).

[H] But we also recite on Tannaitic authority, *"[If a person says to his slave], 'Receive this writ of divorce on behalf of my wife' or 'Take this writ of divorce to my wife,' and then later wishes to retract the divorce, he may do so"* (M. Giṭ. 6:1).

[I] Now is this slave in any way eligible to deliver the writ of divorce? [No! Yet in the cited passage of the Mishnah he acquires the writ on behalf of the wife. It seems clear, then, that one need not himself be eligible to gather an object in order to acquire it on behalf of another.]

[J] [The cited objection is irrelevant,] for one must interpret this Tannaitic teaching disjunctively.[88] [That is, when speaking of delivery of a divorce document, we assume that the householder is speaking to a free man, but when speaking of delivery of an emancipation document, we assume that the householder is speaking to a slave. In both cases, because the agent himself would be eligible to receive the writ of divorce or emancipation, the agent too may acquire the writ for another. At any rate, the operative criterion is that one must be eligible to gather the poor offerings himself in order to acquire them for another, which proves the point aimed at from H on.]

[K] Does the following Tannaitic teaching dispute the one who holds that "Anyone who is eligible to receive [poor offerings] may acquire [them for another poor person]"?

88. See Lieberman, *About the Yerushalmi*, p. 48, for this sense of *li-ṣedādîn*. See also Jastrow, vol. 2, p. 1261, s.v. *ṣedâd*.

[L] For in another context we recite on Tannaitic authority, *"[Once Rabban Gamaliel and the elders were traveling on a ship (when the time for removal of agricultural dues arrived). (Said Rabban Gamaliel), "The tenth I intend to measure out (and dedicate as first tithe) should be given to Joshua (who is a Levite), and the place (in which it is located) is rented to him].*[89] *The other tenth that I intend to measure out [and designate as poor person's tithe] is given to Aqiva b. Joseph, who will acquire it on behalf of the poor, and the place [in which it is located] is rented to him"* (M. M.S. 5:9). Now was R. Aqiva eligible to receive [poor person's tithe]? [Certainly, as a rich person, he should not have been eligible; hence, this passage of the Mishnah seems to contradict the opinion that only a poor person can acquire poor offerings for others. Rather, anyone who is in a position to set aside the offerings may acquire them for another.]

[M] One ought to interpret this case as referring to the time before [R. Aqiva] became rich. [Since at that time he was a poor man, he was eligible himself to collect poor person's tithe, and so could acquire it for others.]

[N] But even if you would claim that [the incident took place] after [R. Aqiva] became rich, [still it does not disprove the point at hand, namely, that those who are in a position to set aside poor offerings may acquire them for others]. For one could then interpret [the incident to refer to the time] when [R. Aqiva] was a manager [of the Israelite community's charity]. For such a manager is accorded the same status as a poor person.

[O] The opinion of R. Joshua b. Levi proves that "Anyone who is eligible to gather [poor offerings] may acquire [them for others]." For **R. Joshua b. Levi said, "[In M. Peah 4:9, Eliezer and sages] dispute [with regard to] a rich householder [who attempts to gather some of the corner offering for a poor friend]. But [they agree that] if the householder himself is a poor person, since he himself is eligible to gather [the poor offerings, he] may acquire [the poor offering on behalf of his friend]"** (Y. Peah 4:61.A).

89. The first portion of the quote of the Mishnah is added by the translator for clarity.

Y. M.S. 5:5 (M. M.S. 5:10–15)

M. M.S. 5:10

[A] *During the Afternoon Service* (minhah) *of the last festival day [of Passover during the fourth and seventh years of the Sabbatical cycle, farmers] would recite the Confession [Deut. 26:13–15, stating that they had properly distributed or destroyed all consecrated produce].*

[B] *What is the meaning of the Confession?*

[C] "I have cleared out the consecrated portion"—*i.e., second tithe and fourth year produce—*

[D] "from the house"—*i.e., the dough offering.*[90]

[E] "I have given it to the Levite"—*i.e., the tithe of the Levites, [first tithe].*

[F] "And I also gave it"—*i.e., heave offering and heave offering of the tithe—*

[G] "to the stranger, the fatherless, and the widow"—*i.e., poor person's tithe, gleanings, forgotten sheaves and the corner offering, although these offerings are not a prerequisite for saying the Confession*[91]*—*

M. M.S. 5:11

[A] "Just as you commanded me"—*but if he had separated second tithe before first [tithe], he may not recite the Confession.*

[B] "I have neither transgressed"—*i.e., I did not separate [agricultural gifts] from one kind [of food] on behalf of another kind, and not from harvested produce on behalf of unharvested produce, and not from unharvested produce on behalf of harvested produce, and not from new produce [harvested after this spring's first-sheaf offering] on behalf of old produce [harvested before the first-sheaf offering], and not from old produce on behalf of new produce—*

[C] "nor neglected any of your commandments"—*i.e., [I did not*

90. Mishnah has this stich following F. I move it here to correspond to the order of the biblical verse.

91. Cf. Haas, *Maaser Sheni*, p. 184.

forget] to praise you, [O God], and to mention your name [in connection with my crop].[92]

M. M.S. 5:12

[A] "I have not eaten of it while in mourning"—*but if he ate [second tithe or fourth-year produce] while in the mourning period [before a close relative's burial], he may not*[93] *recite the Confession.*

[B] "I have not cleared out any of it while I was unclean"—*but if he separated [the agricultural gifts] while in a state of cultic uncleanness, he may not recite the Confession.*

[C] "And I have not deposited any of it with the dead"—*i.e., I did not [use its value] to buy a coffin or shrouds for the dead, and I did not give it to other mourners [whose dead remain unburied].*

[D] "I have obeyed the LORD my God"—*i.e., I brought [the tithes] to the chosen sanctuary, [the Temple in Jerusalem].*

[E] I have done just as you commanded me"—*i.e., I rejoiced and allowed others to rejoice [with the produce].*[94]

M. M.S. 5:13

[A] "Look down from your holy abode, from heaven"—*we did what you required of us, now you do what you promised us.*

[B] "Look down from your holy abode, from heaven,[95] and bless your people Israel"—*with sons and daughters.*

[C] "And the soil You have given us"—*with dew, wind, rain, and offspring of cattle.*

[D] "A land flowing with milk and honey, as you swore to our fathers"—*in order to make the fruit sweet tasting.*[96]

M. M.S. 5:14

[A] *On the basis of this [reference to God's gift of the land (M. M.S. 5:13)], they ruled, "Israelites and those of impaired lineage may*

92. Cf. ibid., pp. 184–85.
93. Romm edition: 32b.
94. Cf. Haas, *Maaser Sheni*, p. 185.
95. The Talmud reduplicates this phrase, lacking in Mishnah itself.
96. Cf. Haas, *Maaser Sheni*, pp. 185–86.

recite the Confession, but aliens and freed slaves may not, for they do not [hold] a portion of the land."

[B] *R. Meir says, "Also: priests and Levites do not [recite the Confession], since [as a tribe] they did not acquire a portion of the land."*

[C] *R. Yose says, "[Priests and Levites do recite the Confession, for] they possess the [Levitical] cities of refuge."*[97]

M. M.S. 5:15

[A] *Yoḥanan the High Priest [i.e., John Hyrcanus] (1) did away with [the recitation of] the Confession concerning [the removal of] tithes.*

[B] *Also: he dismissed (2) those who sing the psalm of awakening [in the Temple, i.e., Ps. 44:24], and (3) those who stun [the sacrificial animals before slaughter].*

[C] *(4) Until his time, hammers would pound [i.e., work was done] in Jerusalem [during the intermediate days of Passover and Sukkot].*

[D] *(5) And in his time, no one had to ask whether [agricultural gifts] had been separated [from produce one wished to purchase].*[98]

[**I**.A] Perhaps[99] one should make the Confession on the first day of the holiday of Passover? To assure that, throughout the holiday, one will have [an ample supply of food that must be] consumed [in Jerusalem in any case, such as second tithe, allow him to make his Confession only at the end of the holiday].

[B] Perhaps one should make the Confession during the Morning Service (*shaḥarît*) [of that last day]? Since one is commanded to eat [full meals throughout the holiday], on through [to the last evening, allow him to make his Confession in the late afternoon of the last day].

[**II**.A] It has been recited on Tannaitic authority: *[(As for produce in the status of) second tithe] and first fruits, [(these are) to be destroyed under all circumstances]* (cf. M. M.S. 5:6)—whose

97. Cf. ibid., p. 186.
98. Cf. ibid., p. 190.
99. In the Bomberg edition, this unit is numbered Y. M.S. 5:7.

opinion is it that first fruits [are subject]? The rabbis. And whose opinion is it that first fruits are exempt? R. Simeon. For we have recited on Tannaitic authority: *"[First fruits] . . . are subject to the law of Removal; R. Simeon exempts [first fruits from this law]"* (M. Bik. 2:2).

[III.A] *"I have given it to the Levite"* (Deut. 26:13)—on this basis, [one should conclude] that people may not give first tithe directly to the priestly caste, [but must give it to Levites, who will properly distribute it].

[B] Said R. Jonah, "The [declaration, *'I have given it to the Levite'*] implies that if his produce caught fire and was completely burned before he separated [first tithe], he may not make the Confession, [even if he did properly distribute other, non-Levitical tithes]."

[IV.A] [*"I have neither transgressed nor neglected any of your commandments"*]—there are Tannaitic authorities who teach that [failure to comply with] *any* of the Torah's commandments [therefore] disqualifies [a person from making the Confession]. And there are Tannaitic authorities who teach that only [failure to comply with] any one of the commandments within this passage disqualifies [a person from making the Confession].

[B] R. Aḥa bar Papa inquired of R. Zeira: "[Does the stricter reading of this phrase mean that], even if one put the phylactery upon his head before putting the other phylactery upon his arm—[a nearly trivial infraction—he is disqualified from making the Confession]? [R. Zeira] said to him, "I do indeed think so."

[V.A] Said R. Yose b. R. Bun, "[Rather than designating an entire crop consecrated as heave offering or as dough offering], one must [divide off some portion, however large or small, and] state, **'This is dough offering for the whole' or 'This is heave offering for the whole.' [For Scripture says], *'[When . . . you eat of the bread of the land, you shall raise some as a heave offering]*[100] *to the LORD' (Num. 15:18–19)—[meaning that the dough offering—'when you eat of the bread of the land'*—and heave offering—*'you shall raise some up as a heave offering'*—each must have a] specific designation."**

100. NJPST renders the more limited biblical context of dough offerings: *"You shall set some aside a gift to the LORD."*

[B] **From what [scriptural source may we derive] that it is invalid if one [designates an entire crop as heave offering or as dough offering], without leaving at least a miniscule amount [unconsecrated]? Scripture explicitly states, "*[You shall make a gift to the LORD] from the first yield [of your baking]*" (Num. 15:21); [Scripture does not specify], "All of the yield [of your baking]"** (Y. Ḥal. 1:6).

[VI.A] On what clear [scriptural basis can we derive] that [one who anoints with second-tithe oil outside of Jerusalem has transgressed] the positive commandment [to consume the second tithe within the city limits]?

[B] **R. Eleazar in the name of R. Simai: "[Scripture states], '*[When you have set aside in full the tenth part of your yield . . . you shall declare before the LORD your God: "I have cleared out the consecrated portion from the house; . . . I have not cleared out any of it while I was unclean], and I have not deposited any of it with the dead"*' (Deut. 26:12–14). How shall we understand this? If the verse means only to exclude procuring a casket or shrouds for [the deceased]—items prohibited [for purchase with consecrated funds, since they cannot be eaten] by the living—[the phrase turns out to be superfluous]. For if [utilizing second-tithe money to buy] something is prohibited to the living, then [the same purchase] surely is prohibited for the dead, [and so there must be a different meaning for the verse]! What then in fact might be permitted for the living, but prohibited for the dead? I would say: this [verse must mean] anointing [with oil in the status of second tithe]"** (cf. Y. M.S. 2:1.I.Z).

[VII.A] R. Huna bar Aḥa[101] in the name of R. Alexander, "Come and see what greatness is attributed to those who fulfill the commandments![102] For anytime the Torah [uses the term] *'Look down'* [humanity stands] accursed; but in this [one case, when one proudly declares how carefully one has observed God's commandments, *'Look down'* is used as] a request for a [heavenly] blessing."

[B] Said R. Yose b. Ḥanina, "What's more, while [describing the relationship between God and the Israelites who keep the com-

101. In the Bomberg edition, this unit is numbered Y. M.S. 5:8.
102. Romm edition: 33a.

mandments], it is written [in Scripture], *'this day,'* [as follows: *'The LORD your God commands you this day to observe these laws and rules. . . . You have affirmed this day that the LORD is your God. . . . And the LORD has affirmed this day that you are, as He promised you, His treasured people who shall observe all His commandments, and that He will set you, in fame and renown and glory, high above all the nations that He has made'* (Deut. 26:16–19)]. This teaches that [God's blessing is a] daily [matter, in direct response to the Israelite's needs and actions]."

[VIII.A] R. Judah b. Pazzi opened [an exegetical discourse]: "[Scripture states]: *'I shall approach with praise for Your mighty acts, O LORD God'*[103] (Ps. 71:16), [which will reverse the fortunes of the Israelites]. It is also written [in Zech. 4:14], *'They are the two anointed dignitaries who attend the LORD of all the earth,'* [and who carry out God's plan to improve the Israelites' situation]."

[D] R. Abbahu said, "R. Yoḥanan and[104] R. Simeon b. Laqish disputed [the identity of the anointed dignitaries who work God's plans for bettering Israel]. One said, 'They are ones invested with political power derived from the Holy, Blessed One, [i.e., the high priest and the king].'[105]

[E] "The other said, 'They are ones invested with the merit of commandments and good deeds [accomplished] before the Holy, Blessed One.'

[F] "[The following story shows that the latter view, herein to be attributed to Simeon b. Laqish, is correct]: Rav had some [worm]-infested flax seed and asked R. Ḥiyya the Elder, 'What is your ruling as to my slaughtering a bird and treating the flax seeds with some of its blood, [which should keep worms away until I plant the seed]?" [R. Ḥiyya] said to him, '[This is permitted only with the blood of an] improperly slaughtered [bird; otherwise, one must *"pour out its blood and cover it with earth"* (Lev. 17:13)].'—And why did he not instruct him [to use the blood of a bird that, upon slaughter, turns out to have] an organic disease, [so that it is forbidden for human consumption]?

103. NJPST renders this as a present-imperfect: "I come with praise of Your mighty acts, O Lord God." I follow PM's lead in highlighting the change in Israel's fortunes due to God's intervention on their behalf, which links this unit to the preceding.

104. Bomberg edition: 56d.

105. For this identification, see NJPST, note to Zech. 4:14 and 3:8–9.

Because of R. Meir, for R. Meir[106] ruled, '[The blood of an animal that, upon slaughter, turns out to have] an organic disease requires the covering [mentioned by Scripture].'—Did not R. Ami say, attributing to R. Simeon b. Laqish, 'When those in Babylonian exile returned [to Israel], their flax was not worm-infested and their wine did not turn to vinegar, for they looked forward over many centuries toward the eventual leadership of R. Ḥiyya the Elder and his descendants.' "

[G] As for Rav, [he linked the improvement in Israel's fortunes (Ps. 71:16) not to the actions of God's anointed dignitaries (Zech. 4:14), but to Isa. 46:12], as follows: *"Listen to Me, you stubborn of heart, who are far from victory: [I am bringing My victory close. . . . I will grant triumph in Zion to Israel, in whom I glory]."*

[H] R. Abbahu[107] said, "R. Yoḥanan and R. Simeon b. Laqish disputed [the meaning of singling out Israel—those far from victory—for God's special intervention]. One said, 'All others who enter the world come [to victory] through [their collective] righteousness; but these [Israelites] are drawn [into victory by God's own outstretched] arm.'

[I] "The other said, 'All goodness and pleasantries are found in the world by the merit of a few, who themselves benefit not a whit.'

[J] "For example: When Mar Zutra prayed on others' behalf, [his requests] were immediately fulfilled; but on his own behalf, [his requests] were never fulfilled."

[**IX.**A] *[On the basis of the (reference to God's gift of the land [M. M.S. 5:13]) . . . R. Meir says, "Priests and Levites do not (recite the Confession), since (as a tribe) they did not acquire a portion of the land." R. Yose says, "(Priests and Levites do recite the Confession, for) they possess the (Levitical) cities of refuge"]* (M. M.S. 5:14): It has been recited on Tannaitic authority: " '[The cities of refuge] were given [to the Levites during] the apportionment [of the Land of Israel as their tribal entitlement],' the opinion of R. Judah. R. Meir[108] says, 'The [cites of refuge] were

106. See B. Ḥul 85a–86a.

107. See B. Ber. 17b.

108. So the parallel in Y. Mak. 2:7 and as emended thereon by PM. The Romm edition, apparently confusing the dispute within the Mishnah and that under discussion in the Talmud, reads: "R. Yose." See also Y. Soṭ. 9:2 and B. Mak. 13a.

given [to the Levites] as an area to dwell in, [but not as an everlasting legacy].'"

[B] It turns out that R. Judah accords with the opinion of R. Yose [in the dispute at M. M.S. 5:14; both hold that Levites do in fact possess a portion of the Land of Israel—the cities of refuge—and so may validly make the Confession]. [Likewise], R. Meir accords with his own opinion [in that dispute; in both contexts, he rules that Levites should not make the Confession, for they do not in fact possess a portion of the Land]. [Further support that this is in fact R. Meir's view may be found in] that which we have recited on Tannaitic authority: *"As regards a manslaughterer who went into exile in a city of refuge]—'He must pay rent to the Levites, [who own the cities],' the opinion of R. Judah. R. Meir*[109] *says, 'He need not pay rent to [the Levites, for they in fact do not own those cities]'"* (M. Mak. 2:8).

[**X**.A] R. Jeremiah;[110] R. Ḥiyya in the name of R. Simeon b. Laqish: "The current Tannaitic teaching, [which explains that Yoḥanan the High Priest abolished the Confession (M. M.S. 5:15), was enacted] because people were suspected of giving first tithe to the priestly caste, [rather than directly to the Levites; in such a case, people who recited the Confession—*'I have given it to the Levite'*—would be committing perjury, and hence the entire practice was done away with]."

[B] In one respect, this [enactment by Yoḥanan the High Priest] supports the opinion of R. Yoḥanan, but in another respect, it disputes his opinion. The dispute [concerns his view that one may in fact give first tithe directly to members of the priestly caste, which Yoḥanan the High Priest obviously wished to discourage]: For we have recited on Tannaitic authority: *"[A Levite girl*[111] *betrothed to a priest, pregnant by a priest, awaiting levirate marriage with a priest], or even a priestly girl married to a Levite—eats neither heave offering nor [first] tithe"* (M. Yev. 9:4). [That she may no longer consume] heave offering is clear enough: [she no longer is a member of a priest's household]. But how do you figure that [she may not eat] first tithe? If as a priestly

109. So M. Mak. 2:8 itself. The Talmud's citation reads: "R. Yose," apparently through the same confusion as above at A.

110. In the Bomberg edition, this unit is numbered Y. M.S. 5:9. The entire unit also appears verbatim in Y. Soṭ. 9:11.

111. See Y. Yev. 9:4, Y. Sot. 9:10, and B. Yev. 85a–b.

girl she could eat [heave offering], now, as a Levite's wife, she should be permitted to eat [first tithe]! R. Illa in the name of R. Yoḥanan: "[The objection to her eating first tithe] accords with the opinion of those who rule that people must not give first tithe to the priestly caste."[112] [Since R. Yoḥanan does not include himself in the group that rule against the Levite's wife, we may] infer that he would allow giving first tithe directly to members of the priestly caste, [precisely counter to Yoḥanan the High Priest's enactment].

[C] [Yoḥanan the High Priest's abolition of the Confession] supports [R. Yoḥanan], for he has ruled [that all rabbinic enactments must increase Israel's] praiseworthiness.

[D] For R. Yoḥanan said, "Yoḥanan the High Priest sent [his functionaries] to observe [tithing practices] in all Israelite villages. He discovered that all of the people were properly separating heave offering, but only some were separating first and second tithe, while others were not. He proposed, 'Since [failure to separate] first tithe is a capital offense [because the heave offering of the tithe is not given to the priests],[113] and [failure to separate] second tithe entails a direct misuse of untithed produce, let each person designate heave offering and thereby heave offering of the tithe, giving these directly to a priest; let each person deconsecrate his own second tithe with money [to be spent in Jerusalem]; let each person leave poor person's tithe unharvested, and it will be up to anyone who claims [such produce] to prove [poverty]. Then, let the person make the Confession.' "

[E] Said R. Hila, "It would anger the Omnipresent if one said, 'I did it,' even though he had not." For this reason, [Yoḥanan the High Priest enacted the ruling that] only one who properly separates [all the requisite tithes] may make the Confession; but anyone who fails [to comply with even a small detail of the] tithing procedures is not [required] to make the Confession; [by thus avoiding divine anger at the false boast of following all the commandments, Yoḥanan the High Priest, like R. Yoḥanan, acted to preserve Israel's praiseworthiness].

[F] This [notion that the Confession should not give occasion for an individual to feel shame] accords with the following, which has

112. Romm edition: 33b.
113. So Haas.

been recited on Tannaitic authority: "Up to, *'Look down from your holy abode, from heaven,'* [i.e., in the section that asserts complete compliance with the commandments], people should recite the Confession in a whisper, [thus not making a public scandal out of those who cannot recite this portion]. From *'Look down'* to the end [of the Confession, i.e., the part that both the observant and transgressors could equally say] people may recite aloud."

[**XI**.A] *Also: [Yoḥanan the High Priest] dismissed those who sing the psalm of awakening [in the Temple]* (M. M.S. 5:15B)—those who used to recite, *"Rouse Yourself; why do You sleep, O Lord? Awaken, do not reject us forever!"* (Ps. 44:24).

[B] Is "sleep" really appropriate as an attribute of the Omnipresent? Has it not already been clearly stated [in Scripture], *"See, the guardian of Israel neither slumbers nor sleeps!"* (Ps. 121:4)?

[C] And [furthermore], why does Scripture state, *"The Lord awoke as from sleep"* (Ps. 78:65)? [The term *"as from sleep"* makes clear that these images] are figurative. It is as if He sleeps when Israel has problems and when the nations of the world prosper. And so [Scripture] says, *"[Surely mocking men keep me company], and with their provocations I close my eyes"* (Job 17:2), [as if asleep].

[**XII**.A] *[Also: he dismissed] . . . those who stun [the sacrificial animals before slaughter]* (M. M.S. 5:15B)—those who would strike a heifer between its horns[114] [to stun it for slaughter]. Yoḥanan the High Priest said to them, "How long will you supply the altar with [animals whose brain membranes have been] pierced?" So he had yoke-rings installed; [since the animals now could be restrained properly, he dismissed those who used to stun the animals].[115]

[B] R. Ba[116] in the name of R. Judah: "The yoke-rings he had made were wide at the bottom, [so the animal's head could be inserted easily], but narrow at the top, [so that the neck would be held firmly in place]."

114. Codex Vaticanus reads: "between the loins." As Haas jocosely notes, however, "This cannot be correct."

115. So PM and Haas.

116. The Leiden Codex attributes this stich to: "Rabbi in the name of."

[XIII.A] *Until his time, hammers would pound [i.e., work was done] in Jerusalem [during the intermediate days of Passover and Sukkot]* (M. M.S. 5:15C)—until the beginning of his office, [but not throughout].

[XIV.A] *And in his time, no one had to ask whether [agricultural gifts] had been separated [from produce one wished to purchase]* (M. M.S. 5:15D)—for he appointed pairs [of overseers who could assure everyone that all of the tithing regulations had been followed through the Land].

[XV.A] The opinion of R. Joshua b. Levi has it that some [of Yoḥanan the High Priest's legislative initiatives redound] to his discredit, while some [redound] to his credit.

[B] [An example of something that redounds to Yoḥanan's credit is as follows]: For R. Yose in the name of R. Tanḥum bar Ḥiyya; R. Ḥezekiah, R. Eleazar b. R. Yose, R. Tanḥum bar Ḥiyya in the name of R. Joshua b. Levi: "At first, [from Ezra's time to the administration of Yoḥanan the High Priest], one who was tithing [his produce] would [separate the consecrated foodstuffs] into three lots, one-third for confidants of priests or Levites, [who could then hand over the tithes]; one-third for [deposit] in the [Temple] treasury, [to pay for public works], and one-third for poor or needy students[117] in Jerusalem." Said R. Yose b. R. Bun, "One who would travel to Jerusalem to seek a judgment from the rabbinic court was required to pay the expenses attending the first three summons connected with his case. From that point on, however, [all such court costs were to be paid] out of the treasury, [which had adequate funds because of the tithing practices endorsed by Yoḥanan]."

[C] [An example of something that redounds to Yoḥanan's discredit is as follows]: When Eleazar b. Paḥhora and Judah b. Petora,[118] [both priests, not Levites], came and took the tithes by force, [Yoḥanan and his supporters] had the power to protest, but did not; [this led Yoḥanan] to abolish the Confession regarding tithing, which redounds [to Yoḥanan's] discredit.

[D] But [Yoḥanan's initiatives in dismissing] *"those who sing the*

117. So PM, on the basis of Y. M.S. 5:5.II, which claims that first tithe may be given to those who busy themselves in Torah.

118. Codex Vaticanus lacks this name.

psalm of awakening [in the Temple] and those who stun [the sacrificial animals before slaughter]" (M. M.S. 5:15B) redound to his credit.

[**XVI.**A] ***Until his time, hammers would pound [i.e., work was done] in Jerusalem [during the intermediate days of Passover and Sukkot]* (M. M.S. 5:15C)—until the beginning of his office, [but not throughout]** (Y. M.S. 5:5.XIII.A): R. Ḥisda asked R. Ḥezekiah, "[Given the wording, 'Until his time'], wouldn't it make more sense [to assert that this practice continued throughout his administration, to be abolished only] at the end?" [R. Ḥezekiah] said to him, "I do indeed think so."

[**XVII.**A] [And in his time, no one had to ask] whether . . . Demai (M. M.S. 5:15D)—R. Yose in the name of R. Abbahu; R. Ḥezekiah in the name of R. Judah b. Pazzi: "*Demai* means 'perhaps' (*dāʾ mai*):[119] 'perhaps' he did separate tithes, 'perhaps' he did not."

119. So GRA and PM, interpreting *demaʾi* as built of two particles, *dāʾ* and *maiʾ* as "this" and "what." Printed editions simply repeat the word *demaʾi* twice. Haas comments: "Jastrow (vol. 1, p. 312) gives 'talk' as one possible translation of '*demaiʾ*,' . . . [and so] translates this passage: 'There is talk he has given tithes, there is talk that he has not.' His rendering of the word appears, however, to be based on his interpretation of the passage and not vice versa."

Abbreviations and Bibliography

Albeck, *Studies:* Ḥanokh Albeck. *Meḥqarim ba-Veraita ve-Tosefta ve-Yaḥasan la-Talmud (Studies of Baraita and Tosefta in Relationship to the Talmud).* Jerusalem: Mossad HaRav Kook, 1969; original ed., 1944.

Arakh: ʿArākhin

Avery-Peck, *Terumot:* Alan Avery-Peck. *The Talmud of the Land of Israel.* Vol. 6: *Tractate Terumot.* Chicago: University of Chicago Press, 1988.

A.Z.: ʿAvôdâh Zārâh

b.: *ben = bar,* "son of"

B.: bavlî; Babylonian Talmud

B.B.: Bāvāʾ Batrāʾ

Bekh.: Bekhorôt

Ber.: Bᵊrākhôt

Beṣ.: Bêṣâh

Bik.: Bikkurîm

B.M.: Bāvā Mᵊṣîʿāʾ

Bokser, "Annotated Bibliography": Baruch Bokser. "An Annotated Bibliographical Guide to the Study of the Palestinian Talmud." In Wolfgang Haase, ed., *Aufstieg und Niedergang der römischen Welt: Geschichte und Kultur Roms im Spiegel der Neuren Forschung. Principat* (II, 19.2), pp. 139–256. Berlin: Walter de Gruyter. Reprinted in Jacob Neusner, ed., *The Study of Ancient Judaism.* Vol. 2: *The Palestinian and Babylonian Talmuds,* pp. 1–119. New York: KTAV, 1981.

Bomberg edition: Daniel Bomberg, ed. *Talmud Yerushalmi.* Venice, 1523–24.

B.Q.: Bāvā Qamāʾ

Brooks, *Support for the Poor:* Roger Brooks. *Support for the Poor in the Mishnaic Law of Agriculture: Tractate Peah.* Brown Judaic Studies 43. Chico, Calif.: Scholars Press, 1983.

Brooks, Peah: Roger Brooks. *The Talmud of the Land of Israel.* Vol. 2: *Tractate Peah.* Chicago: University of Chicago Press, 1990.

Chron.: Chronicles

Codex Vaticanus: Talmud Yerushalmi. Codex Vaticanus 133

(Vat. Ebr. 133), with an introduction by Saul Lieberman. Includes Division of Agriculture, plus tractate Soṭah; thirteenth century.

Dem.: Dᵊmaʾi

Deut.: Deuteronomy

Ed.: Edduyôt

Eruv.: ʿErûvîn

Ezek.: Ezekiel

Frankel: Zechariah Frankel. *Ahᵃvat Zîôn, Talmud Yerushalmi.* Vol. 1. *Berachot and Peah.* Vienna, 1874; reprinted Jerusalem, 1971. Includes a semicritical version of the Bomberg edition, notes, and commentary.

Frankel, *Introduction:* Zecharias Frankel. *Mᵊvô Ha-Yᵊrûshalmî (Introduction to the Yerushalmi).* Breslau, 1870; reprinted Jerusalem, 1967.

Gilyonei Ephraim: Ephraim Dov Ha-Kohen Lof. *Gilyonei Ephraim;* digest of Joshua Isaak Shapiro, *Noam Yerushalmi.* Vilna, 1863 and 1869; reprinted in Vilna edition.

Ginzberg: Louis Ginzberg, ed. *Yerushalmi Fragments from the Genizah.* Vol. 1: *Texts with Various Readings from the Editio Princeps.* New York, 1909; reprinted 1969.

Giṭ.: Giṭṭîn

GRA: Elijah b. Solomon Zalman, Gaon of Vilna (Lithuania, 1720–1797). *Commentary to Yerushalmi Zeraʿim.* Edited in two versions, A and B, by separate students. Reprinted in Vilna edition.

Haas: Peter J. Haas. Draft translation of Yerushalmi Maaser Sheni.

Haas, *Maaser Sheni:* Peter J. Haas. *A History of the Mishnaic Law of Agriculture: Tractate Maaser Sheni.* Brown Judaic Studies 18. Chico, Calif.: Scholars Press, 1980.

Ḥal.: Ḥallâh

Ḥul.: Ḥullîn

Isa.: Isaiah

Jaffee, *Theology of Tithing:* Martin S. Jaffee. *The Mishnah's Theology of Tithing: A Study of Tractate Maaserot.* Brown Judaic Studies 19. Chico, Calif.: Scholars Press, 1981.

Jastrow: Marcus Jastrow. *A Dictionary of the Targumim, the Talmud Bavli and Yerushalmi, and the Midrashic Literature.* 2 vols. New York, 1903; reprinted New York, 1973.

Ker.: Keritôt

Klein, *Ha-Yishuv:* Samuel Klein. *Sefer Ha-Yishuv* (The Book of Settlement). Vol. 1. Jerusalem, 1939.

Kohut: Alexander Kohut. *The Aruch Completum of Nathan b. Yeḥiel: An Expanded Critical Version in 8 Volumes.* Vilna, 1878–92; reprinted Jerusalem, 1971.

Lam.: Lamentations

Leiden Codex: *Palestinian Talmud. Leiden MS. Cod. Scal. 3. A Facsimile of the Original Manuscript, with an Introduction by Saul Lieberman.* 4 vols. Jerusalem: Kedem Publishing, 1970.

Lev.: Leviticus

Levy: Jacob Levy. *Wörterbuch über die Talmudim und Midraschim.* 4 vols. 2d ed. with additions by H. L. Fleischer and L. Goldschmidt. Berlin, 1924; reprinted Darhmstadt, 1963.

Lieberman: Saul Lieberman. *Ha-Yərûshalmî Ki-feshuto (The simple meaning of the Yerushalmi): A commentary based on manuscripts of the Yerushalmi and works of the Rishonim and Midrashim in MSS. and rare editions*. Jerusalem, 1934.

Lieberman, *About the Yerushalmi:* Saul Lieberman, *ʿAl Ha-Yərûshalmî (About the Yerushalmi)*. Jerusalem, 1929.

M.: Mishnah
Maas.: Maʿasrôt

Maimonides, *Commentary:* Joseph David Qapheḥ, ed. *Mishna, with Commentary by R. Moses b. Maimon*. 3 vols. Jerusalem: Mossad Ha-Rav Kook, 1976.

Mak.: Makkôt

Mareh Ha-Panim: Moses Margoliot (d. 1780). *Mareh Ha-Panim, Additions to Commentary on the Yerushalmi*. Reprinted in Vilna edition.

Meil.: Meilah

Men.: Menāḥôt

Mid.: Middôt

Miq.: Miqvaôt

M.Q.: Môʿēd Qāṭān

M.S.: Maʿasēr Shēnî

Naz.: Nazir

Neh.: Nehemiah

Neusner, *The Mishnah:* Jacob Neusner. *The Mishnah: A New Translation*. New Haven: Yale University Press, 1988.

Neusner, *The Talmud of the Land of Israel:* Jacob Neusner, gen. ed. *The Talmud of the Land of Israel*. 35 vols. Chicago: University of Chicago Press, 1982– .

Neusner, *The Tosefta:* Jacob Neusner. *The Tosefta Translated from the Hebrew*. 6 vols. New York: KTAV, 1977–86.

Newman: Louis Newman. *The Sanctity of the Seventh Year: A Study of Mishnah Tractate Shebiit*. Brown Judaic Studies 44. Chico, Calif.: Scholars Press, 1983.

Nid.: Niddah

NJPST: *TANAKH: The Holy Scriptures. The New Jewish Publication Society Translation according to the Traditional Hebrew Text*. Philadelphia: Jewish Publication Society, 1988.

Num.: Numbers

Pes.: Pəsaḥîm

PM: Moses Margoliot (d. 1780). *Pənê Mōshe: Commentary on the Yerushalmi*. Amsterdam, 1754; Leghorn, 1770; reprinted in Vilna edition.

Ps.: Psalms

Qid.: Qiddûshîn

Qorban Ha-Eidah: Elijah b. Judah Loeb of Fulda. *Qorban Ha-Eidah*. Commentary to the Yerushalmi. Dessau, 1743; Berlin, 1757, 1760–62; reprinted in Vilna edition.

R.: Rabbi
RiDVaZ: *Pērûsh Ha-Ridvaz*. Commentary of R. Jacob David of Slotz (1479–1573). Reprinted in Vilna edition.

Romm edition: Vulgate or "standard" edition of Talmud. Vilna, 1922, and many reprints.

Sanh.: Sanhedrin

Sarason, *Demai:* Richard Sarason. *A History of the Mishnaic*

Law of Agriculture: A Study of Tractate Demai. Leiden: E. J. Brill, 1979.

Schwab: Moise Schwab, trans. *Le Talmud de Jérusalem: Traduit pour la première fois en français*. Vol. 2. Paris, 1871; reprinted 1932–33.

Shab.: Shabbāt

Sheq.: Shᵊqālîm

Shevi.: Shᵊvîᶜît

Shevu.: Shᵊvûᶜôt

Sifra: Isaac Hirsch Weiss, ed. *Sifra de-be-Rav, Hu Sefer Torat Kohanim*. Vienna, 1862; reprinted New York, 1946.

Sif. Deut.: Eliezer Finkelstein and Hayyim Horowitz, eds. *Sifre al Sefer Devarim: With Textual Variants and Notes*. Berlin, 1939; reprinted New York, 1969.

Sirillo: Solomon b. Joseph Sirillo (d. 1558). *Commentary to Yerushalmi Zeraᶜim*. Ca. 1530; reprinted in Vilna edition.

Sot.: Sôṭâh

Sperber: Daniel Speber. *Roman Palestine 200–400*. Vol. 2: *The Land*. Ramat Gan, 1976.

Steinsaltz: Adin Steinsaltz. *Talmud Yerushalmi: Tractate Peah. Explained, Translated, and Pointed*. Jerusalem: Israel Institute for Talmudic Publications, 1987.

Suk.: Sûkkâh

T.: Tosefta

Taᶜan.: Taᶜᵃnit

Tem.: Temurah

Ter.: Tᵊrûmôt

Toh.: Tohorôt

Y.: *Yerushalmi*, Talmud of the Land of Israel

Yev.: Yᵊvāmôt

Zech.: Zechariah

Zev.: Zevaḥîm

Index to Scripture and Rabbinic Literature

Index of Rabbinic Authorities

General Index

Added fifth, penalty, xiii, 78–79, 115–120, 130, 163–164; avoiding payment of, 109–110, 120–127
Albeck, Ḥanokh, 5
Anointing: compared with drinking, 42; under rubric of "eating," 41–43. *See also* Second tithe oil
Avery-Peck, Alan, 47

Bar Kokhba, coins issued by, 17
Bertinoro, Ovadiah ben Abraham of, 49
Bible, ix–xv. *See also* Scripture
Bokser, Baruch, xxxiii, 5
Bread, baked from second tithe wheat, 25–26

Cities of refuge, levitical, 189–190
Coins: Bar Kokhba, 17; bathhouse tokens not legal tender, 16; copper, 17, 61–66; damaged or out of date, 16–17; *dinar,* silver, 18, 69; *dinar,* gold, 111; *dupondium,* value of, 135–136; gold, used to redeem silver coins, 63–66; illegal coins, used to deconsecrate second tithe, 17; Israelite contrasted with Babylonian, 17–18; *issar,* value of, 135–136; *maneh,* 141–143; *perutah,* items worth less than, 12–13, 113, 116–117; poorly minted, 15–18; *selaᶜ*, silver, 4, 116–117, 128–130; silver, deconsecrated with copper or gold, 62–66; silver weights used as, 16; *zuz,* doubtful status, 141–143
Communion-meal sacrifice, 23–29; compared with Passover sacrifice, 80–81; purchased with second tithe coins, 79–81
Confession, at removal of tithes, xiii, 185–187, 188; abolition of, 190–192; text of, 183–187
Containers: marked "consecrated," 139–141; purchased together with second tithe, 20–21, 104–107
Contrived distinctions, xxxii, 71–75
Cultic purity. *See* Uncleanness

Davidic monarchy, reestablishing, xxxii, 158
Day of Atonement, 41–42
Divorce, 130–134, 181
Dream-visions, interpretation of, xxxii, 60, 142–146
Drinking: compared with anointing, 42; under rubric of "eating," 37–41

Elijah b. Solomon Zalman, Gaon of Vilna (GRA), 16–17, 26, 32, 39, 47, 54, 62, 64, 66, 87–88, 91, 107, 111–113, 129, 132, 194
Ephraim Dov Ha-Kohen Lof (*Gilyonei Ephraim*), 25

Fermented grape juice, 21–22
First fruits, compared with second tithe, 3
Firstlings, 1; as betrothal gift, 13–15; compared with tithe of cattle, 10–11
Fourth-year produce, xiii; comparison to second tithe, 147–155, 159–169; deconse-